LICENSE PLATES

OF THE UNITED STATES

A PICTORIAL HISTORY
1903 - TO THE PRESENT

by James K. Fox

Text photographs by Straight Shooter

Text composition by Carole Gilligan

Designed by William Cummings

Interstate Directory Publishing Company, Inc.
New York

PLATES IN FRONT COVER PHOTOGRAPH : By Straight Shooter

Top row : 1941 Georgia, 1951 Tennessee, 1918 Texas radiator seal, 1950's porcelain F.B.I. plate. This was the personal plate of F.B.I. Director J. Edgar Hoover.

Second row : 1908 Pennsylvania porcelain, 1906 West Virginia, 1990 Idaho Centennial (optional plate), 1958 Colorado.

Third row: 1909 West Virginia porcelain, 1935 Louisiana, 1910 Ohio porcelain, 1939 California.

Fourth row : 1928 Idaho, 1911 North Dakota, 1922 Georgia, 1938 Wyoming.

Fifth row : 1920 Nevada flat, 1903-1907 Massachusetts porcelain, 1917 Texas radiator seal, 1937 Ohio Governor's plate, used by Governor Martin L. Davey.

PLATES IN BACK COVER PHOTOGRAPH : By Paul Tepley

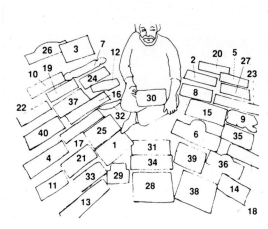

1. Andorra
2. Australia 1956 Olympics
3. Bangladesh
4. Belgium Army
5. Bhutan
6. Burma
7. California 1906
8. Cambodia
9. Canadian Northwest Territories
10. China 1930s
11. Christmas Island
12. Cincinnati 1907
13. Denmark
14. District of Columbia 1933 Presidential Inauguration
15. East Germany U.S. Military Mission
16. Egypt 1914
17. Ethiopia Transit
18. European Economic Community
19. Georgia 1941
20. Hawaii 1921
21. Iceland
22. Idaho 1928
23. Israel West Bank
24. Jordan (Diplomatic)
25. Kiribati
26. Latvia
27. Mexico 1936
28. Nepal
29. North Korea
30. Ohio 1908
31. Ohio Governor (Davey 1937)
32. Pakistan motorcycle
33. Papua New Guinea
34. Queensland, Australia
35. Saudi Arabia Air Force
36. Saudi Arabia Royal Family
37. Solomon Islands
38. Switzerland
39. Syria
40. Yemen Arab Republic

Library of Congress Catalog Card Number: 93-061330

Hardcover edition ISBN 0-9629962-5-4

Softcover edition ISBN 0-9629962-6-2

To my wife, Diane,
who has put up with this obsession for nearly 25 years.

To our daughters, Allison and Andrea,
who have learned to live amongst the "tin."

Contents

Photographs and History

Color Codes

Introduction

Why? That is the question people usually ask when they first learn about my hobby. I can understand it to some degree. Not everyone can appreciate the fineries of a rusting hunk of old steel. I have collected license plates since 1954, the year the Automobile License Plate Collectors Association was founded. However, I was just seven years old then, and I didn't find about ALPCA until 1971. In the interim, I discovered music and dropped all other interests in life in favor of a set of drums. When my band became active in the late 1960s, I was again intrigued by all the plates I would see while we traveled, and my interest was rekindled. Once I discovered ALPCA and realized that I was not the only nut out there, there was no turning back. Though this book covers only private automobile license plates from the United States, my own collecting interests range from the unusual types of non-passenger plates from the U.S. to all types of plates from the various countries of the world.

A part of my interest in license plates stems from the people I have met along the way. This hobby attracts people from all walks of life, from farmers to politicians, from undertakers to entertainers. It has allowed me to get to know people from every corner of the globe, many of whom I have personally visited or who have visited me and seen my collection. But, when it gets right down to it, I still cannot tell you *why* I chose license plates to collect over, say, stamps or coins, or statues of elephants, for that matter! In some ways, it seems almost as if the hobby chose me rather than vice versa, because I can barely recall a time when license plates did not interest me.

License plates are changing today, too. With the advent of the process of silk-screening onto reflective material, designs are getting more and more intricate and attractive, no longer limited to what could be embossed onto a sheet of metal. These colorful plates are attracting more attention today than ever before, and that makes the interest in our hobby run high. Many optional issues are now being introduced, whereby for an additional fee, vehicle owners have a choice of a wider range of more colorful and attractive plates from which to choose. Some make an environmental statement, some call attention to colleges and universities, and some are available only to raise more money for the state treasuries. Regardless of motive, this small revolution has made for a more attractive and diverse group of choices in license plates to the consumer, and thus eventually to the collector.

This book has three sections for each state. First, there is a page of text. This will help to provide an overview of the history of plates in that state. Then, there is a full-color photograph of each state run, from the beginning date to the present (or close to the present). Lastly, there is a color code list to help determine the exact colors of each plate. Like beauty, the names of colors are in the eye of the beholder, and in this case, it is *me* doing the beholding! ALPCA has offered color code sheets to members for many years, and I have had the pleasure (and pain) of working on more than one revision and update. The colors included here are the "official" ALPCA colors, but this does not mean that they are carved in stone. People see colors differently and sometimes silver versus gray, yellow-orange versus orange-yellow, etc. can be bones of contention. For many years, we referred to the colors of the 1927 Tennessee plate as "white on *heliotrope*"! I have tried to avoid the "puces" and "fuchsias," but sometimes, no other description will do. So, if you are using this book as a means to learn the colors in order to repaint a rusted plate, it is strongly suggested that the repainter try to locate an example with original paint, just for accurate reference.

Some definitions of terms seem useful here, so that the reader will more easily understand the chapters of text. A "run" refers to a group of plates, usually from a given state, dating from the earliest issue to the most recent issue, or any segment thereof. A "base" refers to a plate that is issued with the intent of having its validation period extended beyond the first period of use. When the word "undated" is used to describe a plate, it refers to a plate that was actually used with no date on it. By this, I mean that if an undated plate is used with a date sticker or tab, it is no longer undated. A "date tab" is a small piece of metal, designed to be placed on a plate so as to cover a previous date (or to date an undated plate) and validate the plate for an additional period of time. A "sticker" is a piece of paper or synthetic material used for the same purpose. A "windshield sticker" does the same, but is used on the windshield, not directly on the plate. A "date strip" is an elongated tab.

It is hoped that this book will give the reader some idea of the history and usage of license plates. Further, it is hoped that the reader will enjoy this subject, and perhaps will one day have an interest in becoming a collector, too.

Pre-states

There is an area of license plate collecting which focuses on the period before plates were state-issued. These plates represent the pioneering era of motoring in a time when the horseless carriage was not all that far removed from the horse and buggy. In those days, license plates were often made by a local blacksmith. Plates of this era are generally referred to as "pre-states," meaning that they predate the issue of plates by the state itself. Since the making of these plates was very often the responsibility of the vehicle owner, the methods used are diverse and limited in some cases only to the imagination of the owner. These plates are made from leather pads, pieces of wood, pieces of metal with numbers painted on them, or any other material which might serve the purpose of displaying the number on a vehicle. One common method (though not a favorite of license plate collectors) was to paint the assigned number directly onto the body or bumper of the vehicle. In other cases, the issuing authority provided plates for the owner, and these were mainly made of porcelain, though other methods were used, judging from the diverse examples which survive today. Some cities issued plates concurrently with the states, creating a dual form of registration. The 1909 Pittsburgh plate in the accompanying photograph, then, is not a *true* pre-state, because the state was already issuing properly made plates by 1909. I've included it here because it is a good example of an early, non-state-issued plate.

Semantics also come into play here. In the cases of Alaska, Arizona, Hawaii and New Mexico, vehicles were licensed before these places became states. In the case of Alaska, all issues before 1959 date to the period before Alaska became a state. Thus, these plates can properly be viewed as *territorial* issues. City plates are also known to have existed in early Alaska registrations, an example being the 1931 Wrangell plate in the accompanying photograph. In Arizona, plates in use before the territory became a state would fall into two categories. Before 1912, the issues were territorial. Then, between 1912, when Arizona became a state, and 1914, when the first plates were state-issued, the plates of that period should be considered pre-states. In New Mexico, the plates issued prior to 1912 are territorial issues. It is a bit more complicated with Hawaii. Registrations date to 1905, but from then until 1922, these issues are more correctly referred to as "pre-territorials." The territorial issues began when the islands consolidated their registration systems in 1922. The Hawaii territorial issues continued until statehood in 1959.

A few explanations are in order concerning some of the terms used to describe the plates of the pre-state era (and sometimes beyond). "Porcelain" refers to a process whereby porcelainized enamel is placed over steel and baked at a high heat. These plates chip like glass when fractured. "Leathers" are most often leather pads with metal digits attached to them. Some leathers have a metal wire sewn into the borders to help keep the shape intact, but other leathers are simply a leather slab. "Kit plates" are plates made of individual components. Most often, they consist of a metal base with grooves on the top and bottom edges so that individual characters of metal or porcelain squares can be slipped into the edges to make a number which corresponds to the registration number.

Regardless of construction, pre-states are often among the most interesting of all license plates. Though I have touched on pre-states in each chapter, I have also included a photograph of a group of pre-states from various jurisdictions. Many state plate collectors do not consider the pre-states to be a necessary part of a state run because they were not issued by the state. Still, it is hoped that the accompanying photo will give the reader some idea of the diversity of this era of registration.

Pre-state Plates in Photograph

96: Alaska, city of Wrangell, 1931 (territorial issue), embossed steel
7814: California, circa 1906, porcelain
92644: California, circa 1912, porcelain
4: Colorado, city of Salida, circa 1910, porcelain
1664: Washington, D.C., circa 1906, leather pad with aluminum characters
118: Florida, Dade County, 1916, porcelain
628: Florida, Volusia County, 1913-1914, porcelain
800: Hawaii, city of Honolulu, 1916 (pre-territorial), porcelain
562: Hawaii, city of Honolulu, 1921 (pre-territorial), embossed steel with
    brass date tab
139: Illinois, city of Chicago, 1906, brass with steel backing plate
32487: Illinois, circa 1909, alloy with steel backing plate
1841: Indiana, circa 1909, die-cut brass
15687: Iowa, circa 1910, leather pad with aluminum characters
1892: Louisiana, city of New Orleans, 1914, porcelain
1901: Maryland, circa 1907, leather pad with aluminum characters
5026: Michigan, circa 1908, leather pad with painted characters
57400: Nebraska, circa 1914, kit with steel backing and aluminum characters

79559: New York, circa 1908, fiberboard base with aluminum characters
23: Ohio, city of Cincinnati, 1907, brass backing plate with cast brass numbers
3534: Ohio, city of Cleveland, circa 1906, leather pad with aluminum numbers
569: Ohio, city of Columbus, 1907, porcelain
96: Ohio, city of Hamilton, 1907, brass with steel backing plate
148: Ohio, city of Warren, 1908, porcelain
252: Oklahoma, city of Tulsa, 1913, porcelain
REB 28 Pa: Pennsylvania, circa 1903, leather pad with aluminum characters
        The letters "REB" are believed to be the owner's initials.
3135PA: Pennsylvania, circa 1905, kit with aluminum panels that slid into a
    steel backing plate
497: Pennsylvania, city of Pittsburgh, 1908, porcelain
852: South Dakota, circa 1907, leather pad with aluminum numbers and brass letters
13054: South Dakota, circa 1911, leather pad with aluminum characters
206: Texas, date uncertain, leather pad with aluminum numbers
370: Texas, county of Lavaca, circa 1912, kit made with porcelain squares on steel
    backing plate
381: Utah, 1914, solid steel, date is hand painted, possibly unofficially by the owner

ALABAMA

ALABAMA

PRE-STATES

Alabama state law called for the registration of vehicles as early as 1903. However, no license plates were required to be displayed on the vehicles. Various Alabama cities rushed to fill that gap, passing laws requiring their own vehicle registration and ordering motorists to provide their own plates. City registrations date to 1905 for Mobile, and other cities soon followed. By 1909, cities were issuing annual porcelain plates in Birmingham, Mobile and Montgomery. The city issues ended in October of 1911, when the 1912 plates were first issued.

SLOGANS

THE HEART OF DIXIE was introduced with the 1955 plate and has been a fixture through 1993 on Alabama plates.

GRAPHICS

In 1955, a large heart was introduced with the county number inside. In 1956, the county number was removed and put back in as part of the serial, and the size of the heart was reduced. The smaller heart was placed at the lower left corner of the plate and remained there until 1976. The 1977 issue had a heart at upper left that contained the *HEART OF DIXIE* slogan inside. It also had the State Capitol at center, the state flag at lower left and the Bicentennial star at lower right. The 1983 issue simplified the style, showing the heart with the slogan inside at upper left. The 1987 issue showed the slogan across the top with red hearts in the upper corners. The 1992 issue had *ALABAMA* across the top, with a small *HEART OF DIXIE* immediately below. The word *OF* is inside a heart.

OTHER FEATURES

The word *PRIVATE* was used on all private automobile issues from 1922 through 1927. For 1937, the front plates had the word *FRONT* embossed on them. In the late 1930s, an arrow was used to mark the space of missing digits on the low-numbered plates.

FIRST YEAR OF ISSUE
1912 (Actually issued in October of 1911)
UNDATED ISSUES
1912, 1913, 1914, 1915, 1916
PORCELAINS
1912, 1913, 1914, 1915
WINDSHIELD STICKERS
1943
METAL DATE TABS
None

ALASKA

ALASKA

TERRITORIALS

There were laws in the Alaska Territory pertaining to vehicle registration that predate the 1921 territory-issued plates, but they seem to be directed at vehicles "for hire," and in any event, no examples of plates have surfaced. Though no hard evidence exists, it seems reasonable that the first private automobile plates used in Alaska were the plates issued by the territory in 1921.

SLOGANS

The 1966 base had *1867 NORTH TO THE FUTURE 1967* along the bottom. This slogan was used without the dates *1867* and *1967* from 1970 through 1975. The 1968 issue had *THE GREAT LAND* across the bottom of the plate. The 1981 base carries the slogan *THE LAST FRONTIER* and this base remains valid today.

FIRST YEAR OF ISSUE
1959 (Territorials in 1921)

UNDATED ISSUES
None

PORCELAINS
None

WINDSHIELD STICKERS
None

METAL DATE TABS
1944, 1954, 1955, 1957, 1958, 1959, 1961, 1963

GRAPHICS

The Alaskan state flag first appeared on the 1948 issue and has appeared ever since with two exceptions: (1) the 1966 issue bore an intricate totem pole at left, and (2) the 1976 base featured a large brown Kodiak bear standing in front of a graphic mountain range! This latter design will be recorded as one of the most attractive of its era.

OTHER FEATURES

Because Alaska did not become a state until 1959, previous issues are technically territorial issues—not state issues. Still, serious collectors of American plates do try to include them in their year runs. This makes us gluttons for punishment, because the earliest Alaskan plates are about as rare as *any* United States plates! In the 1920s and 1930s, several Alaskan cities issued their own plates. These include Fairbanks, Juneau, Ketchikan and Wrangell. The city issues were used on the front bumpers of the vehicles. Later city issues for Anchorage and Haines in the 1940s and 1950s are also known to collectors. From 1921 through 1931, Alaska territorial issues were small, measuring 3-7/8" x 7-1/8". The 1945, 1946 and 1947 plates were fiberboard, as well as the extremely rare 1944 plate, which was issued only to new registrants.

Alaska plates 1921 -1929

1921 1922 1923 1924

1925 1926 1927 1928 1929

ARIZONA

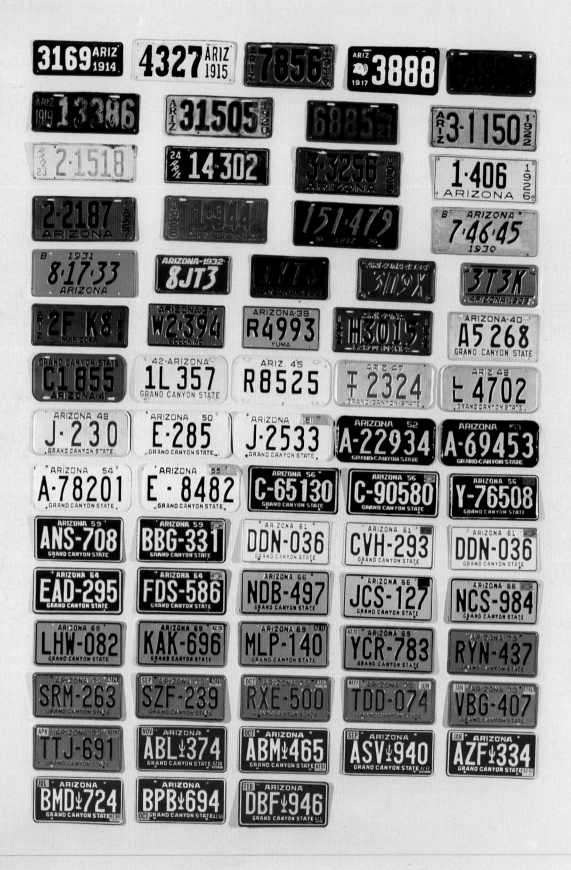

ARIZONA

TERRITORIALS AND PRE-STATES

Cities in the Arizona Territory as well as in the state of Arizona were responsible for registering vehicles in the early days of motoring. The earliest registrations date to about 1909. Plate-making was the owner's responsibility, and city-registered plates of various materials are known to collectors. City plates from this period include examples from Douglas, Phoenix, Prescott and Tucson. The earliest known of these plates are unusual because Arizona did not become a state until 1912; thus any issues that precede statehood are not really state issues but territorial issues.

SLOGANS

In 1939, the slogan *MARCOS DE NIZA* and the dates *1539* and *1939* were used. This plate commemorated the arrival of the Franciscan monk in 1539, in search of the legendary Seven Cities of Cibola. The slogan *GRAND CANYON STATE* first appeared in 1940 and has been used each year through 1993.

FIRST YEAR OF ISSUE
1914

UNDATED ISSUES
None

PORCELAINS
None

WINDSHIELD STICKERS
1943, 1944, 1946

METAL DATE TABS
1951, 1953, 1955

GRAPHICS

A steer head was placed at the left of the 1917 issue, making it the first United States plate to carry any graphics—certainly the first plate to illustrate livestock! Beginning in 1980, a small cactus was used to separate the letters from the numbers.

OTHER FEATURES

Copper plates were used in 1932, 1933 and 1934. These plates are unique in American platedom, and in fact, the 1934 plate has a patent number along the bottom edge. County names were spelled in full along the bottom of the plates in 1936, 1937 and 1938. A waffled texture was embossed into the aluminum plates of 1949 to give strength to the metal. Interestingly, the small letters used at the upper left of the 1930 and 1931 plates remain unexplained today.

ARKANSAS

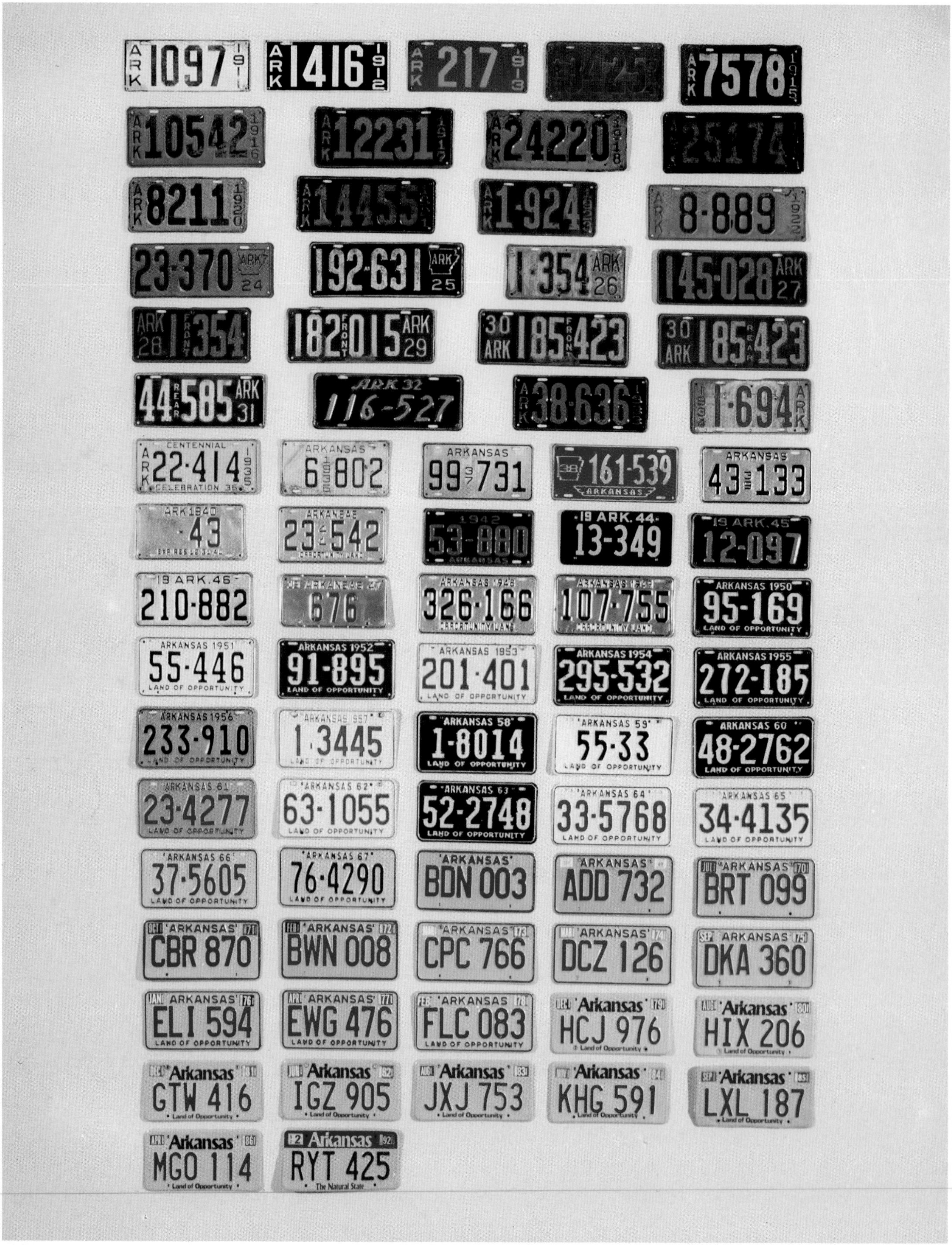

ARKANSAS

PRE-STATES

No state motor vehicle registration laws existed in Arkansas until the first state-issued plates were introduced in April of 1911. Prior to that date, Arkansas cities handled vehicle registration. Porcelain city plates of the 1909 to 1911 period are known from Little Rock, Fort Smith and Pine Bluff. Other city plates are rumored to exist as well.

SLOGANS

The 1935 issue noted the Arkansas *CENTENNIAL CELEBRATION* in the state. The 1941 issue proclaimed *OPPORTUNITY LAND* along the bottom. This phrase was also used on the 1948 base. In 1950, the slogan was modified to read *LAND OF OPPORTUNITY*, and was used yearly through 1967. The slogan returned with the 1975 issue and continued with the 1978 base. A new slogan, *THE NATURAL STATE,* was introduced for the 1989 issue.

FIRST YEAR OF ISSUE
1911
UNDATED ISSUES
1968
PORCELAINS
1911, 1912, 1913
WINDSHIELD STICKERS
1943
METAL DATE TABS
1949

GRAPHICS

In 1924, 1925 and 1938, the dates appeared in a border shaped like the state. The 1938 issue also enclosed the state name in a shield-shaped border. On the 1978 issue, the state name appeared in a stylized graphic design, and this style was carried through on the 1989 base.

OTHER FEATURES

The 1914 Arkansas plate is particularly difficult to collect. For years, a rumor circulated that in order to receive a 1915 plate, the motorist was required to surrender his 1914 plate. This rumor may be true, but no proof has surfaced to date. In 1928, 1929, 1930 and 1931, plates were used with *FRONT* and *REAR* embossed on them. The 1944 plates were made of fiberboard. It is worth noting that Arkansas experimented with some unusually shaped dies over the years, specifically, the 1932, 1955 and 1956 plates.

CALIFORNIA

CALIFORNIA

PRE-STATES

The California State Legislature passed a law requiring motorists to register their vehicles with the state in 1905. However, they did not begin to issue license plates until 1914. This span of nine years in which motorists were required to provide their own plates allowed a variety of styles to be used, both manufactured and homemade. Most examples carried the abbreviation *CAL* at some location on the plate, and the numbers were consecutively issued, beginning with number 1 and ending at well over 100,000. Plates were made of metal, porcelain, wood, aluminum digits on flat steel, and many other materials. In a unique situation, the Automobile Club of Southern California provided porcelain plates to members upon request for a fee.

SLOGANS

CALIFORNIA WORLD'S FAIR 39 appeared on the 1939 issue, the first slogan ever to grace a California plate. The only other slogan, *THE GOLDEN STATE*, appeared on the 1984 base.

FIRST YEAR OF ISSUE 1914
UNDATED ISSUES 1943 tab
PORCELAINS 1914, 1915, 1916-1919
WINDSHIELD STICKERS 1944
METAL DATE TABS 1916, 1917, 1918, 1919, 1942 (strip), 1943, 1946, 1948, 1949, 1950, 1952, 1953, 1954, 1955

GRAPHICS

The 1984 issue displayed a large golden sun, with the state name in stylized characters across the top.

OTHER FEATURES

California may have been short on slogans and graphics, but the interesting series of date tabs used between 1916 and 1919 helped make up for that! Each tab had a specific shape as follows:

1916 – Bear	1917 – Poppy	1918 – Bell	1919 – Star

The lead 1916 tabs differed between front and rear, with the rear carrying the base plate number, while the front carried a space in which the owner was required to scratch his name...and you thought personalized plates were relatively new! The dated 1942 plates had a yellow area made to look as if the 1942 date strip was added, even though it was actually a part of the plate. The 1943 tabs carried a simple red *V* instead of a date.

COLORADO

COLORADO

PRE-STATES

City or county-registered, Colorado pre-states come in a variety of styles, including leather, porcelain, metal kit plates and even some embossed issues. By 1910, Denver alone had registered over 5,000 vehicles (though many were motorcycles). Besides Denver, plates are known from Alamosa, Boulder, Colorado Springs, Salida and others.

SLOGANS

The slogan *COLORFUL* was used on Colorado plates from 1950 through 1955, 1958, 1959, and again in 1973 and 1974. *CENTENNIAL* was used for the 100th anniversary of statehood in 1975 and 1976.

FIRST YEAR OF ISSUE 1913
UNDATED ISSUES None
PORCELAINS 1913, 1914, 1915
WINDSHIELD STICKERS None
METAL DATE TABS 1919, 1920, 1944, 1952

GRAPHICS

The 1958 plate featured an embossed skier at right. Beginning in 1960, a mountain outline appeared on their plates, and that continues through 1993. In 1975 and 1976, a fully graphic Centennial issue was used, featuring the mountain motif, as well as a stylized *76*.

OTHER FEATURES

For 1919 and 1920, Colorado used a rather unusual system. A sheet metal base was manufactured for 1919 with *COLO* embossed at the top. Sheet metal numbers were then spot-welded to the base. Next, a large embossed steel tab was attached. The number on the tab matched the number on the base plate. Further, the tab had a *tab* attached! This smaller tab contained a single letter on it (*A*, *B*, or *C*) that denoted the range of horsepower and thus the registration fee. Just in case that was not complicated enough, the government decided in 1920 to institute pairs of plates. They issued a normal embossed front plate dated 1920 with numbers to match the 1919 plates, and then issued a 1920 tab much like the 1919 tabs to revalidate the existing bases, thereby creating pairs that matched in number but not in any other way. The late issues of 1920 received pairs of the embossed plates.

CONNECTICUT

CONNECTICUT

PRE-STATES

From mid-1903, when the motor laws went into effect, until mid-1905, when the first state-issued plates came into use, approximately 3,000 vehicles were registered. These plates were most often made of aluminum house numbers on a leather pad with the letter *C* at the left.

SLOGANS

Beginning with the 1974 issue, all plates have carried the *CONSTITUTION STATE* slogan, either at the top or bottom.

GRAPHICS

The pickings are slim when it comes to Connecticut graphics, but a small state-shaped figure appeared at the upper left corner of the 1987 issue.

OTHER FEATURES

The highest numbers in the 1905-1909 series were manufactured with a square-shaped *C*. This is in contrast to the round *C* which appeared on the rest of the plates in the issue. The square *C* was used for the duration of all subsequent porcelain issues in Connecticut.

Other than some early state plates, the base issued in 1937 was the first United States plate intended to be used "permanently." It was made of heavy-gauge aluminum with no background paint (thus none to fade or rust). Slots at the bottom were made to accommodate annual revalidation tabs. It was used for 11 years before the next "permanent" plate was issued.

FIRST YEAR OF ISSUE
1905

UNDATED ISSUES
1905-1909, 1910, 1911, 1912, 1913

PORCELAINS
1905-1909, 1910, 1911, 1912, 1913, 1914, 1915, 1916

WINDSHIELD STICKERS
None

METAL DATE TABS
1937 through 1960 inclusive, 1962, 1963

DELAWARE

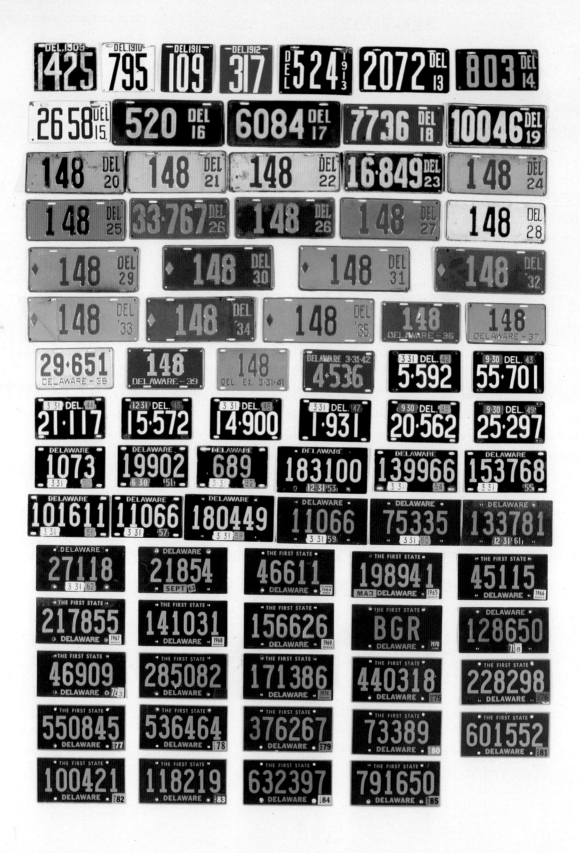

DELAWARE

PRE-STATES

Delaware registered vehicles as early as 1905, and a very few early examples exist, including porcelains dated 1907 and 1908, and a plate with aluminum characters on a type of fiberboard base. Each plate has the abbreviation *DEL* on it.

SLOGANS

The 1963 base carried the slogan *THE FIRST STATE* along the top. This slogan was carried over to the 1970 base and remains current through 1993.

GRAPHICS

Between 1929 and 1935, a diamond-shaped area was embossed to the left of the serial number of the plate.

OTHER FEATURES

Two distinct styles of the 1913 porcelain issue were used that year. One has *DEL* vertically down the left side and the date vertically down the right side. The other has both the state abbreviation and the date horizontally to the right of the serial number. Another interesting feature is the introduction of a porcelain base in 1942, fully 20 years after the other states had abandoned porcelains.

FIRST YEAR OF ISSUE	1909
UNDATED ISSUES	None
PORCELAINS	1909, 1910, 1911, 1912, 1913, 1914, 1915, 1942
WINDSHIELD STICKERS	None
METAL DATE TABS	1942 through 1962 inclusive

DIST. OF COLUMBIA

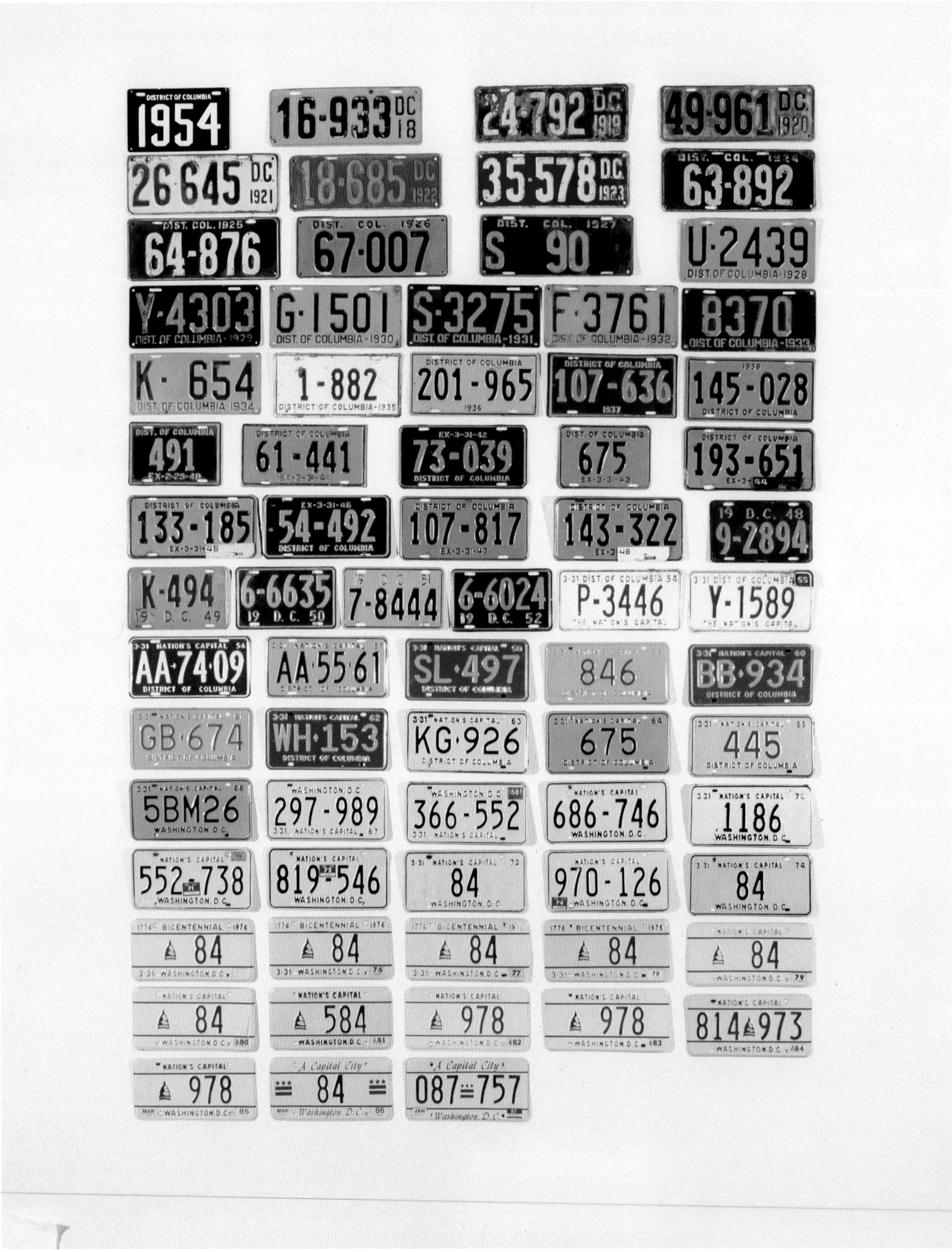

DISTRICT OF COLUMBIA

PRE-STATES

Though approximately 2,000 vehicles were registered in the pioneer era of 1902-1907 in Washington, D.C., there are few surviving plates. Almost all are leather pads with house numbers attached to them. During this period, the government of the District of Columbia required that all vehicles operating on D.C. streets had to have a District of Columbia license along with a license from their home jurisdiction. This ruling chiefly affected the residents of Maryland and Virginia, because of their close proximity to the District.

SLOGANS

The *NATION'S CAPITAL* slogan was first introduced with the 3/31/54 issue and was used through the 3/31/73 issue. The following year, the Bicentennial base was issued, and that carried the slogan *1776 BICENTENNIAL 1976* across the top. In 1979, a version of the Bicentennial base was issued to new registrants, again carrying the *NATION'S CAPITAL* slogan, and by the late 1980s, the Bicentennial bases were gone from the roads. The *NATION'S CAPITAL* slogan lasted this time until the early 1990s. However, a base issued to new registrants in 1985 carried a different slogan, *A CAPITAL CITY*. These bases remain in use through 1993. In 1991, a similar base was given to new registrants, proclaiming *CELEBRATE AND DISCOVER*, and these are also in use through 1993.

FIRST YEAR OF ISSUE
1907

UNDATED ISSUES
1907-1917 issue, 1969

PORCELAINS
1907-1917 issue

WINDSHIELD STICKERS
None

METAL DATE TABS
1944, 1945, 1948, 1955, each expiring on March 31 of their respective years.

GRAPHICS

The Bicentennial issue of 1974 had the Capitol Building embossed on the plate. This graphic continued with the 1979 issue as well. With the 1985 issue, a fully graphic plate was introduced that had the District of Columbia flag screened on the plate. The 1991 *CELEBRATE AND DISCOVER* base was also fully graphic and had the D.C. seal on it.

OTHER FEATURES

The 1907-1917 porcelain was modified during its 10-year run. The early issues had *DISTRICT OF COLUMBIA* in small letters across the top, but the issues from 20,000 upwards had larger, bolder characters. Almost 60,000 numbers were issued in all. It is noteworthy that the District name was abbreviated to read *DIST COL* between 1924 and 1927. The 2/29/40 issue is the first and only embossed plate to carry the added day of a leap year! Low-numbered plates of the 1970s and into the 1980s were issued annual embossed plates—no stickers for the "bigwigs"! By the way, the President of the United States was traditionally issued plate #100. This practice is believed to have ceased in the late 1960s or early 1970s, no doubt because of security considerations.

FLORIDA

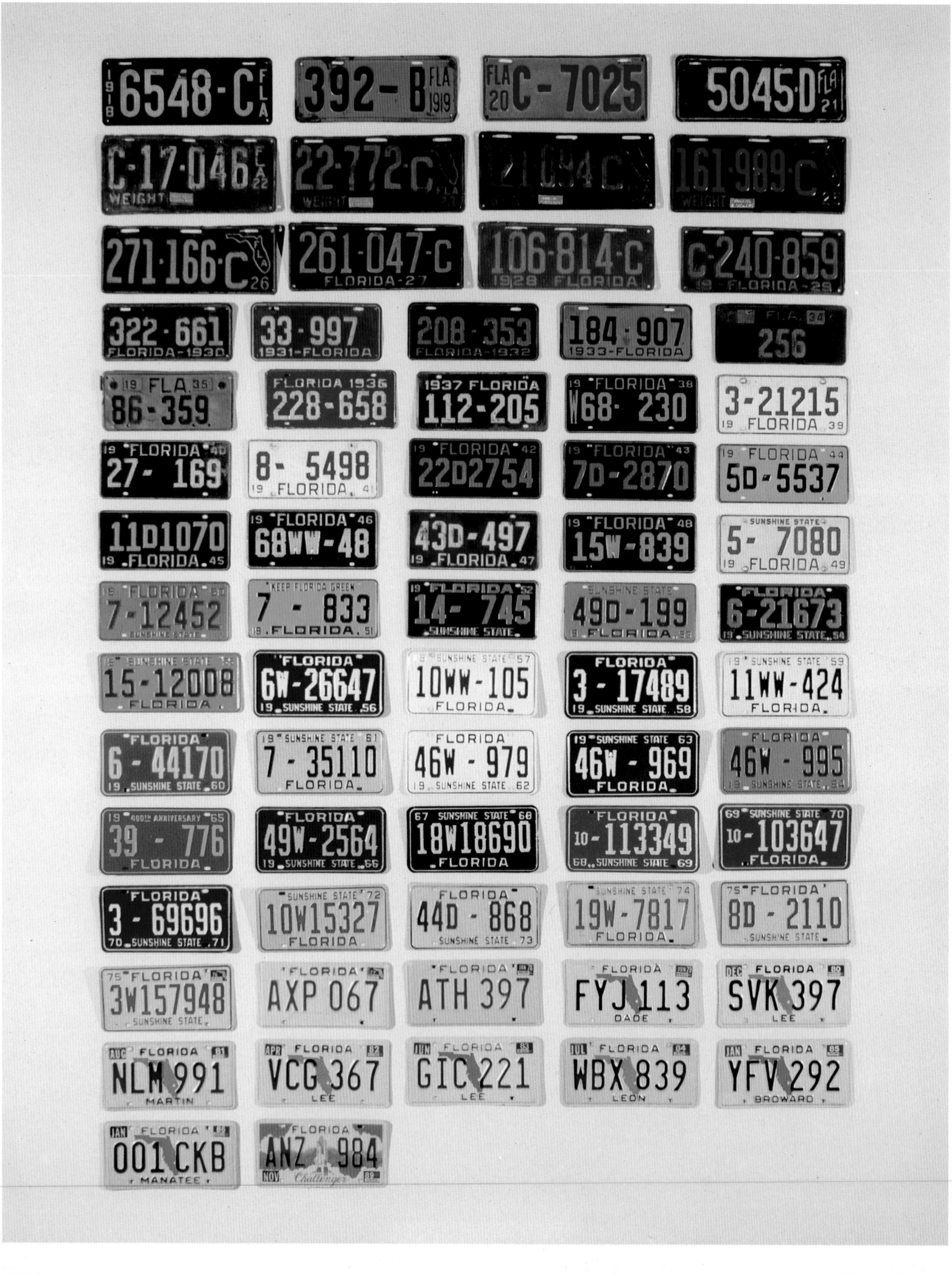

FLORIDA

PRE-STATES

Florida has an unusual and complicated position among the states regarding early issues. In 1905, the state licensing laws went into effect, and by the time the law was discontinued in 1915, over 14,000 vehicles had been registered. However, in late 1911, the state authorized the various counties to issue plates as well, and from then until 1917, a spectacular array of plates, mainly porcelains, were used. The result of this act was that during much of the period from 1911 through 1915, vehicles carried two plates—one from the state and another from the county. In a few instances, the cities were involved as well, leaving a few unfortunate motorists with the dilemma of how to show off *three* plates! A good map of the era would give you the specifics, but as examples, county names (shown prominently on most of the plates) included Alachua, Citrus, Escambia and Suwannee.

FIRST YEAR OF ISSUE
1918
UNDATED ISSUES
None
PORCELAINS
None
WINDSHIELD STICKERS
None
METAL DATE TABS
1943

SLOGANS

The slogan *SUNSHINE STATE* first appeared on the 1949 issue, and continued each year through 1976 with two exceptions: the 1951 plate wore the slogan *KEEP FLORIDA GREEN*, and the 1965 plate commemorated the *400TH ANNIVERSARY* of Florida's "discovery."

GRAPHICS

From 1923 to 1926, an embossed outline of the state appeared at the right of the plates. The 1935 issue had grapefruits embossed in the upper corners of the plate. From the 1978 base to 1993, the plates have had the state image reappear, this time in a silk-screened version in either orange or green.

OTHER FEATURES

A small aluminum tab was added to the plates from 1922 through 1925, denoting the weight class of the vehicle. In 1934 and 1935, a locking date strip was inserted into a special slot on the plates. This strip covered the bolts in an attempt to deter the theft of the plates. Judging from the difficulty in removing that strip today, I'd have to say that it worked!

The 1989 "Challenger" plate
shown is an optional issue.

GEORGIA

GEORGIA

PRE-STATES

Though city registration laws existed in Atlanta and Savannah as early as 1904, pre-state Georgia plates are as scarce today as pre-states from anywhere. Only a couple of examples of leather plates have survived; these have no marking other than the serial number. Proof of their usage lies more with circumstantial evidence (one was found in the trunk of an ancient car in Georgia) than in tangible evidence.

SLOGANS

The slogan *PEACH STATE* was used on the 1940 and 1941 plates, and again between 1947 and 1980.

GRAPHICS

In 1940, a peach was embossed at the center of the bottom of the plates, between the state name and the date. In 1941, a peach decal was placed in the center of the plate, with the serial on either side of it. The peach returned with the 1990 base, where it replaced the letter *O* in the state name, and it remains there as of 1993.

OTHER FEATURES

The 1910-1911, 1912 and 1913 issues appear to be three separately manufactured groups of plates from one continuous series. The plate referred to as the 1910-1911 had a backing plate made to accommodate slide-in numbers secured to the base by means of a groove in the top and bottom edges. The 1912 and 1913 issues were both thin steel plates "enclosed" by a thin steel backing plate crimped over the edges to provide strength. The 1912 and 1913 plates seem to have differed in color only. In 1929, plates were marked *FRONT* and *REAR* in an attempt to minimize misuse. The reflective 1941 plates mark the first general issue of a United States plate to be reflectorized. The peach decal on this plate was the first decal to be used on a plate in United States plate history. County strips were introduced on the 1971 issue and continue as of 1993.

FIRST YEAR OF ISSUE
1910
UNDATED ISSUES
1910-1911, 1912, 1913
PORCELAINS
1915
WINDSHIELD STICKERS
None
METAL DATE TABS
1943 date strip

1910-11

1912

1913

These plates are not included in the display on the opposite page.

The 1976 "Bicentennial" plate
shown is an optional issue.

31

HAWAII

HAWAII

PRE-TERRITORIALS AND TERRITORIALS

Hawaii did not become a state until 1959, so technically, all previous issues are either pre-territorials or territorials. However, as with Alaska, collectors tend to attempt to complete their runs at least back to the point where the four Hawaiian counties consolidated their laws to produce a unified system. This consolidation occurred with the 1922 issue. Prior to that year, each county had its own system, with the counties of Hawaii and Honolulu having annual issues from 1915 to 1921. Motor vehicle laws were written in Hawaii as far back as 1903, and by 1911, laws mentioning the use of homemade plates were enacted. Only a couple of the homemade plates exist today in collections (one being a wooden Maui plate). Beginning with the 1915 issue, both Hawaii and Honolulu counties are at least partly well documented. Hawaii had dated porcelains in 1915 and 1916, embossed steel 1917 plates, and metal plates with unusually shaped metal date tabs (swordfish, automobile and surf rider!) from 1918 to 1921. Hawaii county had dated porcelains in 1915 and 1916, too, and steel plates from 1917 to 1921, though descriptions of the steel plates are incomplete today.

FIRST YEAR OF ISSUE
1959 (Territorials in 1922)

UNDATED ISSUES
1957, 1961 (1953 was an undated plate but was not valid without a 1953 metal date tab attached)

PORCELAINS
None

WINDSHIELD STICKERS
1943, 1944, 1945, 1957 through 1968

METAL DATE TABS
1953, 1954, 1955, 1956

SLOGANS

ALOHA was used from 1957 to 1960. After statehood, the 1961 base carried *ALOHA STATE*, and this slogan has continued through 1993.

GRAPHICS

On the 1922 and 1926 issues, the state name was embossed in a highly stylized design, suggesting a "South Pacific" look. The 1976 graphic was a particularly appealing design, with a red antherium at the upper left and a pale red image of a warrior, palm trees and Diamond Head screened lightly behind the serial. The 1981 base had a bright orange warrior's head in the center of the plate. The 1991 base had a pastel rainbow arching across the top of the plate.

OTHER FEATURES

The 1953 base is undated. Rather than waiting a year to revalidate it, however, a 1953 metal date tab was used to make it valid from the beginning of the issue.

IDAHO

A collection of Idaho license plates arranged by year, from 1914 through 1992:

- 1312 IDAHO 1914
- 7040 IDAHO 1915
- 11083 IDAHO 1916
- 11003 IDAHO 1917
- 16449 IDAHO 1918
- 24812 IDAHO 1919
- 18905 IDA 1920
- 4195 IDAHO 1921
- 45·794 IDA 1922
- 52·941 IDA 1923
- 19·034 IDA X-24
- 39·821 IDAHO X-25
- 24·240 IDAHO X-26
- 54·345 IDAHO-27
- 87·166 IDAHO POTATOES-1928
- 92·106 IDAHO-1929
- 7·686 1930-IDAHO
- 113·909 IDAHO-1931
- K1 768 IDA 1932
- 1K·26·45 19-IDAHO-33
- 1K·24·00 19-IDAHO-34
- 1K·21·30 19-IDAHO-35
- 1K·13·19 19-IDAHO-36
- 1K·13·19 IDAHO-1937
- 1K·13·19 IDAHO-1938
- 1K·13·19 IDAHO-1939
- 1K·13·19
- 1K·13·19 SCENIC IDAHO 1941
- 6R·10·616 SCENIC IDAHO 42
- K·31·95 SCENIC IDAHO 45
- S·290 SCENIC IDAHO 46
- 1J 216 19 IDAHO 47 Vacation Wonderland
- 1O 867 IDAHO 48
- 4B 337 IDAHO 49 World Famous POTATOES
- 1A 14 079 IDAHO 50
- 2T 16 950 IDAHO 51
- 1A 31 787 IDAHO 52
- 1A 29 719 IDAHO 53 WORLD FAMOUS POTATO
- 2J 2 653 IDAHO 1954
- 2C 2 423 IDAHO 55
- 2C 20 710 IDAHO 1956 WORLD FAMOUS POTATO
- 2M 3 224 IDAHO 1957 FAMOUS POTATOES
- 1M 2 575 IDAHO 1958 FAMOUS POTATOES
- 2G 700 IDAHO 59 FAMOUS POTATOES
- K 925 IDAHO 60 FAMOUS POTATOES
- 1O B 1 257 IDAHO 61 FAMOUS POTATOES
- 1O B 1 350 IDAHO 62 FAMOUS POTATOES
- 2M 5 664 IDAHO 63 FAMOUS POTATOES
- N 16 954 IDAHO 64 FAMOUS POTATOES
- K 15 192 IDAHO 65 FAMOUS POTATOES
- 1A 44 728 IDAHO 66 FAMOUS POTATOES
- K 16 571 IDAHO 67 FAMOUS POTATOES
- N 4258 IDAHO 68 FAMOUS POTATOES
- 2C 23836 IDAHO 68 FAMOUS POTATOES 69
- 2C 19938 IDAHO 68 FAMOUS POTATOES 70
- 8B 41 870 IDAHO FAMOUS POTATOES 71
- K 30 165 IDAHO 68 72 FAMOUS POTATOES 71
- K 13504 IDAHO 68 72 71 FAMOUS POTATOES 69
- K 24 599 IDAHO 74 FAMOUS POTATOES
- K 14 539 IDAHO 74 FAMOUS POTATOES 75
- K 22 905 IDAHO FAMOUS POTATOES
- 8B 43 831 IDAHO 74 FAMOUS POTATOES
- 5B 10 886 IDAHO FAMOUS POTATOES
- 1A H 2848 IDAHO FAMOUS POTATOES 78
- 1A K 13 IDAHO FAMOUS POTATOES 79
- 1A H 5092 IDAHO FAMOUS POTATOES 80
- 1A L 7 852 IDAHO FAMOUS POTATOES
- 1A S5 545 IDAHO FAMOUS POTATOES 82
- 2T 94 852 IDAHO 83 Famous Potatoes
- 1F 14 732 IDAHO Famous Potatoes 84
- 1A AD 71 IDAHO 85 Famous Potatoes
- 1A BF 605 IDAHO Famous Potatoes 86
- N 7366 IDAHO Famous Potatoes
- 30406C 1890 IDAHO 1990 CENTENNIAL 8
- 8B 81 808 IDAHO Famous Potatoes 1
- 2J 17 297 IDAHO Famous Potatoes 2

IDAHO

PRE-STATES

From 1909 to 1912, city governments of Idaho had the responsibility for registering vehicles. Several porcelain plates are known to collectors, as well as a few steel and brass representations. Surviving examples of pre-state plates today are from Boise, Hailey, Lewiston, Nampa, Payette and Weiser.

SLOGANS

The 1928 issue proclaimed *POTATOES* along the bottom, just below the potato itself! The 1940 plate commemorated *50 YEARS STATEHOOD* along the top and *1890 IDAHO 1940* along the bottom. The word *SCENIC* was used on all issues from 1941 through 1946. The 1947 issue proclaimed the state a *VACATION WONDERLAND*. The 1948 issue proclaimed their most famous product as *WORLD FAMOUS POTATOES*. In 1953 and 1956 the slogan was modified to read *WORLD FAMOUS POTATO*, but was shortened to *FAMOUS POTATOES* from 1957 to 1993. It would seem that somehow they must have lost the "world" title along the way—to Ireland, maybe?

FIRST YEAR OF ISSUE
1913

UNDATED ISSUES
None

PORCELAINS
None

WINDSHIELD STICKERS
1943, 1944

METAL DATE TABS
1949, 1952

GRAPHICS

The 1928 plate had a most impressive potato embossed on it, filling the entire plate. In 1947, a skier was featured on the plates, but in 1948 and 1949, the potato returned, this time in the form of a decal, complete with a pat of butter inside! In 1983, the screened base had the letter *A* in Idaho capped with snow-covered mountains. The 1985 base was identical to the 1983, but was modified to include more snowcapped mountains to the right of the state name along the top. The 1991 issue, a modification of the optional Centennial base of a couple of years previous, really showed the capabilities of modern silk-screening technique, featuring a panoramic scene of pine trees and mountains under a blazing red sky.

OTHER FEATURES

The 1928 potato plate is among the most striking embossed designs in the history of United States plates. The detail is amazing, right down to the debossed "eyes" in the potato! The two different 1976 stickers are the result of a lost lawsuit over the legality of the staggered monthly registration system. The law was rewritten the following year to alleviate future problems.

1913

This plate is not included in the display on the opposite page.

The 1990 "Centennial" plate shown is an optional issue.

ILLINOIS

A collection of Illinois license plates from 1911 through the early 1980s, arranged chronologically in rows:

- **1293 ILL**, **64152 ILL**, **64152 ILL 1912**, **46334 ILL**, **89798 ILL**
- **1920 ILL 14**, **46315 ILL 15**, **91298 ILL 16**, **303204 ILL 17**
- **360200 ILL 18**, **235820 ILL 18**, **68887 ILL 19**, **36071 ILL 20**
- **100112 ILL 21**, **347-869 ILL 22**, **418-077 ILL 23**, **8883 ILL 24**, **45-929 ILL 25**
- **298-413 ILL 26**, **1043-910 ILL 27**, **139-974 ILL 28**, **335-337 ILL 29**, **8883 ILL 30**
- **263-808 ILL 31**, **27-264 ILL 32**, **143-416 ILL 33**, **102-601 ILLINOIS-1934**, **ILLINOIS-1935 42-793**
- **1386-050 ILLINOIS-1936**, **19 ILLINOIS 37 138539**, **94 961 ILLINOIS 38**, **ILLINOIS 39 63 058**, **214 624 ILLINOIS 1940**, **ILLINOIS 1941 102 601**
- **18 827 ILLINOIS 1942**, **ILLINOIS 43 54 347**, **54 347 ILLINOIS 1944**, **ILLINOIS 1945 146 310**, **97 902 ILLINOIS 1946**, **ILLINOIS 1947 184 014**
- **1806 51 8 ILLINOIS 1948**, **ILLINOIS 1949 1668 165**, **814 688 ILL 1950**, **53 543 1951**, **291 370 ILL 1952**
- **ILL 1953 2537 161**, **2318 012 19 ILLINOIS 54**, **19 ILLINOIS 55 871 437 LAND OF LINCOLN**, **228 443 19 ILLINOIS 56 LAND OF LINCOLN**, **19 ILLINOIS 57 82 454 LAND OF LINCOLN**
- **LAND OF LINCOLN 3010385 19 ILLINOIS 58**, **19 ILLINOIS 59 764 240 LAND OF LINCOLN**, **LAND OF LINCOLN 82 454 19 ILLINOIS 60**, **19 ILLINOIS 61 33 809 LAND OF LINCOLN**, **LAND OF LINCOLN BS 1414 19 ILLINOIS 62**
- **19 ILLINOIS 63 923 814 LAND OF LINCOLN**, **LAND OF LINCOLN 280 396 19 ILLINOIS 64**, **19 ILLINOIS 65 DD 1759 LAND OF LINCOLN**, **LAND OF LINCOLN GG 2781 19 ILLINOIS 66**, **19 ILLINOIS 67 574 924 LAND OF LINCOLN**
- **68 LAND OF LINCOLN LK 1895 19 ILLINOIS 68**, **19 ILLINOIS 69 AY 6059 LAND OF LINCOLN**, **LAND OF LINCOLN AY 6059 19 ILLINOIS 70**, **19 ILLINOIS 71 LJ 7280 LAND OF LINCOLN**, **LAND OF LINCOLN MP 9869 19 ILLINOIS 72**
- **19 ILLINOIS 73 SF 355 LAND OF LINCOLN**, **LAND OF LINCOLN JU 1200 19 ILLINOIS 74**, **19 ILLINOIS 75 WJ 2559 LAND OF LINCOLN**, **1776 TJ 6997 ILLINOIS**, **19 ILLINOIS 77 ZK 1592 LAND OF LINCOLN**
- **LAND OF LINCOLN 403 588 19 ILLINOIS 78**, **ILLINOIS 79 MG 8819 Land of Lincoln**, **ILLINOIS UE 410 Land of Lincoln**, **ILLINOIS JX 8678 Land of Lincoln**, **ILLINOIS HK 2769 ILL**
- **ILLINOIS YZO 606 Land of Lincoln**, **ILLINOIS XBR 268 Land of Lincoln**, **Illinois Land of Lincoln DAU 184**, **Illinois Land of Lincoln VL 5803 MAR**

ILLINOIS

PRE-STATES

From 1899 through 1907, the cities in Illinois handled vehicle registration. Plates made of steel and brass are known to collectors, the most interesting being Chicago's 1904-1907 plates, which were brass wrapped in an alloy backing. Other cities had ordinances, too, and rare examples exist from today Evanston and Oak Park. The first evidence of statewide registrations is in 1907, with the passage of a statewide motor law. These plates were handmade, homemade, and factory-made in leather, steel, kits, etc. They remained in effect until the state decided to provide the plates as well as the registrations in 1911.

SLOGANS

Illinois had no slogans until *LAND OF LINCOLN* first appeared on the 1954 plate. That slogan has appeared faithfully every year through 1993. The 1968 plate commemorated 150 years of statehood with *18...18* in the top corners. The United States Bicentennial was similarly noted on the 1976 issue, with *1776* and *1976* appearing on the plate.

FIRST YEAR OF ISSUE
1911
UNDATED ISSUES
1911
PORCELAINS
None
WINDSHIELD STICKERS
None
METAL DATE TABS
None

GRAPHICS

The 1927 issue featured the state abbreviation *ILL* in an embossed area shaped like the state. The 1976 plate commemorated the United States Bicentennial by using a red, white and blue color scheme, complete with stars and stripes. The 1983 base celebrated no event, but did have a stylized state name as well as a couple of graphic lines meant to enhance the appearance of the plate.

OTHER FEATURES

When the 1911 plates were issued, car owners complained that the front plates blocked their radiators, causing their cars to overheat. In response, the issues from 1912 through 1918 all had front plates made so as to allow air to pass through them. The plate styles varied from screens to silhouetted numbers to slats, but all served the same purpose, apparently successfully. Fiberboard plates, actually made of a soybean composition, were used from 1943 through 1948. This was done to save metal during World War II. License plate lore has it that the local goats used to eat them right off the bumpers, but I have yet to locate a single goat willing to step forward and confess to this heinous crime.

INDIANA

INDIANA

PRE-STATES

The state licensing code was adopted in 1905 in Indiana, but it was written in such a way as to allow other jurisdictions such as cities and counties to register the same vehicles as well. These city and county issues are nearly nonexistent today, with one known example being a leather Anderson plate. However, the state-issued numbers are in good supply, even today. Plates from this era were made mainly in three types. One had cut-out steel characters attached to a flat steel base by means of small tacks. Another had stenciled characters on a flat steel base. The third and most interesting type was made of silhouetted brass numbers with no background present. These plates are die cut from a single piece of brass. All three types had the *IND* abbreviation at the right.

SLOGANS

The plates for 1956, 1957 and 1958 carried the slogan *DRIVE SAFELY*. In 1959, *LINCOLN'S YEAR* was on the plate. *SAFETY PAYS* was the message for 1960, 1961 and 1962. The 1966 issue celebrated their *150th YEAR* of statehood. The 1976 plate proclaimed Indiana *THE HERITAGE STATE* for the Bicentennial. In 1980, the expedition of *GEORGE ROGERS CLARK* was noted. The 1982 base reminded us that Indiana is the *HOOSIER STATE*. In 1985, we were invited to *WANDER* the state. However, by the 1988 base, all were merrily proclaimed *BACK HOME AGAIN*! The 1991 base pointed out the *HOOSIER HOSPITALITY*. The exp. 1994 base highlights the *AMBER WAVES OF GRAIN*.

FIRST YEAR OF ISSUE
1913
UNDATED ISSUES
None
PORCELAINS
1913
WINDSHIELD STICKERS
None
METAL DATE TABS
Date strips for 1943, 1952, 1953 and 1955

GRAPHICS

A minuteman appeared on the 1976 Bicentennial issue, and this ushered in a series of graphic plates that continue today. The exp. 1978 plate issue had the state shape screened in yellow at the center. The exp. 1979 issue had an Indianapolis 500 race car lightly screened beneath its serial with a checkered flag at the upper left. The exp. 1980 plate depicted George Rogers Clark on his expedition. The exp. 1981 plate had a tricolor stripe of red, orange and yellow along the bottom. The exp. 1982 base depicted a pastoral farm scene across the top. The exp. 1985 base had red, green and yellow stripes along the bottom. The exp. 1988 base showed the Statue of Liberty's torch screened lightly in the center. The exp. 1991 issue digressed to having a small screened state shape at the lower left. The exp. 1994 issue came back strong with yet another farm scene, this time a panoramic view, across the top.

OTHER FEATURES

In a gesture to contribute to the war effort, the state asked that the front plates used in 1942 be turned back in so they could be recycled to make the 1944 plates. When the 1943 date strip expired, a small 1944 plate was issued. This wartime issue measured 3-1/4" X 10". *WANDER* proved to be an unpopular slogan among some Indiana residents when it was introduced on the exp. 1985 base. Apparently, there were those who thought it connoted visions of people "wandering aimlessly" around their state.

IOWA

A collection of Iowa license plates arranged in rows by year:

- 28899 IA 1911
- 32258 IA 1912
- 54829 IA 1913
- 27057 IA 1914
- 141573 IA 1915
- 189337 IA
- 296799 IA 19
- 66685 IA 20
- 246777 IA 21
- 94-70 IA 22
- 44-2543 IA 23
- 97-1445 IA 24
- 38-6807 IA 25
- 70-3566 IA 26
- 86-156 IA 27
- 9-2991 IA 28
- 8-14770
- 24-1602 IOWA-1930
- 91-1774 IOWA-1931
- 90-3046 IOWA-1932
- IOWA-1933 33-7371
- 50-7330 IOWA-1934
- IOWA-1935 39-1774
- 90-8654 IOWA-1936
- 33-7750 1937-IOWA
- IOWA-1938 91-1099
- 73-1499 IOWA-1939
- IOWA-1940 97-6223
- 73-4808 IOWA-1941
- IOWA-1942 63-2021
- IOWA-1945 69-3783
- IOWA-1946 50-2089
- 1947-IOWA 84-7431
- 1947-IOWA 91-5189
- 1947-IOWA 81-1
- IOWA-1949 81-1
- 19-IOWA-50 77-76385
- 19-IOWA- 97-8299
- 19-IOWA-52 82-1036
- 19 IOWA 53 97-2594 THE CORN STATE
- 19 IOWA 61-5826 THE CORN STATE
- 19 IOWA 82-54218 THE CORN STATE
- 19 IOWA 56 90-2918
- 19 IOWA 57 9-7322
- 3 5 IOWA 58 6451
- 8 1 IOWA 59 3615
- 3 3 IOWA 60 10590
- 7 IOWA 61 49094
- 3 5 IOWA 62 6796
- 9 2 IOWA 63 8265
- 5 6 IOWA 64 1106
- 1 2 IOWA 65 7841
- 1 2 IOWA 66 8083
- 5 2 IOWA 67 23007
- 1 2 IOWA 68 336
- 5 7 IOWA 69 53592
- 5 1 IOWA 70 7437
- 7 7 IOWA 71 88996
- 7 8 IOWA 72 31238
- 9 0 IOWA 72 20586
- 7 IOWA 72 129166
- 2 3 IOWA 75 BJV681
- 5 5 IOWA 75 76 DGF786
- 7 8 IOWA 75 77 FQB020
- 7 IOWA 75 78 AIJ771
- IOWA 79 JIM 100 CLAY
- IOWA 79 CNE 761 HANCOCK
- IOWA 79 DJB 375 LEE 80
- IOWA 79 ALK 182 BLACK HAWK 81
- IOWA 79 FOX 799 POLK 82
- IOWA 79 GFY 566 SCOTT 83
- IOWA 79 BUP 090 DEC DES MOINES 84
- IOWA 79 BUR 613 OCT DES MOINES 85
- IOWA 86 MVH 523 DES MOINES
- IOWA 86 MWC 635 DES MOINES 87

IOWA

PRE-STATES

Iowa state law called for vehicle registration in 1904, and from then until mid-1911, owners were responsible for providing their own plates. The vast majority of these early plates were leather pads with aluminum characters attached.

SLOGANS

The 1953 base carried the slogan *THE CORN STATE*.

GRAPHICS

No graphic elements have been used in the history of general issue Iowa plates, though a couple of recent optional issues make full use of them.

OTHER FEATURES

In 1916 an undated plate was introduced in order to save metal during World War I. This plate was used through 1918. In 1949 the plates were made of "waffled" aluminum to lend strength to the plates. As an experiment, the 1979 plates were made in two distinct ways. Half the counties were issued plates which were reflectorized and "debossed." The other half received embossed plates with reflectorization only on the raised areas. Since 1911, all Iowa plates have been manufactured in Anamosa, Iowa, at the Men's Reformatory.

FIRST YEAR OF ISSUE
1911

UNDATED ISSUES
1916-1918 plate

PORCELAINS
None

WINDSHIELD STICKERS
1943, 1944, 1945 (the 1945 was used in conjunction with the 1945 rear plate).

METAL DATE TABS
1948, 1951, 1954, 1955, 1957

KANSAS

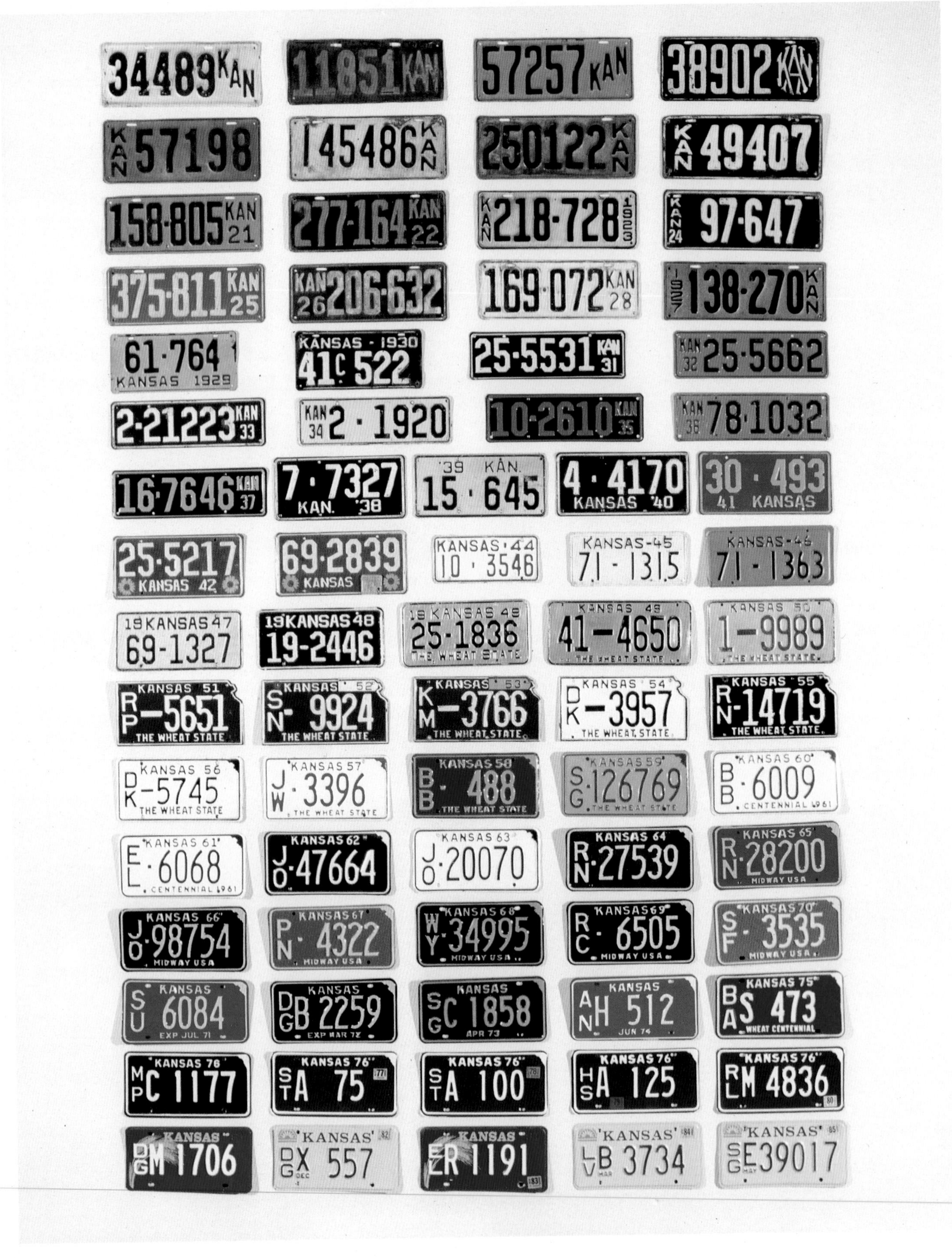

KANSAS

PRE-STATES

As early as 1904, local city and county jurisdictions were registering vehicles. Some authorities issued porcelain plates, while others required registrants to make their own plates. Many examples exist today, in a variety of designs and colors, including porcelains from Great Bend, Girard, Kansas City and Wichita, plus leathers from Manhattan and Wellington.

SLOGANS

The plates from 1949 through 1959 proclaimed Kansas *THE WHEAT STATE*. The 1960 and 1961 plates marked 100 years of statehood by having *CENTENNIAL 1961* along the bottom. Between 1965 and 1970, the slogan read *MIDWAY, U.S.A.* Some of the 1974 issues and all of the 1975 issues had the slogan *WHEAT CENTENNIAL* along the bottom of the plate.

GRAPHICS

The 1942 base had colorful sunflower decals in each of the upper corners. The plates from 1951 through 1955 were die cut in the shape of the state. Even the 1952 and 1953 date tabs were cut to fit the upper right corner of the plate and thus the upper right corner of the state itself. In 1956, faced with United States government standardization of all plates to a uniform 6" X 12", Kansas kept their unique design by embossing the upper right corner to resemble that corner of the state. This continued through the 1976 base, which was validated through 1980 by means of stickers. The 1981 base had screened stalks of wheat to the left of the plate. The 1983 base, which continued through use of stickers through 1988, had a stylized, screened sunflower at the upper left corner. The 1989 base marked the return of the sheaf of wheat, this time screened across the center of the plate. This base is still in use as of 1993. The state name was screened in a curious style, too. The oddly shaped characters proved difficult to read for some and were modified with a more legible style by means of a sticker provided later to cover the original.

OTHER FEATURES

Perhaps Kansas's most interesting feature is the way its first eight undated issues were designed. The date may be identified by two means. The first way is by the colors of the plate, which differed each year. However, identification by color can be rendered useless if the paint is rusted off, or if the plate has been repainted. That leaves only the second method, which is by noting the shape and location of the *KAN* abbreviation. These abbreviations ranged from a circular monogram-style logo to block-print letters, at either the left or right of the plates. Briefly, this method can be stated as follows:

1913 – *KAN* is diagonally downward	1917 – *KAN* vertically down the left side
1914 – *KAN* horizontal but with the *A* slightly higher than the other letters	1918 – *KAN* vertically down the right side
1915 – *KAN* diagonally upwards	1919 – *KAN* vertically down the right side
1916 – *KAN* overlapped and rounded almost into a ball	1920 – *KAN* vertically down the left side

When it comes to determining the 1917 from the 1920 and the 1918 from the 1919, the colors are the most reliable way to determine the correct years of issue.

FIRST YEAR OF ISSUE
1913

UNDATED ISSUES
1913, 1914, 1915, 1916, 1917, 1918, 1919, 1920

PORCELAINS
None

WINDSHIELD STICKERS
None

METAL DATE TABS
1943, 1952, 1953

KENTUCKY

KENTUCKY

PRE-STATES

An early 1904 law in Kentucky pertains to motor vehicles but does not provide for any registration. It was more concerned with not frightening the horses than with anything else! Meanwhile, city issues were taking up the slack, and porcelain, brass and other plates are known to have survived from such cities as Covington, Lexington, Louisville, Newport and Paducah.

SLOGANS

The rear plates of the 1929 and 1930 issues had *FOR PROGRESS* on them. Beginning in 1951, the word *TOUR* was placed before the state name. This brief recommendation continued through the 1957 issue. The 1988 base introduced the slogan *THE BLUEGRASS STATE*, and this base continues in use through 1993.

GRAPHICS

Kentucky's only graphic plate was the 1988 base, still in use as of 1993. It features a silk-screened view of Churchill Downs across the top and two racehorses at the center of the plate.

<table>
<tr><td>FIRST YEAR OF ISSUE
1910</td></tr>
<tr><td>UNDATED ISSUES
1910, 1911, 1912, 1913</td></tr>
<tr><td>PORCELAINS
1910, 1911, 1912, 1913</td></tr>
<tr><td>WINDSHIELD STICKERS
1943, 1945, 1947, 1952</td></tr>
<tr><td>METAL DATE TABS
None</td></tr>
</table>

OTHER FEATURES

The early years of Kentucky state-issued plates remain a mystery after all these years. It is surely the biggest puzzle facing serious students of United States plate history. Though we know the law went into effect in 1910, we do not know the details of the law. Specifically, the meaning of the mysterious letters *B, L, M* and *G*, which appear in the lower right corner of these plates, has been lost. Theories abound as to their meaning, from a guess that the *B* and *G* represent the last names of two early state officials (a Secretary of State named Bruner and an Attorney General named Garnett), to the theory that *L* and *M* stand for 1912 and 1913—the 12th and 13th letters of the alphabet, to the suggestion that the letters stand for cities in Kentucky such as Bowling Green, Louisville, etc. Unfortunately, none of these theories hold true for all four letters. From circumstantial evidence centering around the way many plates were found plus a lot of hard research, it seems likely that *B, L, M* and *G* were issued in that order around 1910, 1911, 1912 and 1913, not coinciding with the calendar year. Apparently, the key lawbooks are misplaced or missing entirely from the state records. The entire collecting community would be indebted to anyone who could solve this mystery.

Front and rear plates differed in the years 1929 to 1932. The front 1929 and 1930 plates had the county name, while the rear said *FOR PROGRESS* in the same place. For the 1931 and 1932 plates, the front plates showed the county name, while the rear plates said *KENTUCKY*. Because of the staggered monthly registration system, the 1978 sticker was issued only to those vehicles whose plates came up for renewal in December of 1978, thus creating a modern rarity—a 1978 Kentucky sticker.

1910

This plate is not included in the display on the opposite page.

LOUISIANA

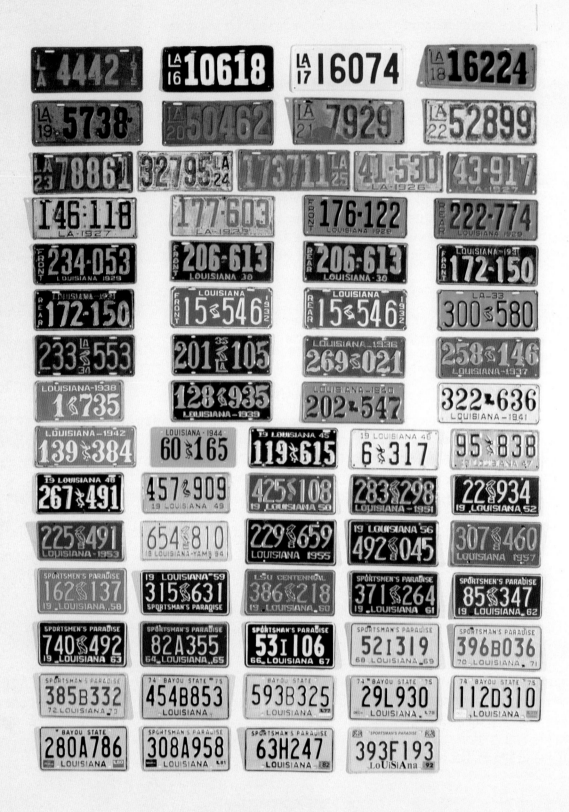

LOUISIANA

PRE-STATES

Cities in Louisiana had the authority to register vehicles as early as 1903, and the earliest city plates known are leathers from New Orleans and Shreveport. Porcelains became the rule later, and examples are known from Alexandria, Monroe, New Orleans, Shreveport and even Houma, a small town near the Gulf of Mexico.

SLOGANS

In 1954, the word *YAMS* appeared on the plates, perhaps a direct challenge to the Idaho potato! The 1958 and 1959 plates carried the slogan *SPORTSMEN'S PARADISE*. The year 1960 saw the commemoration of the *LSU CENTENNIAL*. *SPORTSMEN'S PARADISE* appeared again on the 1961 issue and remained through the 1972/1973 issue. The 1974 and 1977 bases both had the slogan *BAYOU STATE* on them, but the 1980 base saw a return to *SPORTSMEN'S PARADISE* again, and that has continued through the 1984, 1989 and 1993 bases as well.

FIRST YEAR OF ISSUE
1915

UNDATED ISSUES
None

PORCELAINS
None

WINDSHIELD STICKERS
1943

METAL DATE TABS
None

GRAPHICS

A pelican appeared on the 1932 issue. Resting comfortably in the center of the plate, it remained through 1939. In 1940 and 1941, the state outline was embossed in place of the pelican (could he have flown south?), but the 1942 issue saw the pelican return, remaining on each plate through 1963. The pelican was always embossed, with the exception of the 1950 plate, which used a full-color pelican decal at the center. In 1989, the first screened graphic Louisiana plate was issued. This plate depicted a mother pelican on her nest with her young at both upper corners. The state name is positioned along the bottom of the plate in red, but the letters *U-S-A* within the state name are blue and slightly larger. The 1993 base has already earned the nickname "the Lipstick Plate" because the state name is written in script along the top in red, as if done in bright red lipstick, graffiti style.

OTHER FEATURES

In a unique series, the plates dated from 1922 through 1929 were issued in two sets of colors: one for vehicles with up to 23 horsepower, and the other for vehicles with over 23 horsepower. Plates issued from 1929 through 1932 carried *FRONT* and *REAR* designations. The 1944 plate was made of fiberboard.

MAINE

6426 MAINE	3657 MAINE	1085 MAINE	1964 MAINE 1914	1048 MAINE 1915
18747 MAINE 1916	28-955 MAINE 1917	12-029 MAINE 1918	47-432 MAINE 1919	29-803 MAINE 1920
1-118 MAINE 1921	1-818 MAINE 1923	1-118 MAINE 1922	7-647 MAINE 1924	1-818 MAINE 1925
	6-398 MAINE 1926	1-818 MAINE 1927		
90-406 MAINE 1928	1-818 MAINE 1929	1-818 MAINE 1930	29-847 MAINE 1931	40-855 MAINE 1932
	114-730 MAINE 1933			
DT 30 MAINE '34	CK 884 MAINE '35	23-111 MAINE 1936 VACATIONLAND	146-327 MAINE 1937 VACATIONLAND	17-296 MAINE 1938 VACATIONLAND
	110-696 MAINE 1939 VACATIONLAND			
25-192 MAINE 1940 VACATIONLAND	76-660 MAINE 1941 VACATIONLAND	1-133 MAINE 1942 VACATIONLAND	115-755 MAINE 1944 VACATIONLAND	5-579 MAINE 1945 VACATIONLAND
	74-968 MAINE 1946 VACATIONLAND			
5-121 MAINE 1948 VACATIONLAND	38-569 MAINE VACATIONLAND	74-490 MAINE VACATIONLAND	23-365 MAINE VACATIONLAND	74-490 MAINE VACATIONLAND
	245-329 MAINE VACATIONLAND			
333-936 MAINE VACATIONLAND	296-387 MAINE VACATIONLAND	78-531 MAINE VACATIONLAND	274-505 MAINE VACATIONLAND	12-409 MAINE VACATIONLAND
202-716 MAINE VACATIONLAND	205-336 MAINE VACATIONLAND	201-393 MAINE VACATIONLAND	347-143 MAINE VACATIONLAND	466-135 MAINE VACATIONLAND
460-000 MAINE VACATIONLAND	460-000 MAINE VACATIONLAND	541-236 MAINE VACATIONLAND	562-518 MAINE VACATIONLAND	364-032 MAINE VACATIONLAND
403-594 MAINE VACATIONLAND	484-355 MAINE VACATIONLAND	562-927 MAINE VACATIONLAND	554-169 MAINE VACATIONLAND	700-056 MAINE VACATIONLAND
176-364 MAINE 74 VACATIONLAND	345-328 MAINE 74 VACATIONLAND	140-197 MAINE 74 VACATIONLAND	602-012 MAINE VACATIONLAND	782-844 MAINE VACATIONLAND
965-140 MAINE VACATIONLAND	77309 A MAINE	18852 C MAINE VACATIONLAND	45609 B MAINE VACATIONLAND	58397 E MAINE VACATIONLAND
42532 E MAINE VACATIONLAND	53898 G MAINE VACATIONLAND	49480 K MAINE VACATIONLAND	86365 K MAINE VACATIONLAND	81927 R MAINE AUG Vacationland 88

MAINE

PRE-STATES

Like its New England neighbors, the state of Maine was quick to pass a law mandating the registration of vehicles and the issuance of license plates. For this reason, no pre-state plates from Maine are known.

SLOGANS

Beginning in 1936, the word *VACATIONLAND* appeared along the bottom of Maine's plates, and has remained there consistently through 1993.

GRAPHICS

After 82 years of "no frills," the 1987 base was introduced, and the contrast was dramatic. A pinkish-red lobster was screened onto the center of this new plate, marking the first appearance of a crustacean on any plate *anywhere*!

OTHER FEATURES

The original 1905 plate was intended to remain valid for the life of the vehicle. However, by 1911 it became apparent that this plate could not last indefinitely, so a new plate was issued in 1912. Some of the 1916 plates bear a maker's mark on the reverse: the *S.G. Adams Company, St. Louis, MO*. Interestingly, the S.G. Adams Company is still in existence today, though they no longer manufacture plates. A few plates in 1946 and many of the 1948 plates were made of solid brass. This was actually done to save money, for at the time, brass plates were less expensive to manufacture than steel plates. However, the brass plates also proved too expensive to manufacture, and late in the production run of 1948 plates (they were used through 1949), a switch to aluminum was made.

FIRST YEAR OF ISSUE
1905
UNDATED ISSUES
1905-1911, 1912, 1913
PORCELAINS
1905-1911, 1912, 1913, 1914, 1915
WINDSHIELD STICKERS
1943, 1947
METAL DATE TABS
1949, 1950, 1951, 1952, 1953, 1954, 1955, 1957, 1958, 1959, 1960, 1961, 1963, 1964, 1965, 1966, 1967

MARYLAND

MARYLAND

PRE-STATES

From 1904, when Maryland's first motor vehicle regulations went into effect, until 1910, when the first general issue of plates took place, about 9,000 vehicles were registered. The early automobile owners were responsible for securing their own plates. Many varieties of early plate-making are exhibited on surviving examples of Maryland pre-states. These types include wooden plates and metal kit plates, while some registration numbers were painted directly onto the vehicles. The most common types, however, are leather and porcelain.

SLOGANS

In 1934, Maryland celebrated its *TERCENTENARY* (three hundred years of statehood) by using the word on their plates. The issues between 3/31/42 and 3/31/47 implored motorists to *DRIVE CAREFULLY*.

GRAPHICS

It took until 1986 for Maryland to "go graphic" with a general issue plate, but that issue, still in use as of 1993, has a colorful state crest at center.

OTHER FEATURES

The 1910 plate is made of a particularly thin metal, and was lightly embossed by hammering the plate over wooden dies. This manufacturing process produced one of the most primitive of all state issues and has made finding a fine example of a 1910 Maryland plate a real challenge! In the early years, Maryland had no reciprocity laws with other states, and given the closeness to both Washington, D.C. and Virginia, many cars were seen wearing all three plates simultaneously. It took until 1923 for these entities to finally agree to reciprocity.

FIRST YEAR OF ISSUE
1910

UNDATED ISSUES
1976, 1981

PORCELAINS
1911, 1912, 1913, 1914

WINDSHIELD STICKERS
None

METAL DATE TABS
3/31/43, 3/31/44, 3/31/46, 3/31/47, 1949, 1950, 1951, March 1953

The 1980 "Bicentennial" plate is an optional issue. The 1985 and 1986 "350th Anniversary" plates are also optional issues.

MASSACHUSETTS

MASSACHUSETTS

PRE-STATES

Massachusetts was the first state to issue actual plates to motorists, and thus if any types of plates existed before 1903, there is no written record of such activity, nor any surviving examples.

SLOGANS

In 1988, the first fully graphic base in Massachusetts also carried the only slogan ever to be used on Massachusetts plates. *THE SPIRIT OF AMERICA* appeared along the bottom of the plate.

GRAPHICS

The 1928 issue had an embossed codfish on the bottom of the plate. The 1988 base had both the state name and the slogan screened onto the plate in an attractive red "semi-script."

OTHER FEATURES

FIRST YEAR OF ISSUE
1903
UNDATED ISSUES
1903-1907, 1967
PORCELAINS
1903-1907, 1908, 1909, 1910, 1911, 1912, 1913, 1914, 1915
WINDSHIELD STICKERS
1943, 1944, 1950, 1952, 1954, 1956, 1958, 1960, 1962, 1965, 1968, 1969
METAL DATE TABS
None

The first-issue Massachusetts plate displayed the words *MASS AUTOMOBILE REGISTER* along the top. The 1928 plate carries a wonderful story with it. The codfish at the bottom was meant to promote the fact that commercial fishing was a big part of the Massachusetts economy. However, when the plates were issued, the fishermen were horrified to discover that the fish was swimming *away* from the word *MASS*! Being a superstitious lot, they believed that it symbolized bad luck and that it was an omen of poor fishing to come. They raised enough concerns that the fish was removed from the 1929 general issue. However, the fish remained on the 1929 commercial plates, but with the design modified so the fish was now swimming *towards MASS*. This change made everyone happy, with the possible exception of the fish. In an attempt to save steel, no plates were manufactured for new registrants in 1943. Instead, the leftover maroon 1942 plates were painted green and issued to new registrants along with a windshield sticker for 1943. The 1944 windshield sticker revalidated both plates.

MICHIGAN

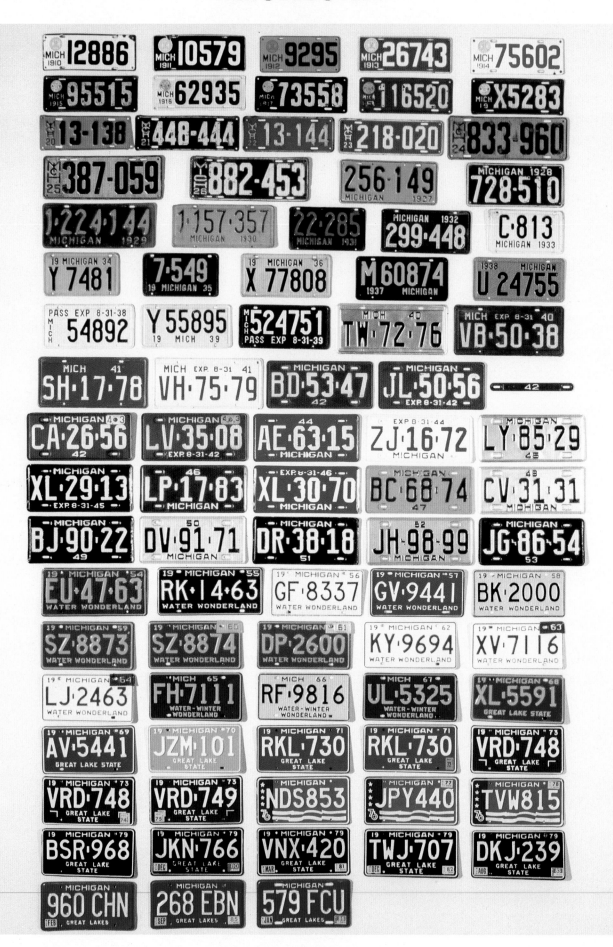

MICHIGAN

PRE-STATES

The Detroit City Council passed legislation to register motor vehicles in 1903, by which time many automobile manufacturers in the area were beginning to establish themselves in the industry. City registrations in Michigan continued until 1905, when the first state laws went into effect. Oddly, there is little evidence of other city registrations for this period, though several Detroit issues survive today, including a leather plate #939, complete with a small plaque attached which reads, "Detroit automobile license made by Automobile Equipment Co., Detroit, Mich." This plate would have been a 1904 issue. In 1905, the state took over the registration of motor vehicles, but the plates were still owner-provided. By the end of 1909, about 12,000 vehicles had been registered. Most surviving plates are made of leather, though other types, especially kit plates, are well known to collectors.

SLOGANS

Beginning with the 1954 plate, Michigan used the slogan *WATER WONDERLAND* on all issues through 1964. The 1965, 1966 and 1967 plates were changed to read *WATER WINTER WONDERLAND. GREAT LAKES STATE* was used on the 1968 plates and continued through 1975. After a break for the Bicentennial during which no slogan was used, that slogan was picked up again and used from 1979 through 1983. The new undated 1983 base, made to expire in 1984, had the words *GREAT LAKES* and, with the aid of expiration stickers, is still in use in 1993.

GRAPHICS

The Bicentennial base, used from 1976 through 1978, had a stylized *76* accompanied by stars and stripes in a red, white and blue color scheme.

OTHER FEATURES

In order to provide an option to those drivers unable to afford to register their vehicles for a full year because of lingering effects of the Great Depression, half-year plates were introduced in 1938, continuing each year through 1946. In 1942, there was an option to extend the half-year plate to a full year through the use of a date strip.

FIRST YEAR OF ISSUE
1910

UNDATED ISSUES
The base introduced in 1983, made to expire in 1984, was undated.

PORCELAINS
1910, 1911, 1912, 1913, 1914

WINDSHIELD STICKERS
None

METAL DATE TABS
1942 half-year date strip (made to extend the 1942 half-year plate to a full year), 1943 tabs for both full and half-year issues, 1960, 1961, 1963, 1964

MINNESOTA

MINN 6136 1909
6456 1910
MINN 9987 1911
MINN 31765
108956
MINN 216584 1918 1919 1920
MINN 327628 1920
A 21 5-849 MINN
A 22 161-112 MINN
B 23 74-494 MINN
MINN 101-323 B 24
A 25 51-675 MINN
B 26 60-142 MINN
A 27 179-996 MINN
A 28 144-899 MINN
B 29 22-963 MINN
B 30 193-794 MINN
B 31 282-558 MINN
B 32 106-277 MINN
B 33 177-552 MINN
B 34 353-397 MINN
B 35 492-365 MINN
B 36 539-711 MINN
B 37 452-045 MINN
B 38 358-046 MINN
B 39 643-552 MINN
702-342 MINNESOTA 1940
408-993 MINNESOTA 1941
180-471 MINNESOTA 1942
737-141 MINNESOTA 1943
208-912 MINNESOTA 1944
554-855 MINNESOTA 1945
287-168 MINNESOTA 1946
103-635 MINNESOTA 1947
790-361 MINNESOTA 1948
MINNESOTA 738-543 1949 CENTENNIAL 1949
10,000 LAKES 728-895 19 MINNESOTA 50
10,000 LAKES 192-510 19 MINNESOTA 51
10,000 LAKES 14-612 19 MINNESOTA 52
10,000 LAKES 764-714 19 MINNESOTA 53
10,000 LAKES 63-832 19 MINNESOTA 54
"10,000 LAKES" CE 6800 19 MINNESOTA 55
10,000 LAKES 3G 4752 19 MINNESOTA 56
10,000 LAKES 57 4Y 3241 MINNESOTA
10,000 LAKES M 1387 19 MINNESOTA 58
10,000 LAKES 59 4Z 5948 MINNESOTA
10,000 LAKES 4X 9250 19 MINNESOTA 60
10,000 LAKES 4X 9250 19 MINNESOTA 61
10,000 LAKES MA 1814 19 MINNESOTA 62
10,000 LAKES 1M 9115 19 MINNESOTA 63
10,000 LAKES MU 3330 19 MINNESOTA 64
10,000 LAKES 7EG 488 19 MINNESOTA 65
10,000 LAKES MDD 259 19 MINNESOTA 65
10,000 LAKES 3VG 885 19 MINNESOTA 65
10,000 LAKES 2DO 270 19 MINNESOTA 68
10,000 LAKES 4ED 556 19 MINNESOTA 68
10,000 LAKES 5EK 426 19 MINNESOTA 68
10,000 LAKES 7DR 473 19 MINNESOTA 71
10,000 LAKES 72 7HQ 604 19 MINNESOTA 71
10,000 LAKES 73 7DR 514 19 MINNESOTA 71
19 10,000 LAKES 74 GX 2173 MINNESOTA
19 10,000 LAKES 74 BN 2420 MAR MINNESOTA 75
19 10,000 LAKES 74 PN 8260 JUL MINNESOTA 76
19 10,000 LAKES 74 GS 9846 JUN MINNESOTA 77
Minnesota DJZ 413 JUL 10000 lakes 78
MINNESOTA AZV 019 SEP 10,000 LAKES 78
Minnesota EJZ 199 APR 10000 lakes 79
Minnesota EQZ 403 APR 10000 lakes 80
Minnesota EPL 805 MAR 10000 lakes 81
Minnesota FJP 995 JUL 10000 lakes 82
Minnesota LFT 472 APR 10000 lakes 83
Minnesota MOD 425 APR 10000 lakes
Minnesota NSD 308 DEC 10000 lakes
Minnesota LHH 921 MAR 10000 lakes
Explore Minnesota 685 BIN DEC 10,000 lakes 87
Explore Minnesota 934 BIP NOV 10,000 lakes
Explore Minnesota 450 AVM APR 10,000 lakes
Explore Minnesota 752 FGZ JUN 10,000 lakes

MINNESOTA

PRE-STATES

The original authority to register automobiles in Minnesota was vested in the state boiler inspectors! The numbers they issued, beginning in 1903, were to be painted on the body of the vehicle to be registered. This authority was shared with local city authorities, and it appears that the vehicle owner had his choice of where to register. In 1905, full authority was turned over to local city clerks, and a dated 1908 Minneapolis plate exists today. It is made of metal characters riveted to a steel base.

SLOGANS

In 1949, the State Centennial was commemorated on Minnesota plates with the slogan *1849-CENTENNIAL-1949* along the bottom. In 1950, the slogan *10,000 LAKES* was introduced, and it has been in use on all issues to date. In 1987, the word *EXPLORE* was placed in front of the state name, and this base remains in use as of 1993.

FIRST YEAR OF ISSUE
1909

UNDATED ISSUES
None

PORCELAINS
1911

WINDSHIELD STICKERS
None

METAL DATE TABS
1943, 1957, 1959, 1961, 1963, 1964

GRAPHICS

The 1978 graphic base depicted a lake scene with a canoe being paddled serenely through the middle. The state shape was embossed between the letters and numbers. While this base has undergone modifications over the years, all graphic elements have been retained and have been used steadily from 1978 through 1993.

OTHER FEATURES

The 1912-1913-1914 plate is unusual in that while the dates were embossed, they remained unpainted, while the other embossed areas were painted black. It is unusual to see all three years of usage noted on a three-year plate, but that is exactly what was done on the 1912-1913-1914, 1915-1916-1917 and 1918-1919-1920 issues. Further, the dated 1920 base, having been issued to only about 1,000 vehicles at the very end of 1920, is a rare plate indeed! The dies used from 1935 through 1954 have a unique look to them and have not been seen elsewhere. The 1949 plates were made of "waffle" aluminum.

MISSISSIPPI

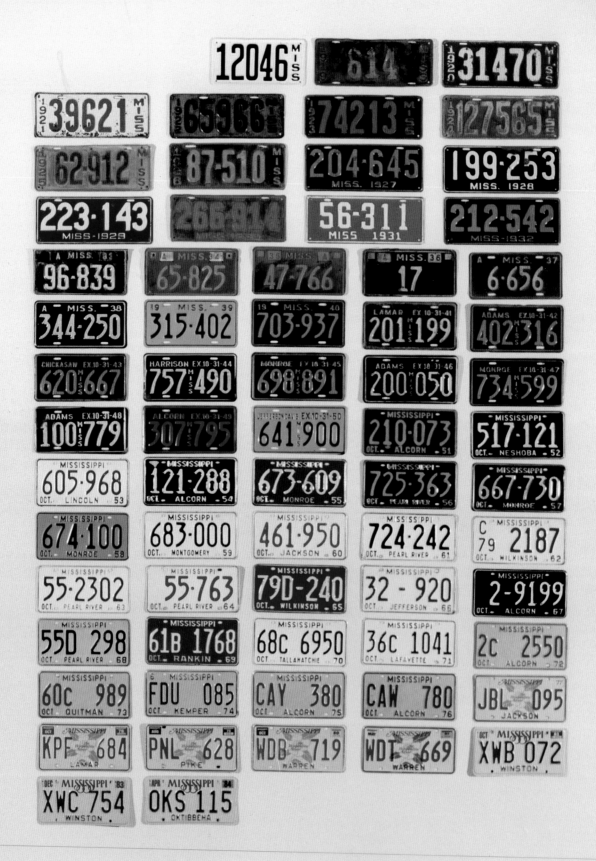

MISSISSIPPI

PRE-STATES

While it seems that there should have been some city or state issues in Mississippi prior to 1912, almost nothing has surfaced. A leather plate with brass characters attached, which reads, *MISS 1907* surfaced in California years ago, and while that seems to fill the bill, no documentation exists. Now, ALPCA archivist Dr. Roy Klotz has just informed me of a new find—a porcelain plate dated 1911 that has the letters *MISS* vertically along the right side of the plate. Nothing like this has been reported to date, but circumstantially, this would seem to be a state-issued number from before the 1912 law took effect.

SLOGANS

With the 1977 issue, the slogan *HOSPITALITY STATE* was added to the Mississippi plates. This slogan continued in use until the base was replaced in 1981.

FIRST YEAR OF ISSUE
1912
UNDATED ISSUES
1914-1918
PORCELAINS
None
WINDSHIELD STICKERS
None
METAL DATE TABS
None

GRAPHICS

The 1977 issue had a silk-screened magnolia at the center of the plate that was used until the base was replaced in 1981. The 1981 issue had the state name screened across the top in a very stylized way with the *S*'s enlarged and intertwined. In 1992, a new base was issued with the same graphics as the 1981 base, but with a different color scheme.

OTHER FEATURES

The discovery, in 1984, of a previously unknown state-issued license plate virtually rocked the plate-collecting community. Popular theory held that an undated 1913-1918 plate followed the dated 1912 first issue. Dr. Klotz's discovery of a dated 1913 Mississippi plate in Jackson, MS, done in the exact style of the 1912, sent collectors and researchers dashing back to the drawing board. It also took our want lists one step in the wrong direction! Two more examples of this plate, discovered within a year, tended to further substantiate this find. It represents the only discovery of an "unknown" state-issued plate since ALPCA was founded in 1954!

From 1933 through 1936, Mississippi used metal locking date strips to denote the date and weight class. These strips could not be removed without obliterating the plate, thus ensuring against theft or improper use. With the 1941 issue, county names appeared on the plates, and this practice continues as of 1993.

1912

1913

These plates are not included in the display on the opposite page.

MISSOURI

MISSOURI

PRE-STATES

In the early years of motoring in Missouri, the cities and counties were so quick to jump on the licensing (thus taxing) bandwagon that the state actually passed a declaration giving the responsibility to them! In 1907, the state came to its senses and required all vehicles to register with them as well. Thus, a dual registration system was created that required motorists to display both plates simultaneously. The earliest city and county examples known were from city of St. Louis and St. Louis County, as early as 1904, and yearly porcelains at that. The state-issued numbers spawned the usual array of homemade plates, with examples surviving in leather, steel, wood and brass, all with the abbreviation *MO* following the numbers.

SLOGANS

To celebrate the U.S. Bicentennial, the 1976 plate had the slogan *200 YEARS* on it. Beginning with the 1980 issue, the slogan *SHOW ME STATE* appeared, and this base is still in use as of 1993.

> **FIRST YEAR OF ISSUE**
> 1911
>
> **UNDATED ISSUES**
> None
>
> **PORCELAINS**
> None
>
> **WINDSHIELD STICKERS**
> None
>
> **METAL DATE TABS**
> 1943 date strip, 1949, 1950, 1951, 1952, 1953

GRAPHICS

The 1976 Bicentennial motif with stylized stripes surrounding the date *76* is the only graphic used in Missouri plate history.

OTHER FEATURES

The 1942 plates were revalidated with a 1943 metal date strip. However, as 1943 neared an end, the state ran out of 1942 plates, and for the duration of the year, a soybean-based fiberboard plate identical to the 1942 metal plate was used. No comment from the goats!

MONTANA

MONTANA

PRE-STATES

In a sparsely populated Western state like Montana, the number of early vehicles was such that registering them was likely not the high priority it would have been in the more densely populated Eastern states. Therefore, it is not surprising that Montana did not require motorists to register their vehicles until a relatively late 1913. Oddly, a couple of plates dated 1912 have surfaced, but these seem not to have been in keeping with any existing law. Additionally, city plates for Butte and Missoula are known, but the dates of these issues have not been determined. The law was modified in 1915, and while that year's plates could still be owner-made, the design restrictions were tightened considerably, and since the state made plates available at 75¢ each, it appears that the majority of motorists chose this option.

FIRST YEAR OF ISSUE
1915
UNDATED ISSUES
None
PORCELAINS
None
WINDSHIELD STICKERS
1943, 1952
METAL DATE TABS
1943, 1954, 1956, 1958, 1960, 1961, 1962, 1964, 1965, 1966

SLOGANS

THE TREASURE STATE first appeared on the 1950 plate, remaining through 1956. After a brief vacation, this slogan returned on the 1963 base. From 1967 through 1975, *BIG SKY COUNTRY* was used along the top of the plates. *BIG SKY* appeared on the 1976 base, which was used until being phased out in 1991. The 1987 base commemorated the statehood Centennial with *100 YEARS* in the lower left corner. The 1991 base, still going strong as of 1993, reintroduced *BIG SKY*.

GRAPHICS

In 1933, the outline of the state first appeared on Montana plates, and with the exception of the 1957 issue, it has appeared ever since, either embossed or silk-screened. A small embossed steer head was used on the 1938 plate and has made a comeback on the 1973 and 1975 plates as well as the 1976 and 1991 bases. The 1976 base also had the stylized *76* Bicentennial logo as well as a small mountain scene. The 1987 base had a panoramic mountain outline across the top as well as a "Montana Centennial" logo inside the letter *O* of the state name. The 1991 base had a very colorful panoramic mountain outline across the top.

OTHER FEATURES

Though it is widely known that license plates are often made in state prison facilities, Montana chose to publicize that fact by having the words *PRISON MADE* stamped into the plate. This stamp first appeared in 1939 and was used on most, though not all, issues through 1962. The 1943 date tab was larger than most, measuring 2-3/4" x 5-3/4". It covered the extreme left side of the plate. The 1944 plate was made of soybean composition fiberboard. No comment from the *mountain* goats.

NEBRASKA

NEBRASKA

PRE-STATES

Early motor vehicle laws in Nebraska are difficult to track down today. Reports of statutes from both 1903 and 1905 are rumored, but hard evidence is scant. However, this state is a case where there is no shortage of physical evidence, and a relatively large number of early Nebraska pre-states survive today. Made most often from metal kits or of leather, surviving examples have numbers as high as 60,000. Most of these plates have the letters *NEB* running vertically to the right of the number.

SLOGANS

THE BEEF STATE first appeared on the 1956 issue and continued through the 1965 issue. In 1966, the state *CENTENNIAL* was noted across the top of the plates and remained until this base was replaced at the end of 1968. In 1969, *1776-BICENTENNIAL-1976* was screened across the bottom of the plate in keeping with the country's 200th birthday celebration, and remained until the base was replaced in 1984.

FIRST YEAR OF ISSUE
1915

UNDATED ISSUES
1962, 1982

PORCELAINS
None

WINDSHIELD STICKERS
None

METAL DATE TABS
1920, 1943, 1944, 1947,
1953, 1959

GRAPHICS

For the 1940 and 1941 issues, an embossed likeness of the state capitol in Lincoln was used on the plates. The 1976 Bicentennial issue was the first screened issue in Nebraska, and showed a covered wagon at upper left and the head of an Indian in full headdress at upper right. This graphic continued, with validation stickers, through 1984. The 1987 base had the state name in a stylized script, surrounded by a yellow-orange skyscape with an orange sun and red ribbon-like lines emanating left and right from the state name, adding a horizon-like look. This graphic continued until the 1989 base was introduced, with a design much like the 1987 base, but with a blue sky and a burnt-orange horizon.

OTHER FEATURES

The 1920 tab was a large affair, measuring 3-1/2" x 4-3/4", covering most of the right side of the 1919 plate. An odd feature of this state is that the 1982 date sticker is undated! This unusual sticker came into use at a time when Nebraska was changing to a monthly staggered registration system, and while the month was abbreviated in large letters on these black on blue stickers, no date was shown.

NEVADA

NEVADA

PRE-STATES

Nevada is another one of those states where the best evidence of the early history is found in the plates which survive today. In 1913, the state began registering vehicles, issuing a small round dashboard disc carrying the number assigned to the vehicle. It was then up to the owner to provide the plates to match. Apparently, there was a factory in Carson City that made high quality properly embossed plates to order, and this is an area where Nevada differs from most states. Thus, a great many Nevada pre-states are well made, properly embossed plates. Today, a number of these dated, embossed 1913 Nevada plates survive, as well as a number of embossed but undated plates, believed to have been used in 1914 or 1915. These plates could be a logical extension of the numbers that began in the 1913 series. In addition to the embossed plates, there are surviving examples of flat plates, kit plates and porcelains. Further, one flat plate exists with *RENO* painted diagonally at the right of the number, and is about the only surviving evidence that the cities may have been involved with early Nevada registrations.

FIRST YEAR OF ISSUE
1916

UNDATED ISSUES
1916

PORCELAINS
None

WINDSHIELD STICKERS
None

METAL DATE TABS
1943, June 1964 (date strip)

SLOGANS

The June 1964 date strip commemorated 100 years of Nevada statehood with the legend *1864-NEVADA-1964* above the word *CENTENNIAL*. The 1983 graphic base introduced the slogan *THE SILVER STATE* along the bottom of the plate, and this base is still valid through 1993.

GRAPHICS

The 1983 issue, Nevada's first screened graphic, shows a rugged mountain scene ranging from desert terrain to snowcapped peaks, complete with a mountain goat! Interestingly, as the reflective sheeting was moved in relation to the steel base, revealing more or less of the design at the left side, it appears that the goat was roaming to different mountaintop locations in the scene. Foraging for Illinois soybean plates, no doubt!

OTHER FEATURES

The years from 1917 through 1922 showed a nice array of colors, all on flat plates. The years from 1923 through 1927 also had interesting colors, this time on debossed plates. The June 1964 date strip, which measures 2" x 12", was used to revalidate the 1961 base. This date strip could then itself be extended till year's end with a 1964 sticker, which interestingly was placed on the strip itself, not on the base.

NEW HAMPSHIRE

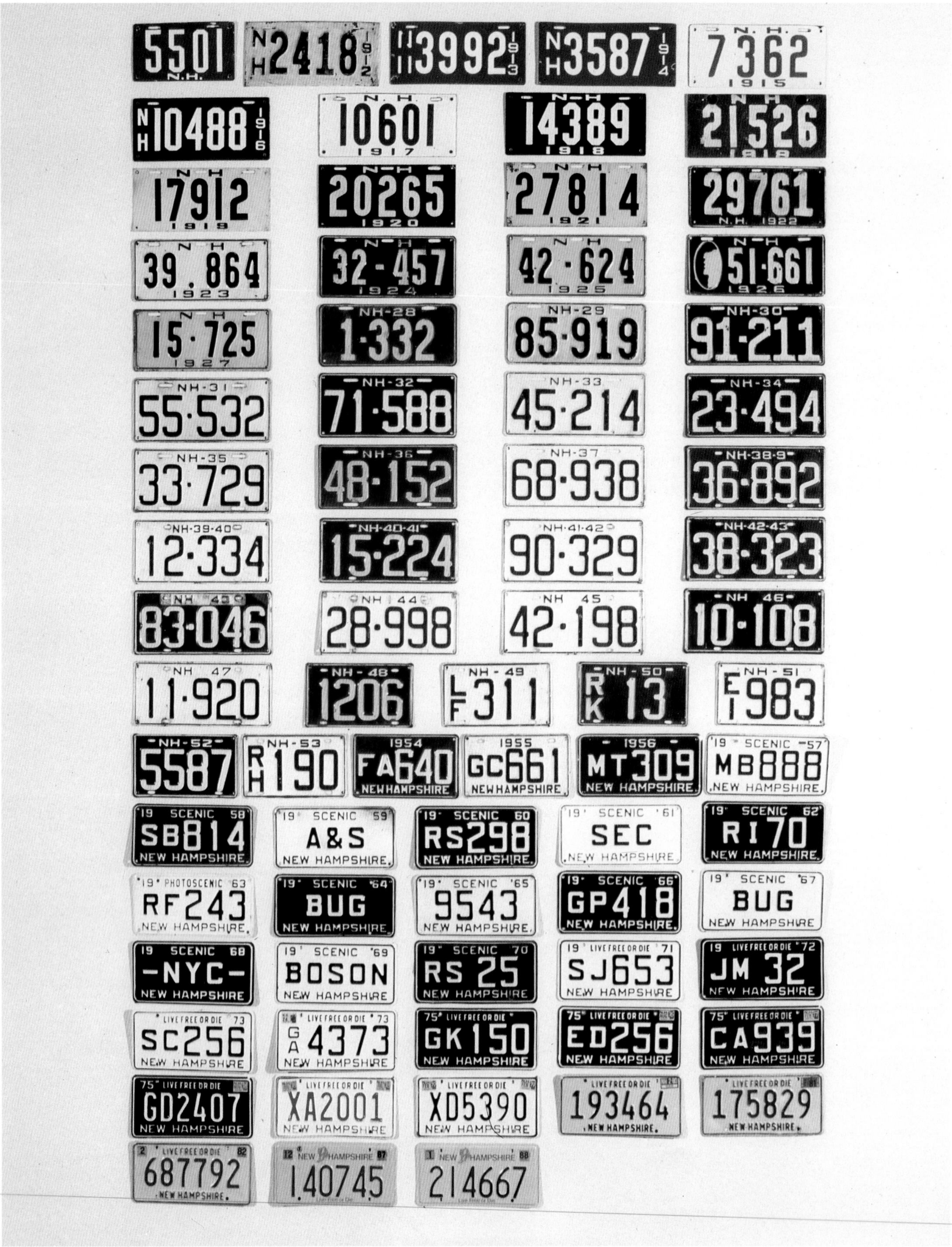

NEW HAMPSHIRE

PRE-STATES

Like other New England states, New Hampshire began to register vehicles and provide the plates to motorists quite early. Therefore, no pre-states are known from this state.

SLOGANS

In 1957, the word *SCENIC* was added to the top of the plates. For the 1963 issue, the word was changed to *PHOTOSCENIC*, but in 1964, it was again shortened to *SCENIC*, and remained that way on all plates through 1970. In 1971, a new slogan was introduced that caused a stir in some circles. Nevertheless, *LIVE FREE OR DIE* has appeared on every normal plate from 1971 through 1993.

GRAPHICS

In 1926, an illustration of The Old Man of the Mountains made its first appearance on New Hampshire plates. This illustration is of a natural rock formation in New Hampshire. When viewed from the proper angle, it resembles the profile of the face of an old man. Because the design so severely crowded the numbers, it was dropped after just this one year. However, the 1987 screened base provided a chance for this design to return, this time in a smaller size, tucked between the words *NEW* and *HAMPSHIRE*, where it resides through 1993.

OTHER FEATURES

In 1912, New Hampshire switched from the porcelain first issue to a steel embossed plate. Sadly, this plate was manufactured very poorly, and as a result, the paint literally fell off the plate almost as soon as it was mounted on the bumpers. This bad paint job caused the government to return to porcelain issues, followed by flat steel plates, and it was not until 1922 that New Hampshire was again willing to try an embossed plate. The *LIVE FREE OR DIE* slogan was actually challenged in court by a couple who felt offended by it and had covered it up on their plate. The United States Supreme Court finally ruled in 1977 that while the state had the right to choose this slogan, the citizens of the state were not compelled to display it!

FIRST YEAR OF ISSUE
1905

UNDATED ISSUES
1905-1911

PORCELAINS
1905-1911, 1913, 1914, 1915, 1916, 1917, 1918

WINDSHIELD STICKERS
None

METAL DATE TABS
1943 date strip

Note the missing crossbars in the letters *N* and *H* on the 1913 plate. This is a manufacturing flaw.

NEW JERSEY

NEW JERSEY

PRE-STATES

The state of New Jersey realized the benefits of motor vehicle registration early on, and in 1903, passed their first motor vehicle law. This foresight provided fertile ground for a proliferation of vehicles, each registered with the state and each given a number to be placed on homemade plates. The usual array of materials was used, with leather leading the pack, followed by kit plates, perforated metal, porcelain, etc. Over 30,000 vehicles were registered in 1906 and 1907 alone!

SLOGANS

The slogan *GARDEN STATE* first appeared on the 1959 base and has appeared on all bases through 1993.

GRAPHICS

The 1979 base had a dividing symbol between the letters and numbers which was embossed in the shape of the state. The background of the 1991 base has a subtle and attractive blending of straw-to-white color running from top to bottom.

FIRST YEAR OF ISSUE
1908

UNDATED ISSUES
1956 base, 1959 base, 1979 base, 1991 base

PORCELAINS
1909, 1910, 1911, 1912, 1913, 1914, 1915

WINDSHIELD STICKERS
Every year from 1956 to 1993

METAL DATE TABS
1943, 1953, 1954, 1955, 1956

OTHER FEATURES

The 1908 issue was a kit plate, though state-issued. It consisted of a metal base with crimped edges meant to accommodate flat painted metal panels. Each digit was assembled and mounted, along with a panel for the state abbreviation, date, and a maker's seal, ostensibly to reduce theft and abuse of the plate. The maker's seal was used on the porcelain plates as well, right through to their last issue in 1915.

NEW MEXICO

NEW MEXICO

TERRITORIALS

Like Arizona, New Mexico began registering vehicles just before the territory became a state. These early registrations produced what should more accurately be called "territorials" rather than "pre-states." Between 1905 and 1911, the New Mexico Territory did indeed require motorists to register their vehicles. Surviving plates of this period are extremely rare, the few known examples being made of metal or wood. One especially interesting survivor from this era is an early hand painted dealer plate. It says *DEALER'S LICENSE* on it, along with the dealer's name, *W.D. Newton*, and the number *14*.

SLOGANS

The slogan *SUNSHINE STATE* appeared on the 1932 issue, predating Florida's use of this slogan by fully 17 years! The 1940 plate celebrates the 400th anniversary of Coronado's expedition by using the slogan *CORONADO QUARTO CENTENNIAL* and the dates *1540-1940*. *THE LAND OF ENCHANTMENT* appeared on the 1941 issue and was used through 1951. For 1952, the *THE* was dropped from that slogan, and from then through 1993, *LAND OF ENCHANTMENT* has been used.

GRAPHICS

Beginning with the 1927 issue, the famous Zia sun sign has appeared on all New Mexico normal plates. Some years had the date inside the Zia sign, and if the plate number consisted of three or fewer digits, a Zia appeared on either side of the number. In 1991, turquoise-colored border trim was added to the yellow plates.

OTHER FEATURES

The 1920 porcelain base was revalidated through 1923 with three tabs. The 1921 tab was red and diamond-shaped. The 1922 tab was a silver octagon. The 1923 tab was a yellow six-pointed star. The 1925 plates had *FRONT* and *REAR* stamped on them respectively. The 1959 plates were revalidated with a metal tab that had a sticker on it.

FIRST YEAR OF ISSUE
1912

UNDATED ISSUES
1912-1913, 1961

PORCELAINS
1920, 1921, 1922, 1923

WINDSHIELD STICKERS
1943

METAL DATE TABS
1921, 1922, 1923, 1960

NEW YORK

28472 NY	72956 NY	61502 NY	71882 NY 1913
NY 1914 F142	NY 1915 20619	154-260 N.Y. 1916	B75-716 N.Y. 1917
N.Y. 1918 670-749	N.Y. 1919 239-844	710-847 N.Y. 1920	639-103 N.Y. 1921
495-552 N.Y. 1922	N.Y. 1923 184-638	1099354 N.Y. 1924	N.Y. 1925 5A-2878
3A-14-27 N.Y. 1926	NY27 1P-10-66	2P-61-44 NY28	H 8 884 NY 29
NY 30 E95-20	2B14-01 NY 31	NY 32 B-26-71	NY 33 2B19-99
2B27-99 NY 34	2H58-18 NY 35	NY 36 4B26-07	NY 37 3X27-20
N.Y. 38 4B57-54 NEW YORK WORLD'S FAIR 1939	NEW YORK WORLD'S FAIR 1939 9E80-90	10-F-4 NEW YORK WORLD'S FAIR 1940	8M78-74 NY 41
NY 42 3J39-05	NY 43 H-19-81	NY 44 X-57-20	NY 45 H-23-13
TX-173 NY 46	9Y66-59 NY 47	NY 48 2H55-47	NY 49 HD-277
NY 50 2B87-09	6Z60-19 NY-THE EMPIRE STATE-51	8D90-22 NY-THE EMPIRE STATE-52	67-89-B NY-THE EMPIRE STATE-53
67-90-B NY-THE EMPIRE STATE-54	NY-THE EMPIRE STATE-55 MV19 35	NY-THE EMPIRE STATE-56 LA47-55	7X-7440 NY-EMPIRE STATE-57

WV-9802 NY EMPIRE STATE-58	3D-8570 NY EMPIRE STATE-59	6118-NR NY EMPIRE STATE-60	537-KP NY EMPIRE STATE-61	6H-4341 NY EMPIRE STATE-62
NG-655 NY EMPIRE STATE-63	9F-5687 NY WORLD'S FAIR-64	FS-940 NY WORLD'S FAIR-64	2096-TP NEW YORK	7978-TG NEW YORK
7979-TG NEW YORK	7980-TG NEW YORK	7981-TG NEW YORK	7982-TG NEW YORK	7983-TG NEW YORK
7984-TG NEW YORK	7985-TG NEW YORK	536-TRB NEW YORK	UUF 376 NEW YORK	

NEW YORK

PRE-STATES

New York was the first state in the Union to require vehicle registrations, beginning on May 25, 1901. The original registration numbers consisted only of the owner's *initials*! These were most often done with metal house numbers on leather. By 1903, this system was becoming unworkable due to duplications, and the system was switched to numbers, which sufficed for the duration of the pre-state era. Most of the initial plates were natural aluminum on black, while most of the numerical plates were black on white. There are known examples of reversed colors in both cases. Virtually all known means of plate-making were used, and by 1910, the numbers reached 100,000, literally forcing the state into making their own plates beginning August 1 of that year.

SLOGANS

NEW YORK WORLD'S FAIR was promoted on the plates in 1938, 1939 and 1940. *EMPIRE STATE* first appeared on the 1951 plate and was used through 1963. The *WORLD'S FAIR* slogan returned for 1964 and 1965.

GRAPHICS

The only graphic used on New York plates is the Statue of Liberty on the current issue, which first appeared in mid-1986.

OTHER FEATURES

The 1910 plate had aluminum characters riveted to a steel background. The 1965 date sticker was actually "strip" shaped, measuring 1/2" x 3-1/2". Interestingly, the state name was abbreviated *NY* from 1910 through 1965. Thus, the state name was not spelled out in full until 1966.

FIRST YEAR OF ISSUE
1910

UNDATED ISSUES
1910, 1911, 1912,
1974 base, 1986 base

PORCELAINS
1912

WINDSHIELD STICKERS
Annual revalidation windshield stickers for the various bases began in 1974 and continues as of 1993.

METAL DATE TABS
1943 (date strip), 1949, 1952, 1954, 1956, 1959, 1961, 1963

NORTH CAROLINA

NORTH CAROLINA

PRE-STATES

The North Carolina state General Assembly passed legislation in 1909 requiring vehicles to display plates. The Secretary of State issued a registration disc to each motorist, and they were expected to acquire front and rear plates bearing the number from the disc. No city plates from the pre-state era are known, but a very few of the early state numbers survive, in leather or other early forms. One surviving plate has brass characters attached to a brass base.

SLOGANS

Some but not all of the 1954 plates carried the slogan *DRIVE SAFELY*. This admonition reappeared in 1956 and remained through 1963. In 1975, *FIRST IN FREEDOM* appeared on the plate, causing comment from some onlookers who questioned whether a state from the "Confederation" had legitimate claim to this slogan. The base was valid (along with later bases) into 1984, so it was seen on some vehicles until that time. The 1981 graphic base first introduced the slogan *FIRST IN FLIGHT*, and this base remains in use as of 1993.

FIRST YEAR OF ISSUE
1913
UNDATED ISSUES
None
PORCELAINS
June 30, 1913; June 30, 1914
June 30, 1915; June 30, 1916
WINDSHIELD STICKERS
None
METAL DATE TABS
1943

GRAPHICS

After experimenting with a logo-like *NC* abbreviation in the early years, the plates for 1939, 1940 and 1941 each had a rather fancy style of embossing the state name. This lettering was the extent of the graphic attempts by the state until the 1981 graphic base, which introduced a silk-screened likeness of the Wright brother' plane at Kitty Hawk.

OTHER FEATURES

The 1913 issue, which actually expired on June 30, 1913, was first issued in April of 1913, thus creating a plate used for only three months. The short life of this plate, combined with the fact that only new registrants received the plate in 1913 (all others kept their homemade plates) makes for one tough plate to collect today! In the early 1930s, a small, single-digit number appeared in a small box at the center of the plate. The meaning of this number is unclear today. The *FIRST IN FLIGHT* bases have been made with either a reflective or non-reflective background.

1913

This plate is not included in the display on the opposite page.

NORTH DAKOTA

NORTH DAKOTA

PRE-STATES

It seems that the registration of the earliest North Dakota plates was left to the cities. Reports of city plates as early as 1905 exist, and examples of leather, embossed metal, porcelain, etc. survive today. City-issued plates are verified from Bismark, Fargo, Minot, Northwood, Valley City and even Devil's Lake.

SLOGANS

The slogan *PEACE GARDEN STATE* refers to the Peace Garden, a 2,300 acre park that straddles the U.S.-Canadian border, celebrating the friendship between the two countries. It was first used on the 1956 plates and has been used on each issue since. In late 1987, the graphic base celebrating the 100th anniversary of statehood was issued, with the word *CENTENNIAL* near the top, the date *1889* in the lower left corner and *1989* in the right corner.

FIRST YEAR OF ISSUE
1911

UNDATED ISSUES
None

PORCELAINS
None

WINDSHIELD STICKERS
1943

METAL DATE TABS
1949 date strip, 1959, 1960, 1961

GRAPHICS

In 1984, the "Teddy Roosevelt" base was issued as an optional plate. It illustrates Theodore Roosevelt and the Rough Riders, along with the Stars and Stripes. These plates were used through 1987 with proper validation. The *CENTENNIAL* issue of 1987 has a fully graphic array of color with the screened background having varying shades of light blue and orange.

OTHER FEATURES

The 1911 issue was a flat steel plate, though with embossed edges. There was an embossed 1943 plate issued to new registrants who did not have a 1942 plate to revalidate with the "normal" 1943 windshield sticker. The 1943 plates began with numbers over 200,000, so as not to duplicate the 1942 numbers. In 1949, initial registrants were issued embossed dated 1949 plates. The dated 1949 plates and some of the 1950 plates were made of pressed aluminum with a "waffled" texture, to lend strength to the plates.

The 1985 "Teddy Roosevelt" plate shown is an optional issue.

OHIO

49 (H)

OHIO 489 1910

OHIO 486 1911

OHIO 489 1912

OHIO 52089 1913

(H) 1914 486

(H) 1915 1462

OHIO 1916 178574

OHIO 1917 9

24350 (H) 1918

(H) 1919 2836

OHIO 192918 1920

OHIO 334860 1921

420.744
OHIO-1922

28.419
OHIO-1923

102-180
OHIO-1924

478-048
OHIO-1925

448-858
OHIO-1926

498-520
OHIO-1927

231-649
OHIO-1928

231-747
OHIO-1929

H21-303
OHIO-1930

H70-966
OHIO-1931

H69-006
OHIO-1932

OHIO-1933
E56-487

E36-201
OHIO-1934

D·826·K
OHIO-1935

G·5938
OHIO-1936

368·PT
OHIO-1937

F·959·G
150 ANNIV. N·W·TERR. OHIO-38

1042·N
OHIO-1939

367·NR
OHIO-1940

N·1174
OHIO-1941

759·QE
OHIO-1942

667·PA
OHIO-1944

MK·473
OHIO-1945

N·5745
OHIO-1946

RU·728
1947-OHIO

L·7246
OHIO·1948

JJ·7165
1949-OHIO

F·362·C
1949-OHIO

F·402·C
OHIO-1950

427·PE
1951-OHIO

769·PB
1803-OHIO-1953

265·PC
OHIO-1954

930·PB
1955-OHIO

574·PC
OHIO-1956

305·PD
1957-OHIO

E·440·S
OHIO-1958

585·PB
1959-OHIO

718·PD
OHIO-1960

291·PB
1961-OHIO

676·PB
OHIO-1962

532·PU
1963-OHIO

912·RA
OHIO-1964

279·QD
1965-OHIO

239 QD
OHIO 1966

9
67 OHIO

294 QE
OHIO 68

283 RD
69 OHIO

649 RC
OHIO 70

275 RE
71 OHIO

JF 776
OHIO 72

SEAT BELTS FASTENED?
H808G
73 OHIO

SEAT BELTS FASTENED?
JF 775
OHIO 74

SEAT BELTS FASTENED?
Z 89332
OHIO 74

CQ 550
OHIO

P 26101
OHIO

P 44575
OHIO

E 90245
OHIO

OHIO
DDV·462

OHIO
EYP·437

OHIO
BYT·332

OHIO
RZQ·194
LUCAS

OHIO
SAS·114
TRUMBULL

OHIO
804·HQA
TRUMBULL

OHIO
595·BNS
TRUMBULL

OHIO
911·GEX
TRUMBULL

OHIO
568·XQS
LAKE

OHIO
UTE·495
LAKE

OHIO

PRE-STATES

Early Ohio registrations were handled by various cities around the state, and the number of survivors today is impressive! Cleveland led the pack, actually registering its first car in 1901. This seems particularly early until one realizes that Cleveland was on par with Detroit in the pioneering of automobile manufacture early in the century. Cleveland's plates were mostly made of aluminum house numbers on leather pads, with no markings other than the actual plate number. Unmarked leathers were also used in Canton and in a few very early Columbus plates as well. Columbus had porcelains for 1907 and 1908. Cincinnati had intricately designed brass plates for 1906, 1907 and 1908. Other cities registering vehicles included Dayton, Delhi (a Cincinnati "suburb" now gone from the map), Hamilton and Warren.

FIRST YEAR OF ISSUE
1908

UNDATED ISSUES
1908-1909, 1976

PORCELAINS
1908-1909, 1910, 1911

WINDSHIELD STICKERS
1943, 1952

METAL DATE TABS
None

SLOGANS

The 1938 plate noted the *150 ANNIV N.W. TERR*, referring to the 150th anniversary of the Northwest Territory, founded in 1788. The 1953 plate commemorated 150 years of Ohio statehood with *1803-OHIO-1953* along the bottom. From 1973 through 1975, the plates asked the question, *SEAT BELTS FASTENED?* along the bottom. In 1991, the new graphic base proclaimed Ohio *THE HEART OF IT ALL* in script below the state name.

GRAPHICS

With the 1908-1909, 1914, 1915 and 1918 through 1921 issues, the state experimented with interesting graphic ways to illustrate the state name. Some had the letters of the name inside the letter *O*, for example. The 1938 plate showed an ox pulling a covered wagon along the bottom, denoting the 150 years of the Northwest Territory. The 1980 base used an embossed shape of the state as a dividing symbol between the letters and numbers, and this symbol has been used on all bases through 1993.

OTHER FEATURES

As the first state-issued plates did not come into use until mid-1908, all vehicles registered locally were exempted from the state registration until January 1, 1909. This law did not sit well with certain Columbus "bigwigs" because it meant that by 1909, all the "good" numbers would have been issued. While it is generally considered that numbers below and including 10,649 were issued in 1908 and those from 10,650 and higher were issued in 1909, it may be that some blocks of low numbers were "reserved" for these influential "latecomers."

OKLAHOMA

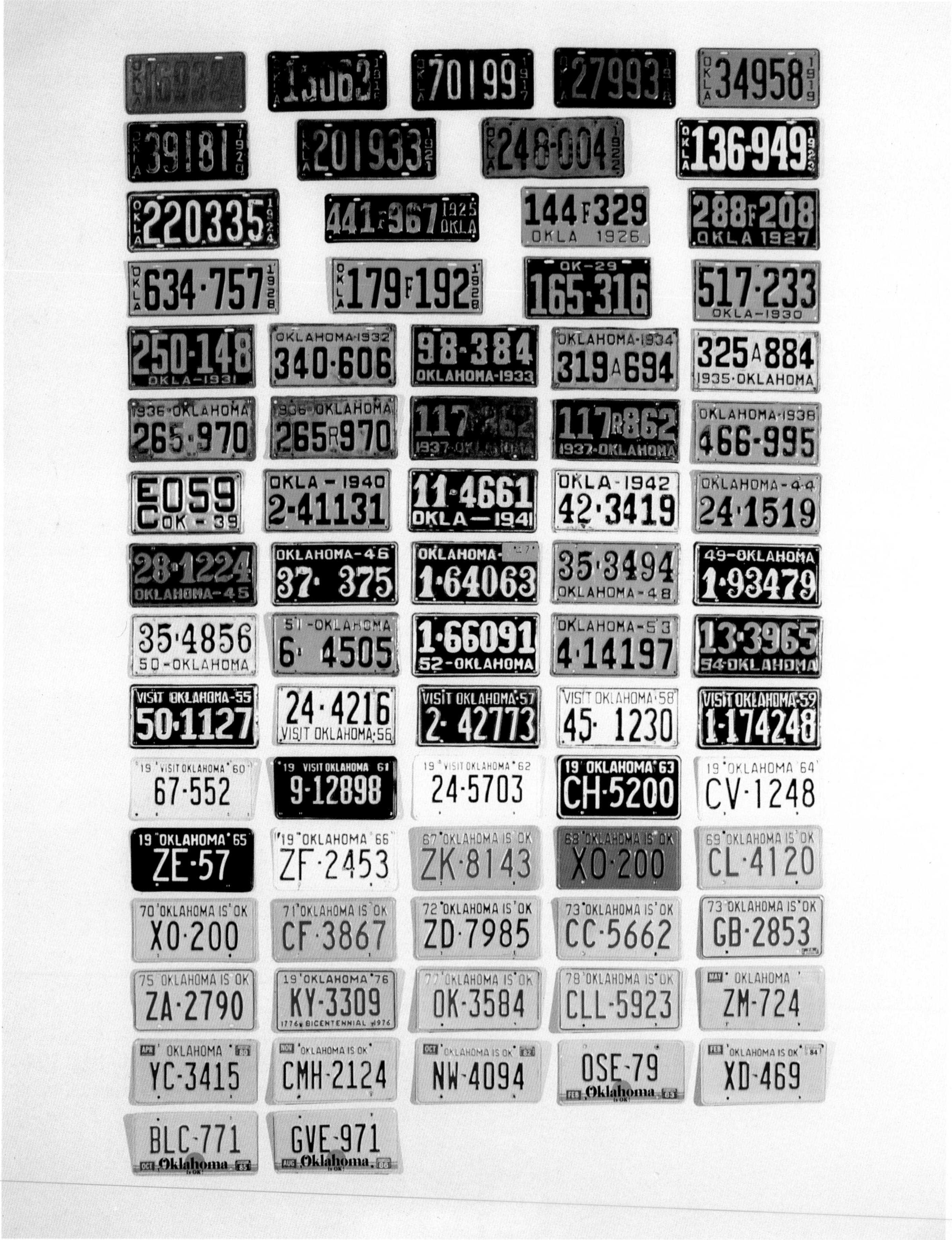

OKLAHOMA

PRE-STATES

Municipal registration was the only game in town when it came to early Oklahoma plates. The earliest known examples seem to date to about 1910 in Tulsa. In fact, a series of Tulsa porcelains exists, dated annually from 1911 through 1914 along with an earlier undated issue. The most interesting fact about Oklahoma pre-states, however, is that nearly all known examples are porcelain! Cities playing this game include Bartlesville, El Reno, Lawton, Mangum, Muskogee, Oklahoma City and Ponca City, along with Tulsa.

SLOGANS

From 1955 through 1962, the word *VISIT* was placed before the state name. From 1967 through 1975, the words *IS O.K.* were placed after the state name. This statement of approval was repeated for 1978 and 1979. The 1976 plate celebrated the nation's 200th anniversary with the slogan *1776 BICENTENNIAL 1976* along the bottom. For the 1981 base, *OKLAHOMA IS O.K.* was brought back. The 1982 base also had *IS O.K.* below the state name, this time silk-screened. The 1989 base used simply *O.K.!* below the state name. The 1981, 1982 and 1989 bases remain valid through 1993.

FIRST YEAR OF ISSUE
1915
UNDATED ISSUES
None
PORCELAINS
None
WINDSHIELD STICKERS
1943
METAL DATE TABS
1947

GRAPHICS

The 1982 base had a yellow sun and horizon line along the bottom of the plate. The 1989 base had a colorful illustration at the center, a silk-screened group of items with an Indian motif. This illustration consisted of an Indian drum, feathers and a peace pipe.

OTHER FEATURES

During the years 1925 through 1937, Oklahoma seemingly went crazy displaying small letters at the center of the plate, dividing the numbers. The 1925 through 1928 issues have either a dash or the letter *F* at center. While first thought to denote a "farm" vehicle, it is now proven that these plates were issued to FORD cars. Fords were so prevalent in those days that they rated their own plate! The plates with the letter *A* seem to have been used to denote "autos," or general-issue private automobile plates. For 1936 and 1937, the plot thickens. Some pairs have a dash on one plate and an *R* on the other. Still, other pairs have an *F* on one and an *R* on the other. These letters could be two ways to designate "front" and "rear" plates, or just maybe the dash was used on the front of all autos except Fords, which used the *F* on the front bumper. Confusing? You bet, but that is what makes license plate collecting so interesting.

OREGON

ORE.3375 | ORE 390 1911 | ORE 4992 1912 | ORE 9505 1913 | ORE 14166 1914

ORE 5198 1915 | ORE 6286 1916 | ORE 17535 1917 | 30485 ORE 1918 | ORE 40686 1919

52656 ORE 1920 | 97719 ORE 1921 | 47157 ORE 1922 | 70932 ORE 1923 | 899 ORE 1924

9-469 ORE 1925 | 50-937 ORE 1926 | 10-813 OREGON-1927 | 8-929 OREGON-1928 | OREGON-1929 29-323

8-688 OREGON EXPIRES JUNE 30 1931 | 115 OREGON JUNE 30 1932 | OREGON JUNE 30 1933 3-115 | 7-407 OREGON DEC 31 1933 | 12-408 OREGON-1934

OREGON-1935 231-492 | 268-278 OREGON-1936 | OREGON-1937 13-192 | OREGON-1938 233-714 | 344-102 OREGON-1939

OREGON-1940 341-926 | 80-765 19 OREGON 41 | 493-132 19 OREGON 42 | 109-483 46 OREGON 46 | 3-369 47 OREGON 47

48 OREGON 48 477-018 | 204-449 19 OREGON 49 | SEP OREGON 50 200-978 | APR OREGON 51 749-705 | JAN OREGON 51 706-018

DEC OREGON 52 861-048 | DEC OREGON 53 822-030 | JUL OREGON 54 880-340 | OCT OREGON 55 281-812 | JUL OREGON 56 1G-3639

FEB OREGON 57 6B-9821 | MAR OREGON 58 8C-3373 | OCT OREGON 59 9K-8489 | DEC OREGON 60 9M-2648 | MAR OREGON 61 2Q-8743 PACIFIC WONDERLAND

AUG OREGON 62 4V-1585 PACIFIC WONDERLAND | MAR OREGON 63 7Q-7593 PACIFIC WONDERLAND | NOV OREGON 64 5Y-7988 PACIFIC WONDERLAND | AAU 257 JAN OREGON 65 | EAV 493 MAY OREGON 66

EAM 479 MAY OREGON 67 | CAZ 689 MAR OREGON 68 | CBV 073 MAR OREGON 68 | LGZ 195 NOV OREGON 70 | BEP 025 FEB OREGON 71

EDR 554 MAY OREGON 72 | KJU 171 OCT OREGON 73 | DGC 203 APR OREGON 74 | KKW 193 OCT OREGON 75 | CJV 716 MAR OREGON 76

DJE 748 APR OREGON 77 | CKA 841 MAR OREGON 78 | LPM 185 NOV OREGON 79 | FLS 755 JUN OREGON 80 | CTE 820 MAR OREGON 81

EPN 610 MAY OREGON 84 | APX 457 JAN OREGON | ARR 956 JAN OREGON 84 | DRQ 053 APR OREGON 85 | JUB 044 SEP OREGON 86

Oregon PTS 644 3 91 | Oregon RRH 587 12 92 | Oregon RQA 100 1 93

OREGON

PRE-STATES

City issues in early Oregon are nearly unknown, the only evidence of them at all being a couple of old photos. One clearly says *DALLES CITY* (now called The Dalles). The same photographic evidence shows that the majority of early registrations were painted directly onto the vehicles. State registrations date to 1905, and early surviving specimens are rare, at least one being made of porcelain. In 1908, a properly manufactured plate was made available to motorists, and between 1908 and 1911, many chose this style of plate.

SLOGANS

The 1961 base, which was used among other bases into the early 1990s, had *PACIFIC WONDERLAND* across the bottom.

GRAPHICS

Oregon used no graphic elements on their plates until the first silk-screened base was issued in 1988. This base featured a Douglas fir tree at center, with a mountain skyline in the background. The plate was somewhat controversial among motorists and other observers, many of whom felt the colors were drab and the serial unintelligible. A modification of the colors has improved the look and readability of this plate.

OTHER FEATURES

In my years of collecting, I have seen the status of the "1908-1910" Oregon plate go from "pre-state" to "first issue" and back to "pre-state" again. This hobby is changing due to "new" discoveries of old information. I feel confident, based on what is now known, that the information provided here is correct: the plate was an optional version of a pre-state, used between 1908 and 1911. The dated 1911 plate was used only from August to December of 1911, making the plate scarce today.

FIRST YEAR OF ISSUE
1911

UNDATED ISSUES
None

PORCELAINS
None

WINDSHIELD STICKERS
June 30, 1930, 1943, 1944, 1945, 1946

METAL DATE TABS
1951, 1952, 1953, 1954, 1955, 1957, 1958, 1959, 1960

PENNSYLVANIA

PENNA 1906 **12397**	PENNA 1907 **11182**	PENNA 1908 **19679**	PENNA 1909 **31029**	PENNA 1910 **10484**
PENNA 1911 **35150**	PENNA 1911 **30737**	PENNA 1912 **1228**	PENNA 1913 **1181**	PENNA 1914 **6356**
PENNA 1915 **8371**	PENNA 1916 **3881**	PENNA 1917 **207528**		PENNA 1918 **147750**
12261 PENNA 1918	**96-632** PENNA 1920	**108-043** PENNA 1921		**355-926** PENNA 1922
276-081 PENNA 1923	**57167** PENNA 1924	**509-351** 1925 PENNA		**16-819** 1926 PENNA
1927 PENNA **452-519**	PENNA 1928 **758-131**	1929 PENNA **50-035**		**CL395** 1930 PENNA
GY490 PENNA 1931	PENNA 1932 **MR779**	PENNA 1933 **61714**	1933 PENNA **J6767**	**C1283** 1934 PENNA
9022H 1935 PENNA	1936 PENNA **916R4**	1937 PENNA **53A2**	1938 PENNA **EG907**	1939 PENNA **NL389**
1940 PENNA **1M061**	1941 PENNA **HV576**	1942 PENNA **86JY8**	1942 PENNA **MM199**	1944 PENNA **AZ711**
1945 PENNA **1PC56**	1946 PENNA **M4038**	1947 PENNA **FU371**	1948 PENNA **YL669**	1949 PENNA **M1389**
1950 PENNA **4LE10**	1951 PENNA **KJ935**	1952 PENNA **KH135**	1953 PENNA **72R93**	1954 PENNA **AB566**
1955 PENNA **6KF69**	1956 PENNA **5099E**	1957 PENNA **63B1**	PA 58 **122-997**	PA 58 **E66-519**
PA 58 **720-96B**	PA 58 **U53-184**	PA 58 **311-90N**	PA 58 **967-52V**	PA 58 **681-33R**
PENNSYLVANIA **950-79F**	PENNSYLVANIA **225-25E**	PENNSYLVANIA **9G8-872**	PENNSYLVANIA **9J1-143**	PENNSYLVANIA **09H-095**
PENNSYLVANIA **30U-211**	PENNSYLVANIA **908-67V** BICENTENNIAL STATE '76	PENNSYLVANIA **2N2-106** BICENTENNIAL STATE '76	PENNSYLVANIA **01D-295** BICENTENNIAL STATE '76	PENNSYLVANIA **48P-129** BICENTENNIAL STATE '76
PENNSYLVANIA **W98-792** BICENTENNIAL STATE '76	PENNSYLVANIA **645-B43** BICENTENNIAL STATE '76	PENNSYLVANIA **0G7-882** KEYSTONE STATE	PENNSYLVANIA **4N0-551** KEYSTONE STATE	PENNSYLVANIA **813-93D** KEYSTONE STATE
PENNSYLVANIA DEC **L78-310** KEYSTONE STATE	FEB PENNSYLVANIA **664-640** KEYSTONE STATE	APR PENNSYLVANIA APR **8Z6-955** KEYSTONE STATE	PENNSYLVANIA APR **620-08S** KEYSTONE STATE	You've Got a Friend in **HAM-363** Pennsylvania
You've Got a Friend in **JXN-322** Pennsylvania	You've Got a Friend in **HND-351** Pennsylvania	KEYSTONE STATE **SUS-556** PENNSYLVANIA	KEYSTONE STATE **TXC-788** PENNSYLVANIA	KEYSTONE STATE **WJV-465** PENNSYLVANIA

PENNSYLVANIA

PRE-STATES

Both state and local governments seem to have been active in the early years of Pennsylvania vehicle registrations. The city of Philadelphia issued dated porcelains as early as 1903, and a state law took effect that year. In some cases, county records exist today, showing names of motorists, their vehicle makes and registration numbers issued. It appears, though, that the counties may have been acting as agents for the state. In any case, early plates are known with the *PA* designation, as opposed to any city name. Besides Philadelphia, city plates are known from Pittsburgh and Scranton, though in both cases, they are dated after the first state-issued plate of 1906. Most city issues are porcelain, while the others are of the usual homemade varieties.

FIRST YEAR OF ISSUE
1906
UNDATED ISSUES
1965, 1977
PORCELAINS
1906, 1907, 1908, 1909, 1910, 1911, 1912, 1913, 1914, 1915
WINDSHIELD STICKERS
None
METAL DATE TABS
1943

SLOGANS

The 1971 base sported the slogan *BICENTENNIAL STATE* to commemorate the coming United States Bicentennial. These remained in use through 1976. The 1977 base, still valid through 1993, had *KEYSTONE STATE* along the bottom. The 1983 base, also still valid, had *YOU'VE GOT A FRIEND* along the top. The 1987 base, also still in use in 1993, returned to *KEYSTONE STATE* at the top.

GRAPHICS

Beginning in 1910, a keystone appeared on the plate in various forms over the years, and with the exception of the 1920 plate, continued through the 1937 plate. After many years of absence, it returned on the 1958 base. Except for the 1971 base, which used a Liberty Bell as a dividing symbol, the keystone has been there ever since. Starting with the 1937 issue and continuing through the 1966 base, the borders of Pennsylvania plates were embossed and painted to match the outline of the state.

OTHER FEATURES

Pennsylvania may have had the first license plate in the United States. Philadelphia's Fairmount Park, in conjunction with its opening to horseless vehicles in 1900, required car owners to register with them and issued a leather plate with painted white numbers to all registrants. It was also suggested then that it "might" be a good idea to require licensing on city roads as well!

The 1911 plates came in two ways—with either flat or beveled edges, a result of different manufacturing runs, no doubt. In 1933, the date appeared either before or after the state name. No explanation is known for this design variation, and again, it appears to be due to two different manufacturing runs.

RHODE ISLAND

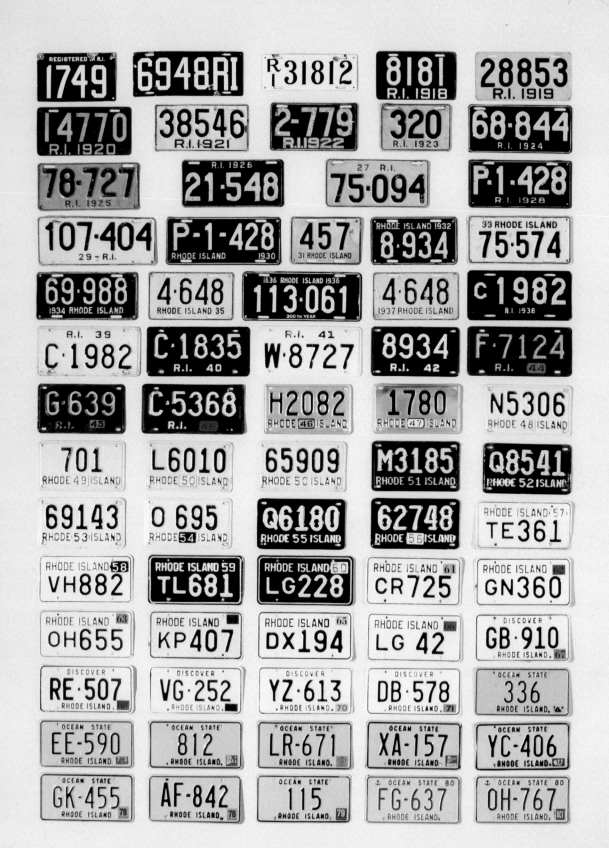

RHODE ISLAND

PRE-STATES

Like Maine and other New England states, the Rhode Island government began licensing vehicles at a very early stage of motoring. Thus, no pre-states are known to have existed here.

SLOGANS

In 1936, Rhode Island celebrated their 300th year of statehood by placing *300th YEAR* at the bottom of their plates and *1636-RHODE ISLAND-1936* at the top. Beginning with the 1967 base, the word *DISCOVER* was added to the top of the plate, which was used until 1981. With the 1972 base, the slogan *OCEAN STATE* came into use, and these bases were also used until 1981. The 1980 base, too, used the *OCEAN STATE* slogan and it continues in 1993 through all the small changes that have occurred in the subsequent variations on this base.

GRAPHICS

The only graphic element to appear on a Rhode Island normal plate is a small anchor, which appeared at the upper left hand corner of the 1980 base, and continues through the variations on this plate through 1993.

FIRST YEAR OF ISSUE
1904

UNDATED ISSUES
1904-1907, 1908-1911, 1912-1917

PORCELAINS
1904-1907, 1908-1911, 1912-1917

WINDSHIELD STICKERS
1943, 1952

METAL DATE TABS
1944, 1945, 1946 (two different issues), 1947, 1948, 1949, 1950, 1951,1954, 1956, 1958, 1960

OTHER FEATURES

Though the 1904-1907 and 1908-1911 issues appear to be totally different, in reality they are both parts of one continuous registration period. In other words, the numbers on the 1908-1911 plates begin where the 1904-1907 plates stopped. The 1904-1907 plates were actually used through 1911, and the 1908-1911 plates, in the purest sense, were for new registrants only.

The 1928 and 1930 plates shown are non-passenger issues. The "P" prefix denotes vehicles used for public service.

SOUTH CAROLINA

SOUTH CAROLINA

PRE-STATES

The cities and counties of South Carolina had the responsibility of registering vehicles in the early years. By far, the most common pre-states are porcelain, and examples from Richland County (Columbia), Greenville, Darlington, Orangeburg and others are known to collectors. There also survives a leather plate with *364 AB* followed by the state abbreviation *SC* vertically. A good guess would place this plate from Abbeville.

SLOGANS

Iodine production was important to the state identity in the early 1930s and was prominently used on South Carolina plates in three different ways. The 1930 issue simply had the word *IODINE* vertically at right. For 1931 and 1932, *THE IODINE STATE* was used. For 1933, *THE IODINE PRODUCTS STATE* was embossed along the bottom. South Carolina celebrated 300 years of statehood with their 1970 issue, with the slogan *1670 300 YEARS 1970* along the bottom. The United States Bicentennial was duly noted at the top of the 1976 plate. The dates *1775* and *1783* also appeared, signifying the first battle of the Revolutionary War to be fought on South Carolina ground (1775) and the year of the Paris Peace Treaty (1783).

FIRST YEAR OF ISSUE
1917
UNDATED ISSUES
1981
PORCELAINS
None
WINDSHIELD STICKERS
None
METAL DATE TABS
1944 date strip

GRAPHICS

The 1926 and 1927 plates both had a palmetto tree embossed at right with the date showing among the leaves and branches and the state abbreviation *SC* on either side of the trunk. The palmetto tree returned to the 1976 base, now silk-screened at the center of the plate. This graphic also depicts a cannon at the foot of the tree. The 1981 issue shows a silk-screened outline of the state with the state seal inside. The 1986 base saw the return (again) of the palmetto tree. The 1991 base, still in use in 1993, illustrates a silk-screened wren sitting on a floral branch.

OTHER FEATURES

Half-year plates were used in 1934, 1935 and 1936. Though the 1937 and 1940 plates are marked, *OCT 31*, there has never been evidence of a half-year plate for those years. To conserve metal during World War II, most 1943 plates were restamped over flattened 1942 plates. Shortly after the 1991 "wren" base came into use, an uproar ensued over the illustration of the wren. In response, a decal was made available which when placed over the existing wren, shows a more acceptable likeness of the bird.

SOUTH DAKOTA

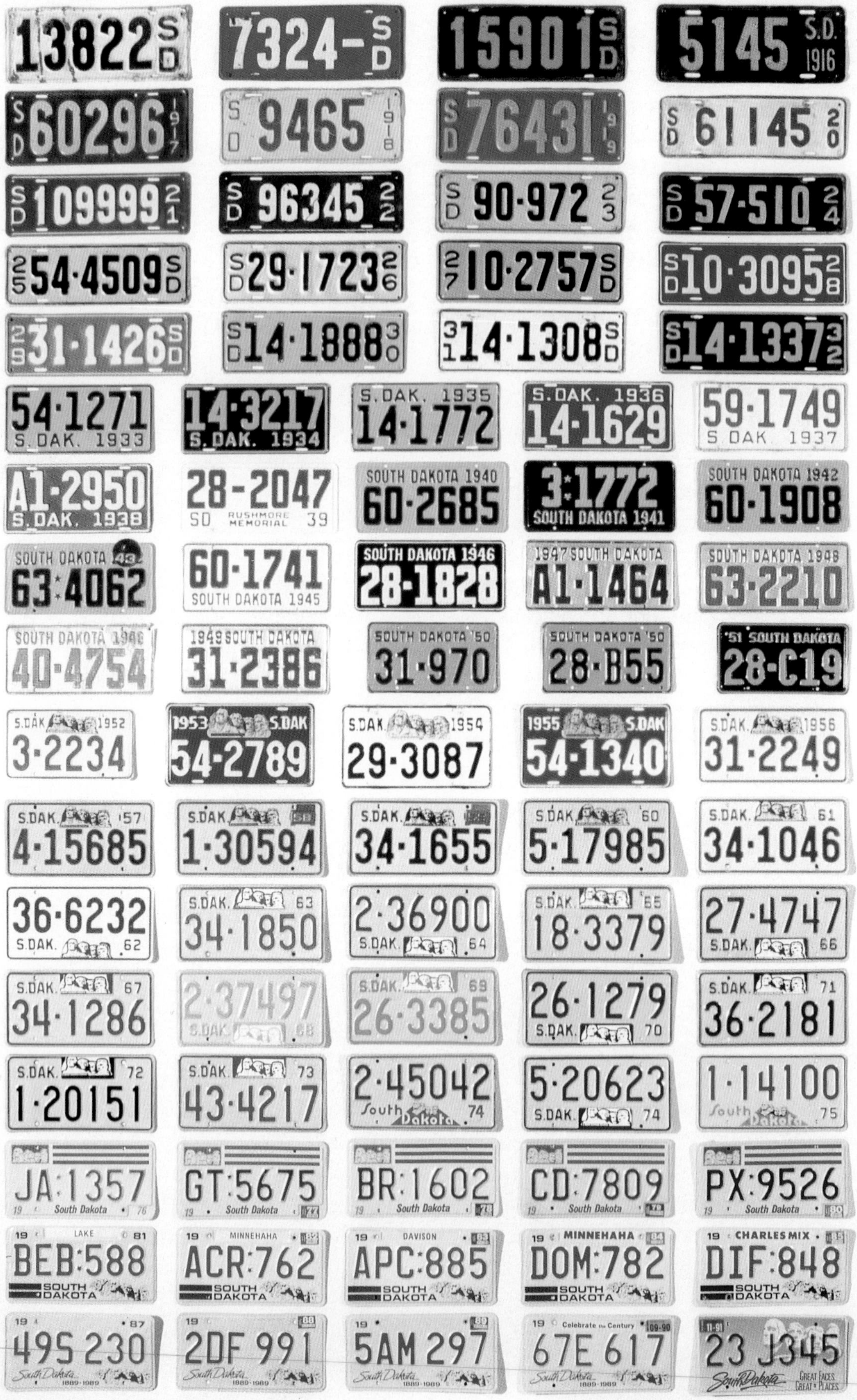

SOUTH DAKOTA

PRE-STATES

It is generally assumed that automobile licensing in South Dakota began in about 1905, though reliable information is scarce. No records remain of city or county issues, nor are any examples known. Rather, all registrations seem to have been handled by the state. All known examples of early South Dakota plates were made from leather bases with aluminum or brass numbers on them. The state abbreviation, *SD,* appeared vertically at the right of all plates. At some point in the pre-state era, dashboard discs bearing the assigned number were issued to registrants.

SLOGANS

In 1939, the words *RUSHMORE MEMORIAL* appeared along the bottom of the plates. In 1987, the dates *1889-1989* were added to commemorate the coming State Centennial. In 1989, an optional sticker was made available with the slogan *CELEBRATE THE CENTURY*. This sticker was intended to be placed along the upper edge of the plate. The new 1991 plates had the slogan *GREAT FACES, GREAT PLACES* at the lower right, and this base continues in use through 1993.

FIRST YEAR OF ISSUE
1913

UNDATED ISSUES
1913, 1914, 1915

PORCELAINS
None

WINDSHIELD STICKERS
1944, 1945 (instead of front plate)

METAL DATE TABS
1943, 1958, 1959

GRAPHICS

Beginning with the 1952 issue, an illustration of the famous Mount Rushmore memorial was placed on the plate, and this design has continued in various forms as of 1993. The 1976 base commemorated the Nation's Bicentennial, using the red, white and blue theme with red and white stripes along the top. The 1981 base had blue and white stripes at bottom left. Beginning with the 1987 base and continuing with the 1990 base, the state name appears in script.

OTHER FEATURES

The 1943 date tab was made in a circular shape. Most tabs and strips were made to cover a specific portion and shape of the base plate, and as such, the round tab is unique. In 1945, a windshield sticker with a number matching the number of the accompanying plate was used. The plate was mounted only on the rear of the vehicle. From 1948 through 1951, some plates were made with the "waffled" aluminum construction.

TENNESSEE

TENNESSEE

PRE-STATES

While no city or county plates are known to collectors today, state registrations in Tennessee date back to about 1905. Plates were homemade or store-bought, and made of every imaginable material, including metal, leather, wood and porcelain. The abbreviation *TENN* appeared vertically following the number. One known pair of porcelains are white on blue and have the car make (in this case, Studebaker) at the bottom of the plate. Placing the vehicle name on the plate is an unusual concept, although for many years, the Australian state of South Australia had their plates embossed with the vehicle make right on them!

SLOGANS

Beginning with the 1977 base, and continuing until the 1984 base was replaced in 1989, the slogan *THE VOLUNTEER STATE* was used on Tennessee plates.

FIRST YEAR OF ISSUE
1915
UNDATED ISSUES
None
PORCELAINS
None
WINDSHIELD STICKERS
None
METAL DATE TABS
1943

GRAPHICS

The 1927 plate had a large embossed outline of the shape of the state, with all but the date inside the outline. Beginning with the 1936 issue, the plates were shaped like the state of Tennessee, right down to the protuberance at the upper line of the northwest corner of the state. By 1938, this protuberance was removed from the design, but the state-shaped plates continued to be issued annually (except for 1943) through 1956. The 1957 issue had the state shape embossed on the plate, surrounding the serial. In 1958, and continuing through 1976, the state shape surrounded the state abbreviation *TENN*. This shape also surrounded the *VOLUNTEER STATE* slogan on the 1984 base. The 1977 base had a large state seal silk-screened at the center of the plate. The artwork on this plate also showed the state name on a scroll-like illustration. The 1989 base had a large round dividing symbol between the letters and numbers. It's three-star design is taken from the Tennessee state flag.

OTHER FEATURES

The 1915 plate was issued in July of 1915 and stated, "EXPIRES DEC. 31, 1915." Thus, this plate was in use for just six months. The 1916 issue had "EXPIRES DEC. 31" on it. For the years 1926, 1927 and 1928, the plates had *FRONT* and *REAR* designations on them. The 1943 tab had no date or state name; only the letter *C*, the meaning of which remains unexplained today.

TEXAS

TEXAS

PRE-STATES

From the earliest days of motoring in 1907, vehicle registration was left to the counties in Texas. At first, most plates were made of leather, wood and other homemade materials. Only the county registration number appeared on these plates. Of course, this created a situation where plates with the same number could exist in more than one county. For the last few years of the pre-state period, most vehicles were using porcelain kit plates which also included a porcelain panel that had the city name, the county name, or just *TEXAS*. These county plates carried such interesting names as *CISCO, LAGRANGE* and *RISING STAR*.

SLOGANS

In 1936, the word *CENTENNIAL* was used on Texas plates to commemorate 100 years of statehood. In 1968, the word *HEMISFAIR* promoted that event. *SESQUICENTENNIAL* appeared in 1985 to celebrate the 150th year of statehood for Texas, which actually took place in 1986. The dates *1836* and *1986* also appeared on the 1985 base.

FIRST YEAR OF ISSUE
1917

UNDATED ISSUES
1917, 1923

PORCELAINS
None

WINDSHIELD STICKERS
None

METAL DATE TABS
1917, 1918, 1919, 1920, 1921, 1922 and 1924 "radiator seals," 1943, 1944 tabs

GRAPHICS

A large "Lone Star" appeared on the 1917, 1918 and 1919 radiator seals. Wherever a dividing device has been used to separate the numbers from the letters, a star was used instead of a dot or a dash. Beginning in 1976, a small outline of the state was substituted for the star. The 1989 base featured the Texas state flag, and this base continues in use through 1993.

OTHER FEATURES

The radiator seals used in 1917, 1918 and 1919 were circular and measured 4" in diameter. The 1920, 1921, 1922 and 1924 radiator seals were rectangular, measuring 3-1/4" X 6". The issues of 1928, 1929 and 1930 all had *FRONT* and *REAR* plate designations on them.

UTAH

3211 U 15
11554 U 16
1520 U 17
3782 U 18
10170 U 19
18047 U 20
10415 U 21
21-777 U 22
UTAH 1923 51-952
66-921 UTAH 1924
UTAH 25 91-063
28-870 26 UTAH
UTAH 27 25-433
89-804 UTAH 28
21-472
27-083 UTAH 30
70-130 31 UTAH
32 UTAH 53-620
UTAH-1933 70-112
82-370 UTAH-1934
137-421 1935-UTAH
79-627 UTAH-1936
UTAH-1937 78-595
71-021 UTAH-1938
UTAH-1939 171-841
P-7479 UTAH-40
N UTAH-41 4574
42 UTAH N4383 CENTER SCENIC AMERICA
H9523 UTAH 44
45 UTAH H2347 CENTER SCENIC AMERICA
46 UTAH A2554 CENTER SCENIC AMERICA
47 UTAH B2475 THIS IS THE PLACE
UTAH 48 N2748 THE FRIENDLY STATE
P 2602 UTAH-49
P UTAH-50 5738
MG UTAH 1951 274
547 MF UTAH 1952
YF UTAH 1953 206
KY 792 UTAH 1954
UTAH 1955 LJ419
AK 7416 UTAH 56
AE UTAH 57 1081
BF UTAH 58 6453
UTAH 59 BC 8230
UTAH 60 AC 8231
UTAH 61 DB 9688
UTAH 62 AH 1825
DE 2528 UTAH 63
UTAH 64 EB 2143
EK 9037 UTAH 65
UTAH 66 DH 8945
BK 9797 UTAH 67
KH 9704 UTAH
KH 9705 UTAH
KH 9706 UTAH
KH 9707 UTAH
KH 9708 UTAH
CKJ 713 UTAH 73
HKH 418 UTAH 73
DDC 358 UTAH 73
MJJ 439 UTAH
NAH 136 UTAH
LDB 752 UTAH
WHE 061 UTAH
VKE 051 UTAH
SWD 985 UTAH
VLC 456 UTAH
MWN 689 UTAH
PVT 618 UTAH
Ski Utah! 572 ALD
Ski Utah! 311 DAE
Ski Utah! 062 EDN
Ski Utah! 424 EEJ

UTAH

PRE-STATES

Utah vehicle registrations began around 1909. All vehicles registered with the state instead of with city or county officials. Plates of the early years from 1909 until about 1913 were homemade and the basic group of materials were used, such as wood, leather and metal. Many numbers were painted directly onto the bumpers of the vehicles. However, by 1913, a Salt Lake City business concern called the Salt Lake Stamp Co. was offering a particularly well made steel plate to motorists, and it appears that many registrants took full advantage of this service. All pre-state plates were required to display the letter *U* after the registration number.

SLOGANS

CENTER SCENIC AMERICA was used on the 1942, 1945 and 1946 plates. *THIS IS THE PLACE* was used on the 1947 plate, and *THE FRIENDLY STATE* was the message in 1948. Slogans were then discontinued until the 1983 base promoted the *GREATEST SNOW ON EARTH* and suggested that we all *SKI UTAH!* This base continues in use as of 1993.

GRAPHICS

In 1975, a dividing symbol was introduced in the center of the base. It was shaped like a beehive. In 1983, the first silk-screened plate came into use, illustrating a skier above the serial and placing an exclamation point after the state name.

OTHER FEATURES

The plates from 1915 through 1922 used only the letter *U* to identify the state. Roads were so primitive then and travel was so restricted, especially in the West, that it is likely that the *U* was widely understood when Utah vehicles ventured across their state borders to neighboring areas. The 1944 plate was made in an unusual way, having a base of masonite with a piece of patterned paper glued to the base. The paper contained the state name, date and serial.

FIRST YEAR OF ISSUE
1915

UNDATED ISSUES
None

PORCELAINS
None

WINDSHIELD STICKERS
1943

METAL DATE TABS
None

VERMONT

844 | 1339 VT. | 1827 VT. 1909 | 1854 VT. 1910

2015 VT. 1911 | 1885 VT. 1912 | VT 1854 13 | 14 2002 VT

VT 6686 1915 | 4654 VT | 20289 V T | 19890 V T

26078 VT 19 | VT 20 18·130 | VT 21 33·385 | 29·914 VT 22 | VT 23 1·226

3·334 VT 24 | VT 25 48·803 | 56·012 VERMONT 1926 | 19·348 VERMONT 1927 | VERMONT 1928 5·760

4·853 VERMONT 1929 | 53·686 VERMONT 1930 | VERMONT 1931 59·737 | 41·600 VERMONT 1932 | VERMONT 1933 698

VERMONT 1934 50·298 | 45·589 VERMONT 1935 | 24·456 VERMONT EXPIRES MARCH 31 1937 | 698 VERMONT TO APR.1 1938 | 6 964 19 VERMONT 38

55 513 19 VERMONT 39 | 52 114 19 VERMONT 40 | 19 VERMONT 41 6 027 | 50 398 19 VERMONT 42 | 23 420 19 VERMONT

1890 VERMONT 44 | 14974 VERMONT 45 | 30052 VERMONT 46 | 77114 47 VERMONT | GREEN MOUNTAINS 600 48 VERMONT | GREEN MOUNTAINS 219 VERMONT 49

GREEN MOUNTAINS 28727 50 VERMONT | BW664 VERMONT 51 | 68518 52 VERMONT | 53062 VERMONT 53 | E6171 54 VERMONT

39591 VERMONT 55 | 65026 56 VERMONT | 2548 SEE VERMONT 57 | 289 SEE VERMONT 58 | 673 SEE VERMONT 59

81452 SEE VERMONT 60 | 9120 SEE VERMONT 61 | 20026 SEE VERMONT 62 | E7456 SEE VERMONT 63 | 38668 SEE VERMONT 64

F8488 SEE VERMONT 65 | 3421 SEE VERMONT 66 | 7700 VERMONT 67 | 2261 VERMONT 67 | G·3006 SEE VERMONT

3951·A SEE VERMONT | 761·C SEE VERMONT | SEE VERMONT R·3540 | SEE VERMONT S·7967 | SEE VERMONT A706B

SEE VERMONT BY·984 | SEE VERMONT A701B | GREEN MOUNTAINS M·8442 VERMONT | GREEN MOUNTAINS 5402·A VERMONT NOV | GREEN MOUNTAINS 763·K VERMONT

GREEN MOUNTAINS 2123·H VERMONT JAN | GREEN MOUNTAINS 3871·X VERMONT SEP | GREEN MOUNTAINS 9006·Y VERMONT FEB | GREEN MOUNTAINS KP409 VERMONT | Vermont 2Y373 Green Mountain State

VERMONT

PRE-STATES

A 1904 state law mandated that all automobiles be registered in Vermont by May 1, 1905. Prior to 1904, no registrations were required, and no Vermont pre-states are known to collectors.

SLOGANS

In 1948, 1949 and 1950, the slogan *GREEN MOUNTAINS* appeared along the top of the Vermont plates. In 1957, the word *SEE* was added to the plate before the state name, and remained through 1966. This short slogan returned in 1969 and remained through 1976. In 1977, *GREEN MOUNTAINS* was again used on the plates, remaining through 1990, when this base was invalidated. The 1985 base, still in use through 1993, says *GREEN MOUNTAIN STATE* across the bottom of the plate.

GRAPHICS

Vermont entered the graphics field with their first silk-screened base in 1985. This plate had a small tree at upper left and is still valid as of 1993.

OTHER FEATURES

The first plate in Vermont said *VERMONT AUTOMOBILE REGISTER* across the top. From May 1, 1905, through the end of 1906, less than 900 *V.A.R.* plates were issued, making this plate a rarity among collectors.

VIRGINIA

A photographic plate showing Virginia license plates from 1937/early through 1986, arranged in a grid by year:

- 3937 VA. | 393 VA. 1910 | 393 VA. 1911 | 377 VA. 1912 | 393 VA. 1913
- 377 VA 1914 | 377 VA 1915 | 32443 VA 1916 | 51892 VA 1917
- 29105 VA 1918 | 31242 VA 1919 | 59148 VA 20 | 90-177 VA 21
- 63676 VA 22 | 46314 VA 23 | VIRGINIA-24 52235 | 146-473 VIRGINIA-1925
- VIRGINIA-26 171-367 | 125-622 VIRGINIA-27 | VIRGINIA-1928 286-203 | 134-229 VIRGINIA-1929
- VIRGINIA 1930 2-673 | 363-403 VIRGINIA-1931 | VIRGINIA-1932 207-844 | 318-876 VIRGINIA-1933
- VIRGINIA-1934 190-457 | VIRGINIA-1935 883 | 99-868 VIRGINIA-1936 | VIRGINIA-1937 229-743 | 263-996 VIRGINIA-1938
- 401-810 VIRGINIA-1939 | 1940-VIRGINIA 408 | 19-VIRGINIA-41 134-475 | VIRGINIA-1942 41-210 | VIRGINIA-1943 68-271
- 408 1944-VA. | 108-565 19-VIRGINIA-45 | 291-081 VIRGINIA-1946 | 19 VIRGINIA 47 332-665 | 1948 VIRGINIA 566-977
- 697-806 VIRGINIA 1949 | 210-184 1950 VIRGINIA | 303-294 19 VIRGINIA 51 | 377-128 19 VIRGINIA 52 | 19 VIRGINIA 53 408
- VIRGINIA 1954 435-322 | 408 1955 VIRGINIA | 889-162 19 VIRGINIA 56 | 408 VIRGINIA 1957 | 1958 VIRGINIA 408
- 19 VIRGINIA 59 408 | VIRGINIA 1960 408 | 408 1961 VIRGINIA | 998-082 19 VIRGINIA 62 | 408 VIRGINIA 1963
- 1964 VIRGINIA 786-655 | 19 VIRGINIA 65 635-634 | VIRGINIA 1966 91-178 | 143-788 1967 VIRGINIA | A406-709 19 VIRGINIA 68
- 17-028 VIRGINIA 1969 | 1970 VIRGINIA 617-329 | 19 VIRGINIA 71 91-668 | VIRGINIA 1972 DWG-048 | VIRGINIA 73 CJT-853
- DEC VIRGINIA 74 FLR-753 | JAN VIRGINIA 75 GAH-882 | JAN VIRGINIA 76 FVV-873 | DEC Virginia 77 426-358 1776 Independence Bicentennial 1976 | JUN VIRGINIA 78 KGL-768
- APR VIRGINIA 79 MCW-298 | NOV Virginia 80 VYV-233 | NOV Virginia 81 XPA-587 | JUN Virginia 82 YYY-590 | OCT Virginia 83 BSR-763
- MAR Virginia 84 CMW-128 | NOV Virginia 85 GEK-978 | JAN Virginia 86 GNU-290

VIRGINIA

PRE-STATES

While there are early porcelain city plates known from Virginia, there is no evidence that any predate the first state issue. It is more likely that a form of dual registration existed, which would account for the porcelain issues from Clifton Forge, Graham and Roanoke. Simply stated, no Virginia pre-state issues are known to exist.

SLOGANS

On the optional 1976 Bicentennial design, the slogan *INDEPENDENCE BICENTENNIAL 1776-1976* appeared. No other slogans have been used in Virginia.

GRAPHICS

The same optional Bicentennial plate had a design with stars and a profile of George Washington. Another optional design, issued in 1985, had the Great Seal of the state of Virginia in the center. No other graphics have been used.

OTHER FEATURES

The 1944 issue was made of a fiberboard composition, in the effort to save metal during the Second World War. This plate differs from other fiberboards in that the plate is fully embossed.

FIRST YEAR OF ISSUE
1906

UNDATED ISSUES
1906-1909

PORCELAINS
1906-1909, 1910, 1911, 1912, 1913

WINDSHIELD STICKERS
None

METAL DATE TABS
1943, 1952

The 1977 "Bicentennial" plate shown is an optional issue.

WASHINGTON

WASHINGTON

PRE-STATES

No city plates are known to collectors from Washington's early days of vehicle registration. The state took the initiative early on, and in 1906, began registering vehicles. These homemade plates were of the usual material, and while the state made no rules about what a plate could be made of, it was required to have the letters *WN* before the number. The majority of plates which have survived this era are leathers.

SLOGANS

In 1939, Washington plates had *1889-GOLDEN JUBILEE-1939* across the top, celebrating 50 years of statehood. The 1987 silk-screened base commemorated the *CENTENNIAL CELEBRATION* to be celebrated in 1989. The base is still in use as of 1993.

GRAPHICS

Washington's only graphic plate is the 1987 base, which shows a lovely version of a snowcapped Mt. Rainier.

FIRST YEAR OF ISSUE

1915 (expired February 29, 1916, and dated 1916)

UNDATED ISSUES

None

PORCELAINS

None

WINDSHIELD STICKERS

1943, 1944, 1946, 1948, 1952

METAL DATE TABS

Exp. February 29, 1920 (dated "20") porcelain, 1951, 1953, 1955, 1956, 1957

OTHER FEATURES

It was unusual for an early plate to show its year of expiration. Yet, the 1916 Washington plate was actually issued in March of 1915, expiring on February 29, 1916. In 1920, a porcelain tab was used to revalidate the 1919 plate. This tab measures 3-7/8" X 4". Initial registrations that year received full-sized plates, either in embossed steel or in porcelain. A small *x* appeared on the 1919 plate, Washington's way of denoting a private automobile registration. This letter continued in use through the 1935 issue. In 1921, a shift from expiration dates to current year dates was initiated, with two different plates dated 1921 in use. The white on green plate expired at the end of 1921.

WEST VIRGINIA

WEST VIRGINIA

PRE-STATES

Like Virginia, early city plates have survived from West Virginia, yet none of these are dated early enough to qualify as pre-states. However, one plate exists today which seems to be in conflict with all laws of that time. It is a small metal plate, clearly embossed with both *WV* and *1905*. Yet, the plate dated 1906 is like the first issue of Washington in that this is an expiration date. In fact, the plate was first issued in March of 1905 and expired in March of 1906. This plate dated 1906 seems to be in keeping with the 1905 law, the first licensing law on the books in West Virginia. The information we have today leaves the plate dated 1905 with no legal basis for its existence. It also leaves today's collectors and historians with an intriguing mystery. The city plates which survive today are mainly porcelains from the period of about 1911 to 1917. The existence of these plates strongly suggests some type of dual registration system between the state and cities. Known city plates include examples from Clarksburg, Fairmont, Parkersburg, Weston and others.

FIRST YEAR OF ISSUE
1905 (dated 1906)
UNDATED ISSUES
1907-1908
PORCELAINS
1907-1908, 1909, 1910, 1911, 1912, July 1914, 1914-1915, 1915-1916
WINDSHIELD STICKERS
1934, 6/30/44
METAL DATE TABS
6/30/43 date strip

SLOGANS

West Virginia celebrated 100 years of statehood with the slogan *1863 CENTENNIAL 1963* on both the 1963 and 1964 plates. From 1965 through 1976, the slogan *MOUNTAIN STATE* appeared along the top of the plates. With the introduction of the graphic base in 1976, the slogan became *WILD, WONDERFUL,* which remains in use as of 1993.

GRAPHICS

The 1921 and 1922 plates had a highly stylized state abbreviation in the shape of a circular monogram. The 1976 silk-screened base had a yellow area with a blue border, shaped like the state. The blue border was dropped on subsequent issues, but the state-shaped graphic remains in use as of 1993.

OTHER FEATURES

The 1906 plate measures 3-7/8" x 6-3/4" and is made of such a thin tin material that it could almost be crumpled in the palm of your hand! In 1909, the state ran out of porcelain plates near the end of the year and issued the last few registrants a thin cardboard plate instead. The early 1961 plates were embossed while later 1961 plates were debossed and reflectorized. The embossed plates had a maroon background while the debossed plates were more red in color. It is difficult to believe, but there were two different 1978 stickers used in West Virginia. The white on red sticker was used as planned. The yellow on green sticker was dated 1978 when it was meant to be used in 1979 because of a manufacturing error. The solution? They used it anyway, despite having the wrong date!

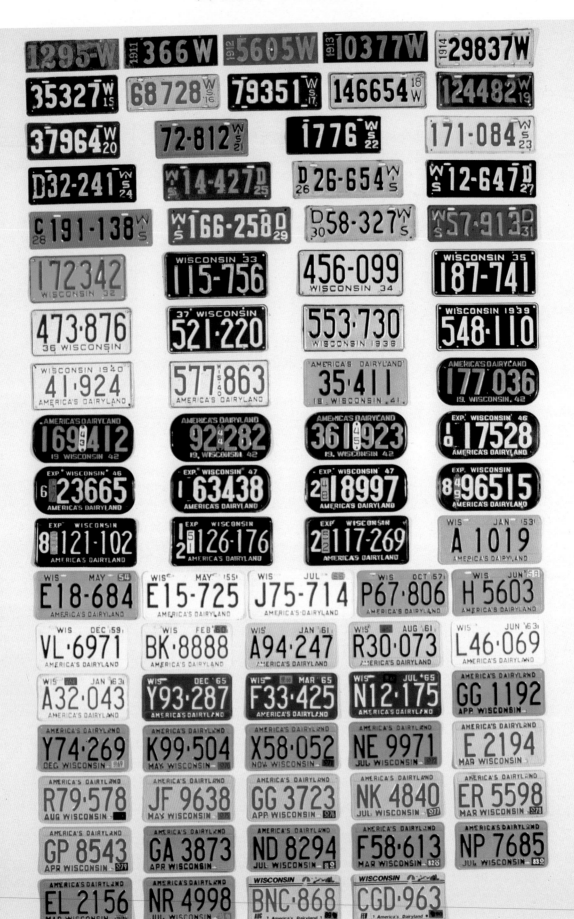

WISCONSIN

PRE-STATES

The cities of Milwaukee and Madison both had motor vehicle registration laws on the books in 1904. If plates were required, they would undoubtedly have been of the home-made variety, but I am unaware of any surviving examples of this era from anywhere in Wisconsin.

SLOGANS

Beginning with the 1940 plate, Wisconsin has used the slogan *AMERICA'S DAIRYLAND* without interruption on all issues, including the current base.

GRAPHICS

Wisconsin's first and only graphic plates were introduced in 1986. At the upper right was a sailboat set against a blazing sun, a couple of geese in flight and a pastoral farm scene, all evidently elements of life in Wisconsin. The registration number on this plate was in blue and apparently it was thought by the motor vehicle department that the plates too closely resembled the plates of Illinois, Wisconsin's southern neighbor. The following year, the graphics remained intact, while the registration number was changed from blue to red. Both bases remain in use as of 1993.

FIRST YEAR OF ISSUE
1905
UNDATED ISSUES
1905-1911
PORCELAINS
None
WINDSHIELD STICKERS
None
METAL DATE TABS
1943, 1944, 1945, 1947, 1948, 1949, 1950, 1951, 1952, 1954, 1956, 1958, 1960

OTHER FEATURES

The 1905-1911, 1912 and 1913 plates all had aluminum characters riveted to a metal base. In July of 1911, new registrants began receiving a plate dated 1911, again made of aluminum characters on a metal base. Though the number of 1911 plates issued is unknown, these plates are very scarce today. The 1940 plates were designed in two different ways. Early issues have the state name and date across the top of the plate. Late issues have the state abbreviation *WIS* down the center of the plate, followed by the date, *40*. The second style allowed room for larger numbers to be used on the plate.

WYOMING

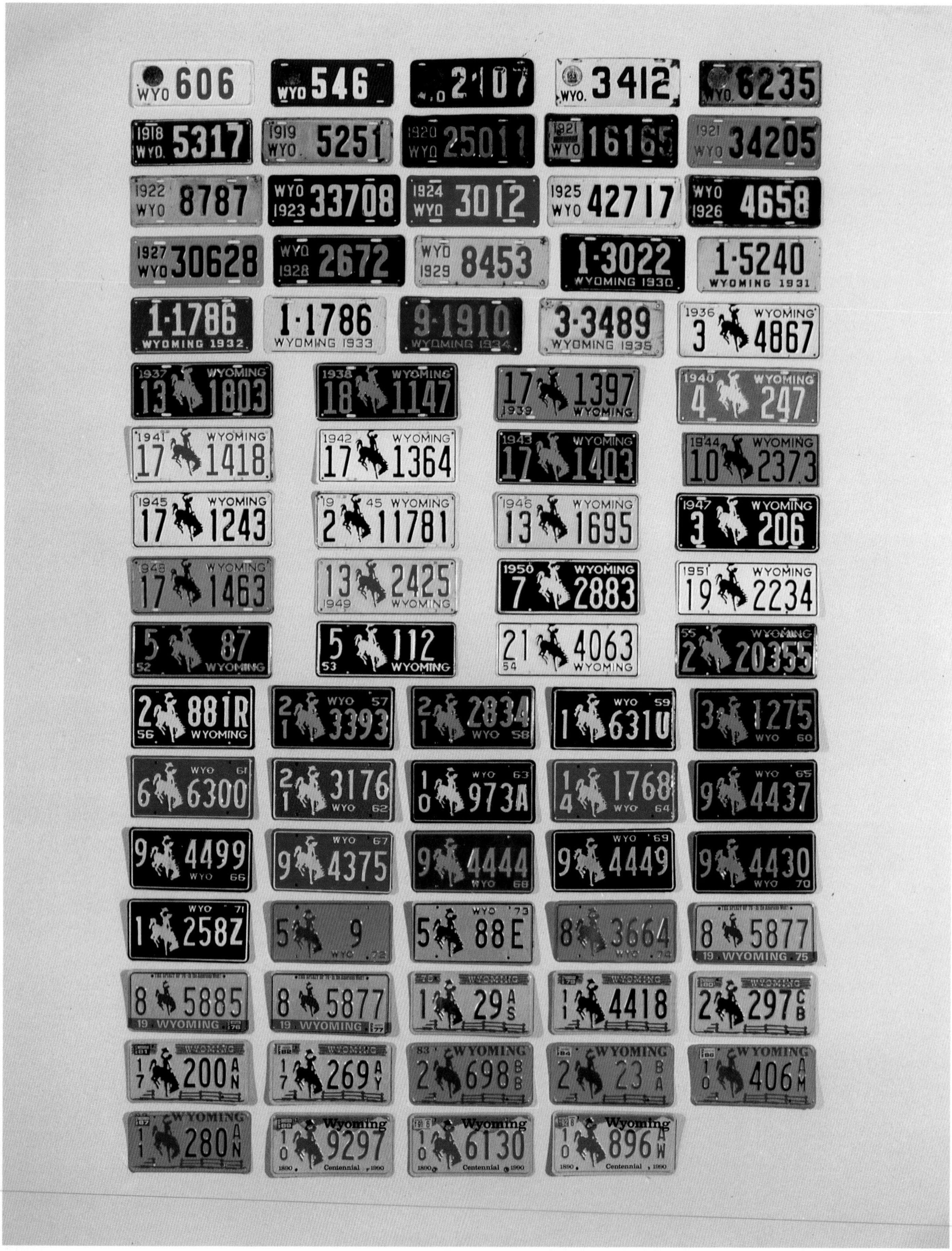

WYO 606
WYO 546
2107
WYO. 3412
WYO. 6235
1918 WYO. 5317
1919 WYO 5251
1920 WYO 25011
1921 WYO 16165
1921 WYO 34205
1922 WYO 8787
WYO 1923 33708
1924 WYO 3012
1925 WYO 42717
WYO 1926 4658
1927 WYO 30628
WYO 1928 2672
WYO 1929 8453
1-3022 WYOMING 1930
1-5240 WYOMING 1931
1-1786 WYOMING 1932
1-1786 WYOMING 1933
9-1910 WYOMING 1934
3-3489 WYOMING 1935
1936 WYOMING 3 4867
1937 WYOMING 13 1803
1938 WYOMING 18 1147
17 1397 1939 WYOMING
1940 WYOMING 4 247
1941 WYOMING 17 1418
1942 WYOMING 17 1364
1943 WYOMING 17 1403
1944 WYOMING 10 2373
1945 WYOMING 17 1243
19 45 WYOMING 2 11781
1946 WYOMING 13 1695
1947 WYOMING 3 206
1948 WYOMING 17 1463
13 2425 1949 WYOMING
1950 WYOMING 7 2883
1951 WYOMING 19 2234
5 87 52 WYOMING
5 112 53 WYOMING
21 4063 54 WYOMING
55 WYOMING 2 20355
2 881R 56 WYOMING
2 1 WYO 57 3393
2 1 2834 WYO 58
1 WYO 59 631U
3 1275 WYO 60
6 WYO 61 6300
2 1 3176 WYO 62
1 0 WYO 63 973A
1 4 1768 WYO 64
9 WYO 65 4437
9 4499 WYO 66
9 WYO 67 4375
9 4444 WYO 68
9 WYO '69 4449
9 4430 WYO 70
1 WYO '71 258Z
5 9 WYO '72
5 WYO '73 88E
8 3664 WYO '74
8 5877 19 WYOMING 75
8 5885 19 WYOMING 76
8 5877 19 WYOMING 77
WYOMING 1 29 AS
WYOMING 1 4418
WYOMING 2 297 CB
WYOMING 1 7 200 AN
WYOMING 1 7 269 AY
83 WYOMING 2 698 BB
WYOMING 2 23 BA
WYOMING 1 0 406 AM
WYOMING 1 1 280 AN
Wyoming 1 0 9297 1890 Centennial 1990
Wyoming 1 0 6130 1890 Centennial 1990
Wyoming 1 0 896 AW 1890 Centennial 1990

WYOMING

PRE-STATES

Hard evidence explaining early automobile registration in Wyoming is difficult to come by today. There were city ordinances in Cheyenne and Laramie, and at least one leather plate survives today with the letters *LAR* on it. Further, plate "PL490" also exists in leather. For want of a better explanation, speculation has it that this plate was issued in Powell, Wyoming, though that number seems improbably high for that town and that time. Several leather plates exist with the letters *WYO*, including one with the letters *branded* into the leather. The letters *WYO* would imply statewide registration of some form, but the earliest state ordinance seems to date to 1912, and deals with the first state-manufactured plates beginning in 1913. More mysteries....

SLOGANS

The 1975 base, used also in 1976 and 1977, had the slogan *THE SPIRIT OF 76-IN THE AMERICAN WEST* across the top. The 1988 base, used through 1992, celebrated Wyoming's first hundred years of statehood with *1890 CENTENNIAL 1990* along the bottom of the plate.

GRAPHICS

Beginning in 1936, a rodeo rider on top of a bucking bronco first appeared in the center of Wyoming's plates. This proved to be extremely popular and has appeared on each plate since. The 1975 issue used a red, white and blue color scheme to emphasize the Bicentennial, accompanying the above slogan. The 1978 base had the state name and date illustrated as if on pieces of driftwood. A split rail fence graced the bottom of the plate. The 1983 base retained the split rail fence across the bottom. The 1988 base featured a blue sky overlooking a panoramic mountain scene. The 1993 base featured an elaborate prairie scene. The plate made full use of current silk-screening technology, showing a multicolored mountain and skyline scene beyond the prairie.

OTHER FEATURES

The 1913 and 1914 plates both had elaborate seals of German silver attached. The seals differ only slightly from each other, and it takes an expert to tell them apart. Further, without paint (and after 80 years, many of these plates have lost their paint), it is almost impossible to tell the 1913 plate from the 1914 plate without their seals. The 1915 seal was embossed into the plate, and the 1916 seal was part of the porcelain. In 1917, an aluminum seal was attached to the plates. The 1921 revalidation tab had a small brass insert containing the registration number. The 1944 issue was a soybean fiberboard plate, but the bronco kept the goats away!

1993 LICENSE PLATES

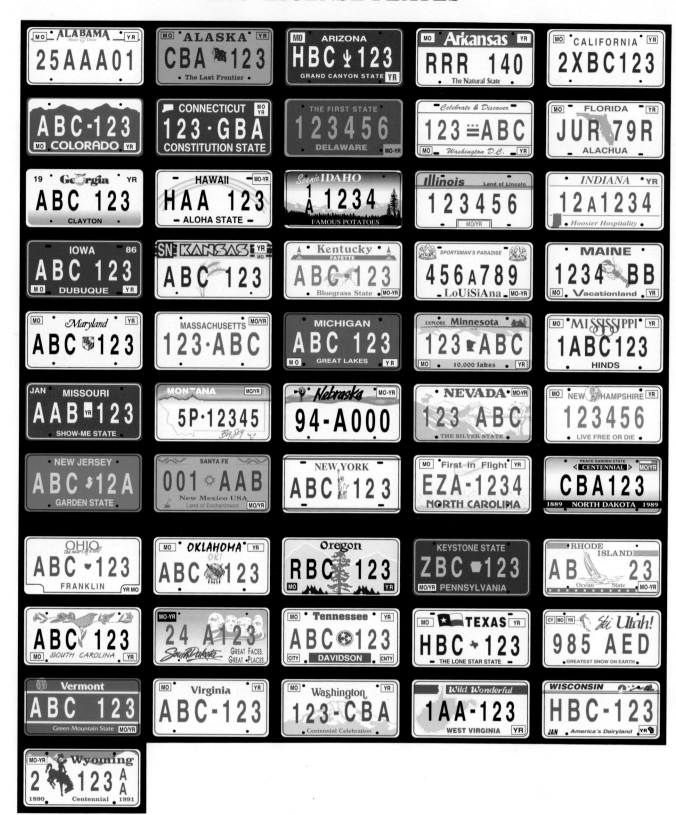

112

The illustrations on the opposite page represent the current crop of United States passenger car plates, at least as of 1993. Some issues have come into use since this was assembled, and others may have been invalidated. However, what this assemblage of goodies really does best is to illustrate how far we have come in plate design. Contrast these designs with any from 25 years ago, and it is plain to see that the silk-screening process has enabled plate designers to make great strides. Several of these designs were voted "Best Plate Design" of their debut years by the members of ALPCA. These are: 1982 North Carolina, 1984 Maryland, 1985 Nevada, 1986 Utah, 1988 Oregon, 1989 Oklahoma, 1990 South Carolina and 1991 Idaho.

It is also worth noting that what you see on the opposite page is not a photograph, but rather a computer-generated image of each plate. With technology such as this, is it any wonder that license plate graphics are getting more complex and attractive, while still maintaining the characteristic that is desired above all others: readability!

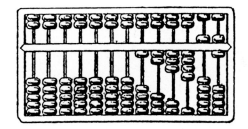

Color Codes

Photo : Joseph E. Daniel / WILDPIC

ALABAMA
COLOR CODE

1912: White on Blue (undated Porcelain)
1913: Black on Orange-Red (undated Porcelain)
1914: Black on White (undated Porcelain)
1915: White on Green(undated Porcelain)
1916: Black on Orange (undated)
1917: Red on White
1918: Blue on Gray
1919: White on Dark Green
1920: Black on White
1921: Red on White
1922: Black on Orange
1923: White on Dark Blue
1924: Brown on Cream
1925: White on Red
1926: White on Green
1927: Ivory on Black
1928: Black on Yellow
1929: Yellow on Black
1930: White on Red
1931: Yellow on Green
1932: Black on White
1933: White on Light Blue
1934: Black on Orange
1935: White on Green
1936: Red on White
1937: Purple on White
1938: Red on Blue-Purple
1939: Black on Silver
1940: Yellow on Black
1941: Blue on Yellow
1942: Yellow on Black
1943: *Windshield Sticker*
1944: Black on Yellow
1945: Yellow on Black
1946: White on Black
1947: Black on Silver
1948: Deep Yellow on Black
1949: Black on Deep Yellow
1950: Yellow on Black
1951: Black on Yellow
1952: White on Blue
1953: Blue on White
1954: White on Blue
1955: White on Green
1956: Black on Deep Yellow
1957: Deep Yellow on Black

1958: White on Blue
1959: Blue on White
1960: White on Blue
1961: White on Black
1962: White on Green
1963: Reflective White on Blue
1964: Reflective White on Red
1965: Reflective Orange on Blue
1966: Reflective White on Black
1967: Reflective Yellow on Medium Blue
1968: Reflective White on Red
1969: Green on Reflective White
1970: Blue on Reflective White
1971: Black on Reflective Lemon Yellow
1972: Black on Reflective Mint Green
1973: Dark Red on Reflective White
1974: Black on Reflective White
1975: Black on Reflective Lemon Yellow
1976: Blue on Reflective White
1977: Blue and Red on Reflective White
1978: *White on Blue Sticker*
1979: *Black on White Sticker*
1980: *Black on Yellow Sticker*
1981: *White on Red Sticker*
1982: *White on Blue Sticker*
New base issued: Blue and Red on Reflective White graphic undated base with 1983 sticker.
1983: *White on Red Sticker*
1984: *Red on White Sticker*
1985: *White on Red Sticker*
1986: *Blue on White Sticker*
1987: *Red on White Sticker*
New registrations received Blue and Red on Reflective White graphic undated base with 1988 sticker.
1988: *White on Blue Sticker* on 1982 and 1987 bases
1989: *Red on White Sticker* on 1982 and 1987 bases
1990: *White on Red Sticker* on 1987 base
1991: *Blue on White Sticker* on 1987 base
1992: *White on Blue Sticker*
New registrations received Blue and Red on Reflective White graphic undated base with 1993 sticker.
1993: *Red on White Sticker* on 1987 and 1992 bases
1994: *White on Red Sticker* on 1987 and 1992 bases

ALASKA
COLOR CODE

1921: Black on Yellow-Orange
1922: Orange on Black
1923: White on Dark Blue
1924: Black on Orange
1925: White on Red
1926: Black on Green
1927: White on Dark Blue
1928: Red on Light Yellow
1929: White on Maroon
1930: White on Dark Blue
1931: Black on Gray
1932: White on Dark Blue
1933: White on Dark Red
1934: White on Green
1935: Black on Orange
1936: Dark Blue on White
1937: White on Blue
1938: Red on White
1939: Black on Silver
1940: Black on Orange
1941: White on Green
1942: Black on White
1943: White on Blue
1944: *White on Black Tab*
New registrations received White
on Black (Fiberboard).
1945: Ivory on Green (Fiberboard)
1946: White on Maroon (Fiberboard)
1947: Yellow on Dark Blue (Fiberboard)
1948: Blue on Yellow
1949: Blue on White
1950: Blue on Orange
1951: Blue on Yellow
1952: Blue on White
1953: Blue on Yellow
1954: *Red on Aluminum Tab*
1955: *White on Black Tab*
1956: Blue on White
1957: *White on Red Tab*
1958: *Blue on Yellow Tab*
1959: *Red on White Tab*
1960: Blue on White
1961: *White on Reflective Blue Tab*
1962: Blue on White
1963: *White on Reflective Blue Tab*
1964: *Blue on Gold Sticker*

1965: *Gold on Blue Sticker*
1966: Reflective Yellow on Blue
1967: *Blue on Yellow Sticker*
1968: Reflective Blue on White
1969: *White on Blue Sticker*
1970: Reflective Blue on Yellow
1971: *White on Blue Sticker*
New registrations received Reflective
Blue on Yellow dated 1970-1971 base.
1972: *White on Green Sticker*
New registrations received Reflective
Blue on Yellow dated 1971-1972 base.
1973: *White on Black Sticker*
New registrations received Reflective
Blue on Yellow dated 1973 base.
1974: *Black on Red Sticker*
New registrations received Reflective
Blue on Yellow dated 1974 base.
1975: *Black on White Sticker*
New registrations received Reflective
Blue on Yellow dated 1975 plate.
1976: Red on Reflective White dated base with
graphic bear in background; previous
bases invalidated.
1977: *Black on Coral Sticker*
1978: *Black on Yellow Sticker*
1979: *White on Green Sticker*
1980: *White on Bronze-Gold Sticker*
1981: *Red on Black Sticker*
New base issued: Blue on Reflective Yellow
graphic undated base with 1982 sticker.
1982: *White on Blue Sticker* on 1976 and
1981 bases
1983: *White on Green Sticker* on 1981 base
1984: *White on Black Sticker*
1985: *Black on Red Sticker*
1986: *White on Brown Sticker*
1987: *Black on White Sticker*
1988: *White on Blue Sticker*
1989: *Black on Red Sticker*
1990: *White on Black Sticker*
1991: *Black on White Sticker*
1992: *White on Blue Sticker*
1993: *White on Red Sticker*
1994: *White on Black Sticker*

ARIZONA
COLOR CODE

1914: White on Blue
1915: Black on White
1916: Black on Copper
1917: White on Black
1918: Blue on Olive-Gray
1919: White on Black
1920: Black on White
1921: White on Black
1922: Green on White
1923: Blue on White
1924: White on Dark Blue
1925: Black on Copper
1926: Black on White
1927: Black on Copper
1928: Red on Copper
1929: Orange on Black
1930: Black on Gray
1931: Black on Orange
1932: White on Natural Copper
1933: Natural Copper on Black
1934: Natural Copper on Turquoise
1935: Black on Copper
1936: Black on Copper
1937: Black on Copper
1938: Black on Yellow
1939: Black on Copper
1940: Blue on White
1941: Black on Copper
1942: Dark Blue on White
1943: *Windshield Sticker*
1944: *Windshield Sticker*
1945: Black on White
1946: *Windshield Sticker*
1947: Red on Aluminum
1948: Black on Aluminum
1949: Green on Aluminum
1950: Black on White
1951: *Black on Aluminum Tab*
1952: White on Black
1953: *Yellow-Orange on Black Tab*
1954: Black on White
1955: *Black on Aluminum Tab*
1956: White on Black
1957: *Black on White Sticker*
1958: *Black on Red Sticker*
1959: White on Blue
1960: *Black on White Sticker*
1961: Blue on White

1962: *Black on Red Sticker*
1963: *Black on Yellow Sticker*
1964: White on Blue
1965: *Black on White Sticker*
1966: Black on Reflective White
1967: *Black on Green Sticker*
1968: *Black on Yellow Sticker*
1969: Black on Reflective Lemon Yellow
1970: *Green on Reflective White Sticker*
1971: *White on Black Sticker*
1972: *Red on White Sticker*
1973: Green on Reflective Copper-Bronze
1974: *White on Green Sticker*
1975: *White on Blue Sticker*
1976: *White on Red Sticker*
1977: *Black on White Sticker*
1978: *White on Blue Sticker*
1979: *Black on White Sticker*
1980: *White on Green Sticker*
New registrations received Reflective White on Maroon undated base with above sticker.
1981: *Red on White Sticker* on 1973 and 1980 bases
1982: *White on Black Sticker* on 1973 and 1980 bases
1983: *Blue on White Sticker* on 1973 and 1980 bases
1984: *Orange on White Sticker* on 1973 and 1980 bases
1985: *White on Green Sticker* on 1973 and 1980 bases
1986: *Black on Yellow Sticker* on 1973 and 1980 bases
1987: *White on Black Sticker* on 1973 and 1980 bases
1988: *Blue on White Sticker* on 1973 and 1980 bases
1989: *White on Blue Sticker* on 1973 and 1980 bases
White on Red Sticker (Emissions) on 1973 and 1980 bases
1990: *White on Orange Sticker* on 1973 and 1980 bases
White on Green Sticker (Emissions) on 1973 and 1980 bases
1991: *Black on White Sticker* on 1980 base
Black on Yellow Sticker (Emissions) on 1980 base
1992: *White on Red Sticker* on 1980 base
White on Blue Sticker (Emissions) on 1980 base
1993: *White on Green Sticker* on 1980 base
White on Black Sticker (Emissions) on 1980 base
1994: *White on Orange Sticker* on 1980 base
Orange on White Sticker (Emissions) on 1980 base

ARKANSAS
COLOR CODE

1911: Black on White (Porcelain)
1912: White on Black (Porcelain)
1913: Yellow on Green (Porcelain)
1914: Black on White
1915: White on Blue
1916: Black on Yellow-Orange
1917: Yellow on Black
1918: Black on Light Green
1919: Light Green on Black
1920: Dark Blue on Light Blue
1921: Silver on Black
1922: Black on Yellow
1923: Yellow on Black
1924: Blue on Gray
1925: White on Black
1926: Black on White
1927: Yellow on Green
1928: Orange on Black
1929: White on Blue
1930: Yellow on Blue
1931: White on Black
1932: Deep Yellow on Black
1933: Green on Black
1934: Red on White
1935: Dark Blue on Cream-Yellow
1936: Blue on White
1937: Black on White
1938: White on Red
1939: Black on Aluminum
1940: Red on Aluminum
1941: Green on Aluminum
1942: Red-Orange on Black
1943: *Windshield Sticker*
1944: White on Black (Fiberboard)
1945: Deep Yellow on Black
1946: Black on White
1947: Red on Aluminum
1948: Black on Aluminum
1949: *Red on Aluminum Tab*
1950: White on Green
1951: Green on White
1952: White on Brown
1953: Blue on White
1954: White on Green
1955: White on Blue
1956: Black on Green
1957: Red on White
1958: White on Blue

1959: Black on White
1960: White on Blue
1961: Red on Gray
1962: Blue on White
1963: White on Blue
1964: Red on White
1965: Blue on White
1966: Red on Reflective White
1967: Blue on Reflective White
1968: Red on Reflective White (undated)
1969: *Green on White Sticker*
1970: *White on Red Sticker*
1971: *White on Green Sticker*
1972: *White on Orange Sticker*
1973: *White on Blue Sticker*
1974: *White on Red Sticker*
1975: *White on Green Sticker*
New registrations received Red on Reflective White undated base with above sticker.
1976: *White on Blue Sticker* on 1968 and 1975 bases
1977: *White on Red Sticker* on 1968 and 1975 bases
1978: *White on Green Sticker* on 1968 and 1975 bases
New registrations received Red and Blue on Reflective White graphic undated base with above sticker.
1979: *White on Blue Sticker* on 1968, 1975 and 1978 bases
1980: *White on Red Sticker* on 1968, 1975 and 1978 bases
1981: *White on Green Sticker* on 1968, 1975 and 1978 bases
1982: *White on Blue Sticker* on 1968, 1975 and 1978 bases
1983: *White on Red Sticker* on 1978 base
1984: *White on Green Sticker* on 1978 base
1985: *White on Blue Sticker* on 1978 base
1986: *White on Red Sticker* on 1978 base
1987: *Blue on Yellow Sticker* on 1978 base
1988: *White on Blue Sticker* on 1978 base
1989: *White on Red Sticker* on 1978 base
New registrations received Blue and Red on Reflective White graphic undated base with above sticker.
1990: *Blue on Yellow Sticker* on 1978 and 1989 bases
1991: *White on Blue Sticker* on 1978 and 1989 bases
1992: *White on Red Sticker* on 1978 and 1989 bases
1993: *Blue on Yellow Sticker* on 1978 and 1989 bases
1994: *White on Blue Sticker* on 1978 and 1989 bases

CALIFORNIA
COLOR CODE

1914: White on Red (Porcelain)
1915: Black on Yellow (Porcelain)
1916: Blue on White (Porcelain) with *Lead Bear Tab*
1917: *Yellow Poppy Tab*
1918: *Green Mission Bell Tab*
1919: *Red Star Tab*
1920: White on Black
1921: Black on Deep Yellow
1922: Blue on White
1923: White on Black
1924: White on Green
1925: Black on Yellow
1926: White on Slate Blue
1927: White on Maroon
1928: Deep Yellow on Blue
1929: Orange on Black
1930: Black on Orange
1931: Orange on Black
1932: Black on Orange
1933: Orange on Black
1934: Black on Orange
1935: Orange on Black
1936: Black on Orange
1937: Orange on Black
1938: Black on Lemon Yellow
1939: Yellow-Orange on Blue
1940: Black on Deep Yellow
1941: Deep Yellow on Black
1942: *Black on Yellow Date Strip* New registrations received Deep Yellow on Black 1942 plate.
1943: *Red on White "V" Tab* (undated) on 1941 and 1942 plates
1944: *Windshield Sticker*
1945: White on Black
1946: *Black on Yellow Tab*
1947: Black on Deep Yellow
1948: *Red on Aluminum Tab*
1949: *Black on Aluminum Tab*
1950: *Red on Aluminum Tab*
1951: Chrome Yellow on Black
1952: *Black on Chrome Yellow Tab*
1953: *Black on White Tab*
1954: *White on Red Tab*
1955: *Black on Gray Tab*
1956: Black on Deep Yellow

1957: *Black on Red Sticker*
1958: *White on Green Sticker*
1959: *Black on White Sticker*
1960: *Silver on Blue Sticker*
1961: *Silver on Red Sticker*
1962: *Green on White Sticker*
1963: Chrome Yellow on Black
1964: *Black on White Sticker*
1965: *Black on Orange Sticker*
1966: *Black on Lemon Yellow Sticker*
1967: *Black on Blue Sticker*
1968: *Black on Pink Sticker*
1969: *Black on White Sticker* New registrations received Yellow on Blue undated base with above sticker.
1970: *Black on Orange Sticker*
1971: *Black on Green Sticker*
1972: *Black on Lemon Yellow Sticker*
1973: *Black on Red Sticker*
1974: *Black on White Sticker*
1975: *Red on White Sticker*
1976: *Blue on White Sticker*
1977: *Red on White Sticker*
1978: *Black on Green Sticker*
1979: *Black on White Sticker*
1980: *Black on Blue Sticker*
1981: *Black on Blue Sticker*
1982: *Black on Yellow Sticker*
1983: *Silver on Red Sticker*
1984: *Black on Green Sticker* New registrations received Blue on Reflective Red, Orange and White graphic undated base with above sticker.
1985: *Black on White Sticker*
1986: *Black on Orange Sticker*
1987: *Black on Blue Sticker* New registrations received Blue on Reflective White base with above sticker.
1988: *Black on Yellow Sticker*
1989: *Black on Dark Red Sticker*
1990: *Black on Green Sticker*
1991: *Black on White Sticker*
1992: *Black on Orange Sticker*
1993: *Black on Blue Sticker*
1994: *Black on Yellow Sticker*

Note: All bases issued since 1963 remain valid.

COLORADO
COLOR CODE

1913: Black on White (Porcelain)
1914: White on Blue (Porcelain)
1915: Black on Yellow (Porcelain)
1916: White on Brown
1917: Black on Pink
1918: White on Black
1919: Silver on Dark Brown (Flat) with *Silver on Dark Brown Tab*
1920: *Silver on Blue Tab*
New registrations received Silver on Dark Brown 1920 plate.
1921: Silver on Dark Blue
1922: Black on White
1923: White on Black
1924: Black on Gray
1925: White on Maroon
1926: White on Light Green
1927: White on Black
1928: Maroon on Gray
1929: White on Maroon
1930: Yellow-Orange on Black
1931: Black on Yellow-Orange
1932: Orange on Black
1933: Black on Orange
1934: Yellow on Black
1935: Black on Yellow
1936: White on Blue
1937: Black on Silver
1938: White on Turquoise
1939: Yellow on Black
1940: Black on Yellow
1941: Yellow on Black
1942: White on Maroon
1943: Yellow on Black
1944: *Black on Yellow Tab*
1945: White on Black
1946: Yellow on Black
1947: Black on Yellow
1948: Black on Natural Aluminum
1949: Yellow on Black
1950: Green on White
1951: White on Green
1952: *Black on Yellow Tab*
1953: Green on Yellow
1954: White on Black
1955: Black on White
1956: White on Black
1957: Black on Orange
1958: Dark Green on Light Green
1959: White on Green
1960: Green on White
1961: *Green on White Sticker*

1962: White on Green
1963: Green on White
1964: White on Green
1965: Green on White
1966: White on Green
1967: Green on White
1968: White on Green
1969: Green on White
1970: White on Green
1971: Green on Reflective White
1972: Reflective White on Green
1973: Green on Reflective White
1974: Reflective White on Green
1975: Red, Light Blue and Dark Blue on ReflectiveWhite graphic
1976: *Blue on White Sticker*
New registrations received Red on Reflective White undated plate with above sticker.
1977: Reflective White on Green (undated)
1978: *Black on White Sticker*
1979: *Black on Orange Sticker* (December only)
Black on Yellow Sticker (other months)
1980: *Black on White Sticker* (December only)
Black on Gold Sticker or
White on Red Sticker or
Yellow on Red Sticker
1981: *Blue on White Sticker*
1982: *Black on Orange Sticker*
1983: *Black on Red Sticker* (1968 and newer)
Black on White Sticker (1967 and older)
1984: *Red on White Sticker* (1968 and newer)
Black on White Sticker (1967 and older)
1985: *Red on White Sticker* (1968 and newer)
Black on Yellow Sticker (1967 and older)
1986: *White on Red Sticker* (1968 and newer)
Yellow on Black Sticker (1967 and older)
1987: *Red on White Sticker* (1968 and newer)
Black on Yellow Sticker (1967 and older)
1988: *White on Red Sticker* (1968 and newer)
Yellow on Black Sticker (1967 and older)
1989: *Blue on White Sticker* (1968 and newer)
Orange on White Sticker (1967 and older)
1990: *Brown on White Sticker* (1968 and newer)
Green on White Sticker (1967 and older)
1991: *Red on White Sticker* (1968 and newer)
Black on White Sticker (1967 and older)
1992: *Blue on White Sticker* (1968 and newer)
Orange on White Sticker (1967 and older)
1993: *Brown on White Sticker* (1968 and newer)
Green on White Sticker (1967 and older)
1994: *Red on White Sticker* (1968 and newer)
Black on White Sticker (1967 and older)

CONNECTICUT
COLOR CODE

1905-09: White on Black (undated Porcelain)
1910: White on Red (undated Porcelain)
1911: Blue on White (undated Porcelain)
1912: White on Green (undated Porcelain)
1913: White on Blue (undated Porcelain)
1914: White on Green (Porcelain)
1915: Yellow on Black (Porcelain)
1916: White on Black (Porcelain)
1917: Blue on White (Flat)
1918: Green on White (Flat)
1919: Black on White (Flat)
1920: Blue on Cream
1921: Orange on Black
1922: Maroon on White
1923: White on Dark Green
1924: Black on Gray
1925: White on Dark Blue
1926: Black on Yellow
1927: White on Dark Red
1928: White on Dark Blue
1929: White on Dark Red
1930: White on Dark Blue
1931: White on Dark Red
1932: White on Dark Blue
1933: White on Dark Red
1934: White on Blue
1935: White on Dark Red
1936: Yellow on Blue
1937: *Black on Aluminum with Yellow Tab*
1938: *Aluminum Tab*
1939: *Green Tab*
1940: *Yellow Tab*
1941: *Aluminum Tab*
1942: *Green Tab*
1943: *Yellow Tab*
1944: *White Tab*
1945: *Green Tab*
1946: *Aluminum Tab*
1947: *Green Tab*
1948: Black on Reflective Aluminum with
    Yellow Tab
1949: *Aluminum Tab*
1950: *Green Tab*
1951: *Yellow Tab*
1952: *Aluminum Tab*
1953: *Red Tab*
1954: *Yellow Tab*
1955: *Green Tab*
    New registrations received Black on Reflective
    Aluminum base with above tab.
1956: *Red Tab*

1957: *White on Blue with White on Blue Tab*
1958: *Blue on White Tab*
1959: *Black on Aluminum Tab*
1960: *White on Metallic Blue Tab*
1961: No dated 1961 issue due to advent of
    staggered expiration system.
1962: *Black on Tan Tab*
1963: *Red on White Tab* or *Red on White Sticker*
1964: *Blue on White Sticker*
1965: *Green on White Sticker*
1966: *Red on White Sticker*
1967: *Blue on White Sticker*
1968: *Green on White Sticker*
1969: *Red on White Sticker*
1970: *Blue on White Sticker*
1971: *Green on White Sticker*
1972: *Red on White Sticker*
1973: *Blue on White Sticker*
1974: *Green on White Sticker*
    New registrations received Blue on Reflective
    White undated base with above sticker.
1975: *Black on White Sticker*
1976: *Blue on White Sticker*
    New registrations received Reflective White
    with Blue undated base with above sticker.
1977: *Green on White Sticker*
1978: *Black on White Sticker*
1979: *Blue on White Sticker*
1980: *Green on White Sticker*
1981: *Black on White Sticker*
1982: *Blue on white Sticker*
1983: *Green on White Sticker*
1984: *Black on White Sticker*
1985: *Blue on White Sticker*
1986: *Green on White Sticker*
1987: *Black on White Sticker*
    New registrations received a Reflective White
    on Blue undated base with above sticker.
1988: *Blue on White Sticker*
1989: *Green on White Sticker*
1990: *Black on White Sticker*
1991: *Blue on White Sticker*
1992: *Green on White Sticker*
1993: *Black on White Sticker*
1994: *Blue on White Sticker*
1995: *Green on White Sticker*

Note: All bases issued since 1957 remain valid, with the
    exception of the 1974 and 1976 bases, which were
    phased out in 1991.

DELAWARE
COLOR CODE

1909: White on Black (Porcelain)
1910: Black on White (Porcelain)
1911: White on Blue (Porcelain)
1912: White on Maroon (Porcelain)
1913: White on Black (Porcelain)
1914: Yellow on Black (Porcelain)
1915: Blue on White (Porcelain)
1916: White on Green
1917: White on Black
1918: White on Brown
1919: White on Blue
1920: Black on Light Green
1921: Red on White
1922: Blue on White
1923: White on Black
1924: Brown on White
1925: Black on Orange
1926: Yellow on Blue
1927: Red on Gray
1928: Black on White
1929: Blue on Yellow
1930: Yellow on Blue
1931: Blue on Yellow
1932: Yellow on Blue
1933: Blue on Yellow
1934: Yellow on Blue
1935: Blue on Yellow
1936: Yellow on Blue
1937: Blue on Yellow
1938: Red on Silver
1939: Silver on Maroon
1940: No dated 1940 issue due to advent of staggered expiration system.
3/31/41: Blue on Yellow
3/31/42: Yellow on Blue
1942: White on Black (undated Porcelain) with *Blue on Yellow Tab*
1943: *Yellow on Blue Tab*
1944: *Blue on Yellow Tab*
1945: *Yellow on Blue Tab*
1946: *Blue on Yellow Tab*
1947: *Yellow on Blue Tab*
1948: *Blue on Yellow Tab*
New registrations received Stainless Steel on Black riveted undated base with above tab.
1949: *Yellow on Blue Tab*
1950: *Blue on Yellow Tab*
1951: *Yellow on Blue Tab*
1952: *Blue on Yellow Tab*
New registrations received Reflective White on Black riveted undated base with above tab.
1953: *Yellow on Blue Tab*
1954: *Blue on Yellow Tab*

1955: *Yellow on Blue Tab*
1956: *Blue on Yellow Tab*
1957: *Yellow on Blue Tab*
1958: *Blue on Yellow Tab*
1959: *Yellow on Blue Tab*
New registrations received Reflective Yellow on Reflective Blue riveted undated base with above tab.
1960: *Blue on Yellow Tab*
1961: *Yellow on Blue Tab*
1962: *Blue on Yellow Tab*
1963: *Blue on Yellow Sticker*
New registrations received Reflective Yellow on Reflective Blue riveted undated base with above sticker.
1964-1970: *Quarterly Expiration Stickers:*
MAR– Black on White
JUN – White on Green
SEP – Black on Red
DEC– Black on Yellow
New registrations in 1970 received Reflective Gold on Blue (Flat) undated base with above sticker.
1971: *White on Maroon Sticker*
1972: *White on Pink Sticker*
1973: *Monthly Expiration Stickers:*
JAN – Black on Gold
FEB – White on Blue
MAR– Black on Orange
APR – Black on Green
MAY– White on Red
JUN – White on Green
JUL – Black on Lemon Yellow
AUG– Black on Silver
SEP – Black on Yellow
OCT– White on Dull Blue
NOV– White on Tan
DEC– Black on White
1974: *Monthly Expiration Stickers* same as 1973 colors
1975: *Monthly Expiration Stickers:*
JAN – Black on Pale Yellow
FEB – Black on Light Blue
MAR– Black on Red-Orange
APR – Black on Green
MAY– Black on Red
JUN – Black on Yellow
JUL – White on Yellow-Green
AUG– White on Blue
SEP – White on Orange
OCT– White on Light Green
NOV– White on Orange-Pink
DEC– White on Lemon Yellow

DELAWARE
COLOR CODE

1976 to date: *Monthly Expiration Stickers:*[*]
   JAN – Black on Red
   FEB – Black on Gold
   MAR– Black on Light Blue
   APR – Black on Orange
   MAY– Black on Green
   JUN – Black on Yellow
   JUL – White on Red
   AUG– White on Brown
   SEP – White on Dark Blue
   OCT– White on Purple
   NOV– White on Green
   DEC– Black on Silver

Note: All bases issued since 1942 remain valid.

---

[*]Since January of 1976 monthly expiration stickers have been similar each year, although the shades differ. For example, February 1980, 1982 and 1985 can be considered off-white.

DISTRICT OF COLUMBIA
COLOR CODE

1907-17: White on Black (undated Porcelain)
1918: Black on Yellow
1919: White on Olive Green
1920: Black on White
1921: Blue on Light Gray
1922: White on Red
1923: White on Brown
1924: White on Black
1925: White on Dark Blue
1926: Black on Yellow-Orange
1927: Deep Yellow on Black
1928: Black on Deep Yellow
1929: Deep Yellow on Black
1930: Black on Deep Yellow
1931: Deep Yellow on Black
1932: Black on Deep Yellow
1933: Deep Yellow on Black
1934: Black on Yellow-Orange
1935: Green on White
1936: Black on Yellow-Orange
1937: Yellow-Orange on Black
1938: Black on Orange
2/29/40: Yellow-Orange Black
3/31/41: Black on Orange
3/31/42: Yellow on Black
3/31/43: Black on Yellow
3/31/44: *White on Black Tab*
3/31/45: *Black on White Tab*
3/31/46: Yellow on Black
3/31/47: Black on Yellow
3/31/48: Yellow on Black
1948: Yellow on Black
1949: Black on Yellow
1950: Yellow on Black
1951: Black on Yellow
1952: Yellow on Black
3/31/54: Green on White
3/31/55: *White on Green Tab*
3/31/56: White on Green
3/31/57: Black on Yellow
3/31/58: Yellow on Blue
3/31/59: Blue on Yellow
3/31/60: Yellow on Blue
3/31/61: Blue on Yellow
3/31/62: Yellow on Blue
3/31/63: Green on Reflective White
3/31/64: Black on Reflective Yellow

3/31/65: Red on Reflective White
3/31/66: Black on Reflective Yellow
3/31/67: Black on Reflective White
3/31/68: *White on Green Sticker*
New registrations received Black on Reflective White undated base with above sticker.
3/31/69: Black on Reflective White (undated)
3/31/70: *Black on Yellow Sticker*
3/31/71: *White on Red Sticker*
3/31/72: *White on Blue Sticker*
3/31/73: *White on Black Sticker*
3/31/74: *White on Green Sticker*
3/31/75: Blue and Red on Reflective White
3/31/76: *Blue on White Sticker*
3/31/77: *Red on White Sticker*
3/31/78: *Blue on White Sticker*
3/31/79: *Black on White Sticker*
New registrations received Blue and Red on Reflective White undated base with above sticker.
3/31/80: *Red on White Sticker* on 1975 and 1979 bases
3/31/81: *Blue on White Sticker* on 1975 and 1979 bases
3/31/82: *Red on White Sticker* on 1975 and 1979 bases
3/31/83: *Blue on White Sticker* 1979 base
3/31/84: *Red on White Sticker* on 1979 base
1985: *Blue on White Sticker* on 1979 base
New registrations received Blue and Red on White base with above sticker.
1986: *Red on White Sticker* on 1979 and 1985 bases
1987: *White on Red Sticker* on 1979 and 1985 bases
1988: *White on Blue Sticker* on 1979 and 1985 bases
1989: *Red on White Sticker* on 1979 and 1985 bases
1990: *White on Red Sticker* on 1985 base; 1979 base invalidated
1991: *Blue on White Sticker*
New registrations received Blue and Red on Reflective White graphic undated base with above sticker.
1992: *Red on White Sticker* on 1985 and 1991 bases
1993: *White on Blue Sticker* on 1985 and 1991 bases
1994: *White on Red Sticker* on 1985 and 1991 bases
1995: *White on Black Sticker* on 1985 and 1991 bases

FLORIDA
COLOR CODE

1918: White on Black (Flat)
1919: Black on Orange
1920: Red on Gray
1921: White on Brown
1922: White on Green
1923: Orange on Dark Blue
1924: White on Black
1925: Orange on Green
1926: Yellow on Black
1927: White on Black
1928: Yellow on Maroon
1929: Yellow on Blue
1930: White on Green
1931: White on Maroon
1932: Orange on Black
1933: Black on Orange
1934: White on Black with
Black on White Lock Strip
1935: Black on Yellow with
Black on Yellow Lock Strip
1936: White on Red
1937: White on Green
1938: Yellow on Black
1939: Red on White
1940: White on Black
1941: Red on White
1942: Orange on Blue
1943: *Yellow on Blue Tab*
1944: Black on Yellow
1945: Yellow on Black
1946: White on Dark Blue
1947: White on Green
1948: Yellow on Black
1949: Red on White
1950: Blue on Orange
1951: Green on Yellow
1952: Orange on Blue
1953: Blue on Orange
1954: Orange on Blue
1955: Blue on Orange or
Reflective Blue on Orange
1956: White on Blue
1957: Blue on White
1958: White on Dark Green
1959: Dark Green on White
1960: Yellow on Blue
1961: Dark Blue on Yellow
1962: Blue on White

1963: White on Blue
1964: Blue on Orange
1965: Reflective Yellow on Red
1966: Reflective White on Blue
1967-68: Reflective White on Black
1968-69: Reflective White on Red
1969-70: Reflective White on Green
1970-71: Reflective White on Blue
1972: Red-Orange on Reflective White
1973: Green on Reflective White
1974: Red-Orange on Reflective White
1975: Red-Orange on Reflective White
1976: *White on Green Sticker*
1977: *White on Blue Sticker*
New registrations received Green on Reflective White undated base with above sticker.
1978: *White on Green Sticker* on 1975 and 1977 bases
New registrations received Green on Reflective White and Orange graphic undated base with above sticker.
1979: *White on Red Sticker* on 1975, 1977 and 1978 bases
1980: *White on Blue Sticker* on 1975, 1977 and 1978 bases; 1975 base invalid after June 30, 1980
1981: *White on Green Sticker*
1982: *White on Red Sticker*
1983: *White on Blue Sticker*
1984: *White on Green Sticker*
1985: *White on Red Sticker*
1986: *White on Blue Sticker*
New registrations received Orange on Reflective White and Green graphic undated base with above sticker.
1987: *Black on Yellow Sticker*
1988: *White on Green Sticker*
1989: *White on Red Sticker*
1990: *White on Blue Sticker*
1991: *Black on Yellow Sticker*
New registrations received Green on Reflective White and Orange graphic undated base with above sticker.
1992: *White on Green Sticker*
1993: *White on Red Sticker*
1994: *White on Blue Sticker*

Note: All bases issued since 1977 remain valid.

GEORGIA
COLOR CODE

1910-11: Black on Aluminum (undated)
1912: New registrations received Black on Yellow undated plate.
1913: New registrations received Black on White undated plate.
1914: Black on White
1915: White on Black (Porcelain)
1916: Blue on White
1917: White on Black
1918: Black on Light Green
1919: Black on White
1920: White on Dark Green
1921: Green on White
1922: White on Black
1923: White on Brown
1924: Black on Gray
1925: White on Dark Blue
1926: White on Red
1927: Black on Yellow
1928: White on Dark Blue
1929: Orange on Black
1930: Black on Gray
1931: White on Green
1932: White on Blue
1933: Blue on Orange
1934: Orange on Blue
1935: Blue on Orange
1936: Orange on Blue
1937: Blue on Orange
1938: Orange on Blue
1939: Dark Blue on Yellow
1940: Orange on Green
1941: Reflective Yellow on Blue
1942: White and Red on Blue
1943: *White on Red Date Strip*
1944: Yellow on Black (3-1/2" X 12-1/2")
1945: White on Black
1946: Black on Silver
1947: Maroon on Cream
1948: Black on Aluminum
1949: Red on Aluminum
1950: Black on Aluminum
1951: Green on Aluminum
1952: White on Black
1953: Orange on Black

1954: Black on Yellow
1955: Yellow on Black
1956: White on Black
1957: White on Dark Green
1958: Black on White
1959: White on Black
1960: Black on White
1961: Black on Deep Yellow
1962: Red on White
1963: White on Dark Red
1964: Peach on Green
1965: Blue on White
1966: White on Red
1967: Red on White
1968: White on Green
1969: White on Black
1970: White on Medium Blue
1971: Blue on Reflective White
1972: *White on Red Sticker*
1973: *White on Blue Sticker*
1974: *White on Green Sticker*
1975: *White on Rust Red Sticker*
1976: Red on Reflective White
1977: *White on Blue Sticker*
1978: *White on Red Sticker*
1979: *White on Green Sticker*
1980: *White on Black Sticker*
New registrations received Red on Reflective graphic base, still with embossed 1976 date, and above sticker.
1981: *Black on Yellow Sticker* on 1976 and 1980 bases
1982: *Red on White Sticker* on 1976 and 1980 bases
1983: Green on Reflective White graphic
1984: *Blue on White Sticker*
1985: *White on Red Sticker*
1986: *White on Blue Sticker*
1987: *White on Green Sticker*
1988: *White on Orange Sticker*
1989: *White on Black Sticker*
1990: Black on Reflective Green, Peach and White graphic
1991: *Dark Green on White Sticker*
1992: *Black on Peach Sticker*
1993: *White on Black Sticker*

HAWAII
COLOR CODE

1922: White on Green
1923: Green on White
1924: Red on White
1925: Black on Orange
1926: White on Green
1927: Black on Silver
1928: Orange on Black
1929: Yellow on Blue
1930: White on Red
1931: White on Black
1932: Yellow on Green
1933: Red on Orange
1934: White on Blue
1935: Black on Yellow
1936: White on Green
1937: Blue on White
1938: Yellow on Black
1939: White on Blue
1940: Black on Yellow
1941: Red on Gray
1942: White on Black
1943: *Windshield Sticker*
1944: *Windshield Sticker*
1945: *Windshield Sticker*
1946: Black on White
1947: White on Green
1948: Black on Yellow
1949: Yellow on Black
1950: Black on Yellow
1951: Yellow on Black
1952: Black on Yellow
1953: Yellow on Black (undated) with *Black on Aluminum Tab*
1954: *Black on Yellow Tab*
1955: *Red on White Tab*
1956: *Black on Yellow-Orange Tab*
1957: Reflective White on Red undated base, with *Windshield Stickers* issued each year from 1957 to 1960

1961: Reflective White on Green undated base, with *Windshield Stickers* issued each year from 1961 to 1968
1969: Black on Reflective Lemon Yellow
1970: *Yellow on Red Sticker*
1971: *White on Green Sticker*
1972: *Black on White Sticker*
1973: *White on Blue Sticker*
1974: *White on Red Sticker*
1975: *White on Green Sticker*
1976: Blue, Light Red and Dark Red on Reflective White graphic
1977: *Sticker – Top and Bottom Black on Reflective Red, Center Black on Reflective White*
1978: *Black on Blue and White Sticker*
1979: *Black, White and Red Sticker*
1980: *Green, White and Yellow Sticker*
1981: Brown and Orange on White graphic
1982: *White on Blue Sticker*
1983: *Black on Yellow Sticker*
1984: *White on Green Sticker*
1985: *White on Red Sticker*
1986: *Black on White Sticker*
1987: *White on Brown Sticker*
1988: *White on Brown Sticker*
1989: *White on Orange Sticker*
1990: *Blue on White Sticker*
1991: *Pink on White Sticker*
New base issued: Black on Reflective White undated base with a Red, Yellow and Blue graphic rainbow across top and 1992 sticker.
1992: *Green on White Sticker*
1993: *Black on Yellow Sticker*
1994: *White on Red Sticker*

IDAHO
COLOR CODE

1913: White on Blue
1914: White on Red
1915: Red on White
1916: Black on Yellow
1917: Yellow on Black
1918: White on Brown
1919: Yellow on Dark Green
1920: White on Blue
1921: Black on Orange
1922: Orange on Black
1923: Orange on Silver
1924: Black on Yellow
1925: Black on White
1926: Black on Orange
1927: Orange on Dark Blue
1928: Green on Tan
1929: Yellow on Black
1930: Black on Yellow
1931: White on Black
1932: Black on Orange
1933: Orange on Black
1934: Black on Yellow
1935: Yellow on Black
1936: Black on Yellow
1937: Black on Silver
1938: White on Maroon
1939: Yellow on Blue
1940: Green on Yellow-Orange
1941: Black on Yellow
1942: Blue on White
1943: *Windshield Sticker*
1944: *Windshield Sticker*
1945: Black on Yellow-Orange
1946: White on Black
1947: White on Blue
1948: Black on Aluminum
1949: *Red on Aluminum Tab*
1950: White on Black
1951: White on Maroon
1952: *Red on Aluminum Tab*
1953: White on Black
1954: Black on White
1955: White on Black
1956: Black on White
1957: White on Light Green
1958: Green on White
1959: White on Green
1960: Green on White
1961: White on Green
1962: Green on White
1963: White on Green

1964: Green on White
1965: White on Green
1966: Green on White
1967: White on Green
1968: Green on Reflective White
1969: *Green on White Sticker*
1970: *Red on White Sticker*
1971: *Black on Yellow Sticker*
1972: *Black on White Sticker*
New registrations received Green on Reflective White undated base with above sticker.
1973: *White on Red Sticker* on 1968 and 1977 bases
1974: Green on White
1975: *Black on Yellow Sticker*
1976: *White on Red Sticker or White on Blue Sticker* on 1974 base
1977: *Black on White Sticker*
1978: *Red on Yellow Sticker*
New registrations received Green on Reflective White undated base with above sticker.
1979: *White on Black Sticker* on 1974 and 1978 bases
1980: *White on Red Sticker* on 1974 and 1978 bases
1981: *White on Blue Sticker* on 1974 and 1978 bases
1982: *Black on Yellow Sticker* on 1974 and 1978 bases
1983: *White on Red Sticker* on 1974 and 1978 bases
New registrations received Green on Reflective White graphic undated base with above sticker.
1984: *Green on White Sticker* on 1974, 1978 and 1983 bases
1985: *White on Blue Sticker* on 1974, 1978 and 1983 bases
New registrations received Green on Reflective White graphic undated base with above sticker.
1986: *White on Black Sticker* on 1974, 1978, 1983 and 1985 bases
1987: *White on Red Sticker* on 1974, 1978, 1983 and 1985 bases
1988: *White on Green Sticker* on 1974, 1978, 1983 and 1985 bases
1989: *White on Blue Sticker* on 1974, 1978, 1983 and 1985 bases
1990: *White on Black Sticker* on 1974, 1978, 1983 and 1985 bases
1991: *White on Red Sticker* on 1985 base
New registrations received Blue on Reflective Red, Blue and White graphic undated base with above sticker.
1992: *White on Blue Sticker* on 1985 and 1991 bases
1993: *Blue on White Sticker* on 1991 base
1994: *White on Red Sticker* on 1991 base

ILLINOIS
COLOR CODE

1910: Black on Aluminum (undated)*
1911: Black on White (undated)
1912: White on Black (Flat, perforated front plate)
1913: White on Blue (Cut out front plate)
1914: Green on White
1915: Blue on Yellow
1916: Black on Silver
1917: White on Black
1918: Blue on Gray
1919: White on Brown
1920: Black on Orange
1921: White on Black
1922: Black on Gray
1923: White on Green
1924: Deep Yellow on Black
1925: White on Brown
1926: White on Blue
1927: Black on Orange
1928: White on Maroon
1929: Red on Black
1930: White on Black
1931: Black on Light Green
1932: Yellow on Dark Blue
1933: White on Blue
1934: Yellow on Black
1935: Blue on Light Gray
1936: White on black
1937: Black on Yellow
1938: White on Green
1939: Yellow on Black
1940: Cream on Brown
1941: Black on Deep Yellow
1942: Deep Yellow on Black
1943: White on Green (Fiberboard)
1944: Cream on Brown (Fiberboard)
1945: Orange on Black (Fiberboard)
1946: White on Maroon (Fiberboard)
1947: White on Green (Fiberboard)
1948: Black on Orange (Fiberboard)
1949: Cream on Blue
1950: Dark Green on White
1951: Maroon on Aluminum
1952: Blue on Orange
1953: Maroon on Cream
1954: White on Green

1955: Orange on Blue
1956: Green on White
1957: White on Red
1958: Purple on White
1959: White on Brown
1960: Orange on Blue
1961: White on Red
1962: White on Orange
1963: Yellow on Dark Green
1964: White on Lavender
1965: Green on White
1966: Red on Reflective White
1967: Black on Reflective White
1968: Red on Reflective White
1969: Dark Blue on Reflective Orange
1970: Red on Reflective Lemon Yellow
1971: Black on Reflective White
1972: Blue on Reflective White
1973: Green on Reflective White
1974: Red on Reflective White
1975: Black on Reflective Lemon Yellow
1976: Blue and Red on Reflective White
1977: Green on Reflective White
1978: Black on White
1979: Dark Blue on Reflective White dated base with *White on Blue 1979 Sticker*
1980: *White on Red Sticker*
1981: *White on Green Sticker*
1982: *White on Brown Sticker*
1983: *White on Orange Sticker* on 1979 base New registrations received Blue on Reflective Light Blue and White graphic base**
1984: *White on Purple Sticker* on 1979 and 1983 bases
1985: *Black on Light Green Sticker* on 1979 and 1983 bases
1986: *Black on Orange Sticker* on 1979 and 1983 bases
1987: *White on Blue Sticker* on 1983 base
1988: *White on Red Sticker* on 1983 base
1989: *White on Green Sticker* on 1983 base
1990: *White on Red-Orange Sticker* on 1983 base
1991: *White on Burgundy Sticker* on 1983 base
1992: *Red on White Sticker* on 1983 base
1993: *White on Blue Sticker* on 1983 base

---

*This plate is not state-issued.

**The base issued in 1983 guadually replaced the 1979 base over a four-year period.

INDIANA
COLOR CODE

1913: Black on Yellow (Porcelain)
1914: White on Blue
1915: Green on Pink
1916: Black on White
1917: Yellow on Black
1918: Black on Green
1919: White on Black
1920: Green on Cream
1921: Black on Tan
1922: White on Dark Blue
1923: White on Brown
1924: Orange on Black
1925: Maroon on Tan
1926: White on Green
1927: White on Black
1928: White on Maroon
1929: Black on Orange
1930: Orange on Blue
1931: Blue on Orange
1932: White on Green
1933: White on Maroon
1934: White on Black
1935: Black on Light Green
1936: White on Red
1937: Yellow on Black
1938: Maroon on White
1939: Blue on Yellow
1940: Silver on Black
1941: White on Blue
1942: Blue on Yellow
1943: *White on Black Strip*
1944: White on Black (3-1/4" X 10")
1945: White on Brown
1946: Yellow on Black
1947: Blue on Yellow
1948: White on Blue
1949: White on Red
1950: Yellow on Black
1951: Black on White
1952: *Black on Yellow Strip*
1953: *Black on Green Strip*
1954: White on Maroon
1955: *White on Reflective Red Strip*
1956: Yellow on Blue
1957: Dark Blue on Yellow
1958: Yellow on Dark Blue
1959: Dark Blue on Yellow
1960: White on Dark Blue

1961: White on Red
1962: Yellow on Black
1963: Yellow on Blue
1964: Reflective White on Dark Red
1965: Reflective White on Dark Olive Green
1966: Black on Reflective White
1967: Red on Reflective White
1968: Blue on Reflective White
1969: Black on Reflective White
1970-71: Red on Reflective White
1971-72: Blue on Reflective White
1972-73: Green on Reflective White
Expires 1974: Red on Reflective White
Expires 1975: Black on Reflective White
Expires 1976: Blue on Reflective White Blue
1976: Red on Reflective White graphic dated plate
1977: No dated 1977 issue due to previous plate.
Expires 1978: Green and Yellow on Reflective White graphic
Expires 1979: Black, Red and Blue on Reflective White graphic
Expires 1980: Brown on Reflective Brown, Yellow and White graphic
Expires 1981: Black on Reflective Red, Yellow, Orange and White graphic
Expires 1982: Brown on Reflective Brown, Black, Yellow and White graphic dated base. Some bases had *White on Black 1982 Sticker.*
Expires 1983: *Green and White Sticker*
Expires 1984: *Blue on White Sticker*
Expires 1985: Black on Reflective Red, Yellow, Green and White graphic undated base with *White on Black Sticker*
Expires 1986: *Orange on White Sticker*
Expires 1987: *White on Green Sticker*
Expires 1988: Blue on Reflective Blue, Gold and White graphic undated base with *Black on White Sticker*
Expires 1989: *White on Red Sticker*
Expires 1990: *Green on White Sticker*
Expires 1991: Red on Reflective Red, Blue and White graphic
Expires 1992: *Red on White Sticker*
Expires 1993: *White on Blue Sticker*
Expires 1994: Black on Reflective Red and Yellow dated graphic

IOWA
COLOR CODE

1911: White on Blue
1912: White on Black
1913: Black on white
1914: White on Dark Blue
1915: Black on Yellow
1916-1918: Cream on Olive Green (undated)
1919: White on Brown
1920: Black on Light Green
1921: Silver on Black
1922: Black on Silver
1923: Yellow on Black
1924: White on Black
1925: Black on Gray
1926: White on Maroon
1927: Orange on Dark Blue
1928: Black on White
1929: Black on Green
1930: White on Dark Blue
1931: Dark Blue on White
1932: White on Maroon
1933: White on Dark Blue
1934: Yellow on Dark Blue
1935: White on Dark Blue
1936: Dark Blue on White
1937: White on Dark Blue
1938: Dark Blue on White
1939: White on Dark Blue
1940: Dark Blue on Orange
1941: Black on White
1942: White on Black
1943: *Windshield Sticker*
1944: *Windshield Sticker*
1945: Black on White rear plate used in conjunction with *Windshield Sticker*
1946: White on Black
1947: Black on White
1948: *Yellow on Aluminum Tab*
1949: White on Black
1950: Black on White
1951: *Red on Aluminum Tab*
1952: White on Black
1953: Black on White

1954: *Black on Aluminum Tab*
1955: *Orange on Aluminum Tab*
1956: White on Black
1957: *Black on Aluminum Tab*
1958: Black on White
1959: Black on Yellow (some reflective)
1960: Black on Gray
1961: Black on Yellow
1962: Black on Gray
1963: Reflective White on Black
1964: Reflective White on Green
1965: Reflective White on Dark Blue
1966: Reflective White on Red
1967: Black on Reflective White
1968: Red on Reflective White
1969: Black on Reflective White
1970: Red on Reflective White
1971: Black on Reflective White
1972: Black on Reflective Lemon Yellow
1973: *Green on White Sticker*
1974: *Rose Red on White Sticker*
1975: Black on Reflective White
1976: *Blue on White Sticker*
1977: *Red on White Sticker*
1978: *Green on White Sticker*
1979: Reflective White on Green (some entirely reflective)
1980: *Blue on White Sticker*
1981: *Red on White Sticker*
1982: *Black on White Sticker*
1983: *Blue on White Sticker*
1984: *Red on White Sticker*
1985: *Black on White Sticker*
1986: Reflective White on Blue
1987: *Red on White Sticker*
1988: *Green on Gold Sticker*
1989: *Black on White Sticker*
1990: *Orange on White Sticker*
1991: *Green on White Sticker*
1992: *Red on White Sticker*
1993: *Green on Gold Sticker*
1994: *Black on White Sticker*

KANSAS
COLOR CODE

1913: Black on White (undated)
1914: White on Blue (undated)
1915: Black on Yellow-Orange (undated)
1916: White on Black (undated)
1917: Black on Light Green (undated)
1918: Green on White (undated)
1919: Dark Blue on Light Blue (undated)
1920: White on Black (undated)
1921: Black on Yellow
1922: Yellow on Black
1923: Black on White
1924: White on Green
1925: White on Red
1926: White on Blue
1927: Black on Gray
1928: Blue on White
1929: Black on Yellow
1930: White on Black
1931: White on Green
1932: Black on Orange
1933: White on Blue
1934: Black on White
1935: Orange on Black
1936: Black on Orange
1937: Yellow on Black
1938: White on Black
1939: Black on White
1940: White on Black
1941: Yellow on Red
1942: White on Green
1943: *Aluminum Tab*
1944: Red on White (4 1/2" X 10")
1945: Black on White
1946: Blue on Butterscotch
1947: Black on Cream
1948: White on Black
1949: Black on Aluminum
1950: Green on Aluminum
1951: White on Blue
1952: *Blue on White Tab*
1953: *Blue on Yellow Tab*
1954: Black on White
1955: White on Black
1956: Black on White

1957: Red on White
1958: Yellow on Blue
1959: Blue on Yellow
1960: Blue on White
1961: Brown on White
1962: White on Green
1963: Green on White
1964: Reflective White on Dark Blue
1965: Reflective White on Red
1966: Reflective White on Black
1967: Reflective White on Pale Blue
1968: Reflective Yellow on Black
1969: Reflective White on Black
1970: Reflective White on Pale Green
1971: Reflective White on Red
1972: Reflective White on Black
1973: Reflective Yellow on Green
1974: Reflective White on Red
1975: Reflective White on Green
1976: White on Dark Blue
1977: *Black on White Sticker*
1978: *Black on Yellow Sticker*
1979: *Black on Red Sticker*
1980: *Red on White Sticker*
1981: White on Reflective Yellow and Blue graphic
1982: *Blue on White Sticker*
1983: *Black on Yellow Sticker*
New registrations received Blue on Reflective Blue, Gold and White graphic undated base with above sticker.
1984: *Green on White Sticker* on 1981 and 1983 bases
1985: *Red on White Sticker* on 1981 and 1983 bases
1986: *Black on White Sticker* on 1983 base
1987: *White on Green Sticker* on 1983 base
1988: *White on Black Sticker* on 1983 base
1989: Blue on Reflective Blue, Brown, Yellow and White graphic
1990: *Blue on White Sticker* on 1989 base
1991: *Red on White Sticker* on 1989 base
1992: *Green on White Sticker* on 1989 base
1993: *Black on White Sticker* on 1989 base
1994: *Red on White Sticker* on 1989 base

KENTUCKY
COLOR CODE

1910: White on Black (undated Porcelain,
B in circle)
1911: White on Black (undated Porcelain,
L in circle)
1912: White on Black (undated Porcelain,
M in square)
1913: White and Red on Black (undated Porcelain,
G in diamond)
1914: Black on White
1915: Red on White
1916: White on Blue
1917: Black on White
1918: Yellow on Black
1919: White on Green
1920: Black on White
1921: White on Brown
1922: Black on Orange
1923: Blue on Gray
1924: White on Dark Blue
1925: White on Green
1926: White on Maroon
1927: White on Blue
1928: White on Green
1929: White on Blue
1930: Red on Cream-Yellow
1931: White on Green
1932: White on Maroon
1933: White on Green
1934: Black on White
1935: Black on Yellow
1936: Silver on Black
1937: Blue on White
1938: Green on White
1939: White on Green
1940: Red on White
1941: Black on Silver
1942: Silver on Black
1943: *Windshield Sticker*
1944: Yellow on Black
1945: *Windshield Sticker*
1946: Silver on Black
1947: *Windshield Sticker*
1948: Orange on Aluminum
1949: Black on Aluminum
1950: White on Green
1951: Black on Silver
1952: *Windshield Sticker*

1953: White on Blue
1954: Blue on White
1955: White on Blue
1956: Blue on White
1957: White on Blue
1958: Blue on White
1959: White on Blue
1960: Blue on White
1961: White on Blue
1962: Blue on White
1963: White on Blue
1964: Blue on White
1965: White on Blue
1966: Blue on White
1967: White on Blue
1968: Blue on White
1969: White on Blue
1970: Blue on White
1971: White on Blue
1972: Blue on White
1973: White on Blue
1974: Blue on White
1975: White on Blue
1976: *Blue on White Sticker*
1977: *White on Rose Red Sticker*
1978: Blue on White undated base with
White on Yellow Sticker
1979: *White on Blue Sticker*
1980: *White on Red Sticker*
1981: *White on Green Sticker*
1982: *Black on White Sticker*
1983: *White on Blue Sticker* on 1978 base
New base issued: White on Blue with "84"
faintly embossed at lower right corner and
White on Green 1983 Sticker.
1984: *White on Blue Sticker*
1986: *Red on White Sticker*
1987: *White on Green Sticker*
1988: *White on Red Sticker*
New base issued: Blue on Reflective White
graphic undated base with above sticker.
1989: *White on Blue Sticker*
1990: *White on Green Sticker*
1991: *White on Red Sticker*
1992: *White on Blue Sticker*
1993: *White on Green Sticker*
1994: *White on Red Sticker*

LOUISIANA
COLOR CODE

1915: White on Blue
1916: White on Green
1917: Blue on White
1918: Black on Orange
1919: Black on Light Green
1920: White on Maroon
1921: Black on Gray
1922-1929 plates were issued in two different color combinations depending upon engine horsepower.

	Up to 23 Horsepower	*Over 23 Horsepower*
1922	White on Green	Maroon on White
1923	Black on Gray	White on Black
1924	White on Blue	Black on White
1925	Red-Orange on Gray	White on Maroon
1926	White on Blue	Maroon on White
1927	White on Green	Black on Cream
1928	White on Blue	Blue on White
1929	Yellow on Black	Black on Orange

1930: Yellow on Orange
1931: White on Dark Blue
1932: White on Red
1933: Black on Orange
1934: White on Blue
1935: Deep Yellow on Purple
1936: Light Blue on Olive Green
1937: Deep Yellow on Maroon
1938: White on Red
1939: Orange on Black
1940: Blue on Orange
1941: Black on White
1942: White on Red
1943: *Windshield Sticker*
1944: Black on Yellow (Fiberboard)
1945: White on Black
1946: Black on White
1947: Black on Aluminum
1948: White on Green
1949: Black on Yellow
1950: Yellow on Blue
1951: Yellow on Green
1952: White on Green
1953: Yellow on Green
1954: Blue on Cream
1955: Reflective White on Black
1956: Reflective White on Green
1957: Reflective Yellow on Purple
1958: Reflective White on Red
1959: Reflective White on Blue
1960: Reflective Yellow on Purple

1961: Reflective Yellow on Green
1962: Reflective White on Brown
1963: Reflective White on Green
1964-65: Reflective White on Blue
1966-67: Reflective White on Green
1968-69: Green on Reflective White
1970-71: Red on Reflective White
1972-73: Blue on Reflective White
1974-75: Black on Reflective White
1976: No dated 1976 issue due to advent of staggered expiration system
1977: *Black on Reflective Yellow Sticker*
New registrations received Black on Reflective White undated base with above sticker.
1978: *Blue on White Sticke*
1979: *Fuchsia on Yellow Sticker*
1980: *White on Red Sticker*
New registrations received Black on Reflective White undated base with above sticker.
1981: *Black on White Sticker*
1982: *Monthly Expiration Stickers:*

JAN – Black on Yellow	*JUL – Black on White*
FEB – Black on Pink	*AUG – Black on Gold*
MAR – Black on Green	*SEP – Black on Fuchsia*
APR – Black on Red	*OCT – Black on Brown*
MAY – None	*NOV – Black on Orange*
JUN – None	*DEC – Black on White*

1983: Same as 1982
1984: Same as 1982
New registrations received Blue on Reflective White graphic undated base with above sticker.
1985: *Black on Yellow Sticker*
1986: *Black on Yellow Sticker*
1987: *Black on Yellow Sticker*
1988: *Black on Yellow Sticker*
1989: *Black on Yellow Sticker*
New registrations received Blue on Reflective Blue, Red and White undated base with above sticker.
1990: No dated 1990 issue due to advent of multiyear registration system.
1991: *Black on Yellow Sticker*
1992: *Black on Yellow Sticker*
1993: *Black on Yellow Sticker*
New registrations received Blue on Reflective Red, Blue and White graphic undated base with above sticker.
1994: *Black on Yellow Sticker*
1995: *Black on Yellow Sticker*

Note: All bases issued since 1974 remain valid.

MAINE
COLOR CODE

1905-11: White on Red (undated Porcelain)
1912: Dark Blue on Yellow (undated Porcelain)
1913: Yellow on Dark Blue (undated Porcelain)
1914: White on Blue (Porcelain)
1915: Blue on White (Porcelain)
1916: White on Dark Blue
1917: Blue on White
1918: Green on White (Flat)
1919: White on Maroon
1920: Maroon on White
1921: White on Maroon
1922: White on Blue
1923: Blue on White
1924: White on Blue
1925: Blue on White
1926: Yellow on Dark Blue
1927: Dark Blue on Orange
1928: Blue on White
1929: White on Dark Blue
1930: White on Red
1931: White on Black
1932: White on Green
1933: White on Black
1934: Black on Orange
1935: White on Blue
1936: White on Black
1937: White on Green
1938: Green on Gray
1939: Silver on Green
1940: Green on Silver
1941: Red on Silver
1942: Black on White
1943: *Windshield Sticker*
1944: Yellow on Black
1945: Blue on White
1946: White on Dark Blue
1947: *Windshield Sticker*
1948: Orange on Black
1949: *Aluminum Tab*
1950: Black on Reflective White with
Aluminum Tab
1951: *Reflective Red Tab*
1952: *Reflective Green Tab*
1953: *Reflective Gold Tab*

1954: *Aluminum Tab*
1955: *Reflective Blue Tab*
1956: Black on Reflective Yellow
1957: *Red Tab*
1958: *Green Tab*
1959: *White Tab*
1960: *Dark Blue Tab*
1961: *Orange Tab*
1962: Black on Reflective White
1963: *Yellow Tab*
1964: *Blue Tab*
1965: *Red Tab*
1966: *Yellow Tab*
1967: *Black Tab*
1968: Black on Reflective Lemon Yellow
1969: *White on Red Sticker*
New registrations received Black on Reflective
Lemon Yellow undated base with above sticker.
1970: *White on Blue Sticker*
1971: *White on Green Sticker*
1972: *Black on White Sticker*
1973: *White on Black Sticker*
1974: Black on Reflective White
1975-86: *Monthly Expiration Stickers* (see page 136)
New registrations in 1975 received Black
on Reflective White undated base with 1975
stickers.
1987: *Black on Yellow Sticker*
Blue on Reflective Red and White graphic base
with "lobster" design began replacing previous
bases with a few plates using the 1987 sticker,
but most using the 1988 sticker.
1988: *White on Red Sticker* on 1974, 1975 and
1987 bases
1989: *White on Blue Sticker* on 1974, 1975 and
1987 bases
1990: *White on Green Sticker* on 1974, 1975 and
1987 bases
1991: *White on Red Sticker* on 1974, 1975 and
1987 bases
1992: *White on Blue Sticker* on 1987 base
1993: *White on Green Sticker* on 1987 base
1994: *White on Red Sticker* on 1987 base

MAINE
MONTHLY STICKER COLORS

OCT 75: Yellow on Dark Red
NOV 75: Blue on White
DEC 75: Black on Yellow
JAN 76: White on Black
FEB 76: Red on White
MAR 76: White on Blue
APR 76: Green on White
MAY 76: White on Red
JUN 76: Yellow on Black
JUL 76: White on Green
AUG 76: Black on White
SEP 76: Green on Yellow
OCT 76: White on Blue
NOV 76: White on Brown
DEC 76: White on Purple
JAN 77: White on Orange
FEB 77: White on Pink
MAR 77: White on Tan
APR 77: White on Red-Orange
MAY 77: Black on Deep Yellow
JUN 77: White on Dark Green
JUL 77: White on Black
AUG 77: White on Green
SEP 77: White on Light Blue
OCT 77: White on Black
NOV 77: White on Red
DEC 77: White on Light Blue
JAN 78: Black on Lemon Yellow
FEB 78: White on Dark Green
MAR 78: White on Brown
APR 78: White on Orange
MAY 78: White on Dark Blue
JUN 78: White on Light Green
JUL 78: White on Maroon
AUG 78: White on Lavender
SEP 78: White on Lemon Yellow
OCT 78: White on Red
NOV 78: White on Light Green
DEC 78: White on Brown

JAN 79: White on Violet
FEB 79: White on Red
MAR 79: White on Light Blue
APR 79: Black on Yellow
MAY 79: White on Purple
JUN 79: White on Dark Green
JUL 79: White on Tan
AUG 79: White on Black
SEP 79: White on Orange
OCT 79: White on Black
NOV 79: White on Maroon
DEC 79: White on Black
JAN 80: Black on Yellow
FEB 80: White on Dark Green
MAR 80: White on Orange
APR 80: White on Lavender
MAY 80: White on Light Blue
JUN 80: White on Tan
JUL 80: White on Green
AUG 80: White on Red
SEP 80: Black on Yellow
OCT 80: White on Green
NOV 80: White on Light Blue
DEC 80: White on Lavender
JAN 81: White on Orange
FEB 81: White on Tan
MAR 81: White on Maroon
APR 81: White on Blue
MAY 81: Black on Yellow
JUN 81: White on Red
JUL 81: White on Brown
AUG 81: Black on Yellow
SEP 81: White on Light Green
OCT 81: White on Blue
NOV 81: Black on Tan
DEC 81: White on Red
JAN 82: White on Brown
FEB 82: Black on Yellow
MAR 82: White on Orange

APR 82: White on Green
MAY 82: White on Light Blue
JUN 82: White on Purple
JUL 82: White on Light Green
AUG 82: White on Tan
SEP 82: White on Maroon
OCT 82: White on Tan
NOV 82: Green on White
DEC 82: Tan on Black
JAN 83: White on Light Green
FEB 83: Orange on White
MAR 83: White on Brown
APR 83: White on Red
MAY 83: White on Purple
JUN 83: Yellow on Black
JUL 83: White on Maroon
AUG 83: White on Blue
SEP 83: White on Dark Blue
OCT 83: White on Light Blue
NOV 83: White on Dark Blue
DEC 83: White on Dark Blue
1984: All months White on Red
JAN 85: White on Blue
FEB 85 to JUN 85: White on Dark Green
JUL 85 to DEC 85: White on Light Green
JAN 86: Blue on White
FEB 86: Green on White
MAR 86: Black on White
APR 86: Red on White
MAY 86: Brown on White
JUN 86: Blue on White
JUL 86: Black on White
AUG 86: Red on White
SEP 86: Green on White
OCT 86: Brown on White
NOV 86: Orange on White
DEC 86: Blue on White

MARYLAND
COLOR CODE

1910: Black on Yellow
1911: White on Black (Porcelain)
1912: Blue on White (Porcelain)
1913: Yellow on Black (Porcelain)
1914: White on Green (Porcelain)
1915: White on Blue
1916: Yellow on Black
1917: Green on White
1918: White on Gray
1919: Black on White
1920: White on Red
1921: Red on White
1922: White on Dark Blue
1923: Black on Yellow
1924: Orange on Black
1925: White on Green
1926: White on Black
1927: Black on White
1928: White on Light Blue
1929: Blue on White
1930: White on Green
1931: White on Red
1932: Red on White
1933: White on Blue
1934: Yellow on Black
1935: Dark Blue on White
1936: White on Black
1937: Black on White
3/31/39: White on Green
3/31/40: Green on White
3/31/41: White on Blue
3/31/42: Black on Silver
3/31/43: *Black on Yellow Tab*
3/31/44: *Silver on Black Tab*
3/31/45: Silver on Black
3/31/46: *Black on Silver Tab*
3/31/47: *Black on Yellow Tab*
1948: Black on Aluminum
1949: *Silver on Black Tab*
1950: *White on Red Tab*
1951: *White on Black Tab*
March 1952: White on Black
March 1953: *Black on White Tab*
1954: Yellow on Black

1955: Black on Orange
1956: Maroon on White
3/31/57: Green on White
3/31/58: White on Green
3/31/59: Blue on White
3/31/60: White on Blue
3/31/61: Black on Light Green
3/31/62: Blue on White
3/31/63: White on Blue
3/31/64: Blue on White
3/31/65: White on Blue
3/31/66: Black on Orange
3/31/67: Orange on Black
3/31/68: Blue on White
3/31/69: White on Blue
3/31/70: Blue on White
1971: White on Blue
1972: *Red on White Sticker*
1973: *Blue on White Sticker*
1974: *Red on White Sticker*
1975: *White on Blue Sticker*
1976: Red on White (undated)
1977: *White on Blue Sticker*
1978: *White on Red Sticker*
1979: *White on Blue Sticker*
1980: *White on Red Sticker*
1981: Black on White (Undated)
1982: *Black on Yellow Sticker*
1983: *White on Red Sticker*
1984: *White on Blue Sticker*
1985: *White on Black Sticker*
1986: *White on Orange Sticker*
New base issued: Black on Reflective White, Yellow and Red graphic undated base with *Black on White Sticker.*
1987: *Red on White Sticker*
1988: *White on Black Sticker*
1989: *White on Red Sticker*
1990: *Black on White Sticker*
1991: *Yellow on Black Sticker*
1992: *Black on Yellow Sticker*
1993: *Yellow on Black Sticker*
1994: *White on Red Sticker*
1995: *Red on White Sticker*

MASSACHUSETTS
COLOR CODE

1903-07: White on Blue (undated Porcelain)
1908: Blue on White (Porcelain)
1909: White on Blue (Porcelain)
1910: Blue on White (Porcelain)
1911: White on Blue (Porcelain)
1912: Blue on White (Porcelain)
1913: White on Blue (Porcelain)
1914: Blue on White (Porcelain)
1915: White on Blue (Porcelain)
1916: Blue on Cream (Flat)
1917: Cream on Blue (Flat)
1918: Blue on Cream (Flat)
1919: White on Blue (Flat)
1920: Blue on White
1921: White on Blue
1922: Blue on White
1923: White on Blue
1924: White on Maroon
1925: White on Black
1926: White on Blue
1927: White on Maroon
1928: White on Green
1929: White on Blue
1930: White on Maroon
1931: White on Green
1932: White on Maroon
1933: White on Green
1934: White on Maroon
1935: White on Green
1936: White on Maroon
1937: White on Green
1938: White on Maroon
1939: White on Green
1940: White on Maroon
1941: White on Green
1942: White on Maroon
1943: *Windshield Sticker*
New registrations received White on
Green dated 1942 plate.
1944: *Windshield Sticker*
1945: White on Blue
1946: White on Black
1947: White on Green
1948: White on Maroon
1949: White on Black
1950: *Windshield Sticker*
1951: White on Maroon
1952: *Windshield Sticker*
1953: White on Black
1954: *Windshield Sticker*
1955: White on Maroon
1956: *Windshield Sticker*

1957: White on Black
1958: *Windshield Sticker*
1959: White on Maroon
1960: *Windshield Sticker*
1961: White on Green
1962: *Windshield Sticker*
1963: White on Black
1964: White on Maroon
1965: *Windshield Sticker*
1966: White on Green
1967: Blue on Reflective White (undated)
1968: *Windshield Sticker*
1969: *Windshield Sticker*
1970: No dated 1970 issue due to advent of
staggered expiration system.
1971: *White on Red Sticker*
A small number of experimental paper Red on
White Stickers were tried without success.
1972: *White on Blue Sticker*
1973: *White on Black Sticker*
New base issued: Maroon on Reflective White
undated base with 1974 sticker.
1974: *White on Green Sticker*
1975: *White on Red Sticker*
1976: *White on Blue Sticker*
1977: *White on Black Sticker*
Some new registrations began receiving a
Green on Reflective White undated base with
1979 sticker.
1978: *White on Green Sticker* on 1973 base
1979: *White on Red Sticker* on 1973 and 1977 bases
1980: *White on Blue Sticker* on 1973 and 1977 bases
1981: *White on Black Sticker* on 1973 and 1977 bases
1982: *White on Green Sticker* on 1973 and 1977 bases
1983: *White on Red Sticker* on 1973 and 1977 bases
1984: *White on Orange Sticker* on 1977 base
1985: *White on Black Sticker* on 1977 base
1986: *White on Green Sticker* on 1977 base
1987: *White on Red Sticker* on 1977 base
1988: *White on Orange Sticker* on 1977 base
New registrations received Red and Blue on
Reflective White graphic undated base with
above sticker.
1989: *White on Black Sticker* on 1977 and 1988 bases
1990: *White on Green Sticker* on 1977 and 1988 bases
1991: *White on Red Sticker* on 1977 and 1988 bases
1992: *Black on White Sticker* on 1977 and 1988 bases
1993: *Black on Blue Sticker* on 1977 and 1988 bases
1994: *Black on Orange Sticker* on 1977 and
1988 bases
1995: *Black on Yellow Sticker* on 1977 and
1988 bases

MICHIGAN
COLOR CODE

1910: Black on White (Porcelain)
1911: White on Black (Porcelain)
1912: Black on Orange (Porcelain)
1913: White on Green (Porcelain)
1914: Red on White (Porcelain)
1915: White on Blue
1916: Blue on White
1917: White on Black
1918: White on Green
1919: White on Brown
1920: Black on Orange
1921: White on Black
1922: White on Red
1923: White on Green
1924: Black on Yellow
1925: Black on Gray
1926: White on Black
1927: Black on Orange
1928: White on Green
1929: Yellow on Black
1930: Black on Orange
1931: Red on Black
1932: White on Dark Blue
1933: Black on Cream
1934: Black on Yellow
1935: Yellow on Black
1936: Black on Gray
1937: Yellow on Blue
1938-1946: Full-year and half-year plates were issued in different color combinations. All half-year plates expired on August 31.

	Full-Year	*Half-Year*
1938	Black on Green	Black on White
1939	Black on Cream	White on Dark Blue
1940	Black on Silver	White on Black
1941	White on Maroon	Maroon on White
1942	White on Dark Green	White on Dark Green with optional *White on Green Date Strip*[*]
1943	*Green on White Tab*	*Black on Yellow Tab*
1944	White on Maroon	Maroon on White
1945	Black on Silver	White on Black
1946	White on Dark Green	White on Maroon

1947: Black on Deep Yellow
1948: Black on Silver
1949: White on Black
1950: Black on Silver

1951: White on Black
1952: Black on Silver
1953: White on Black
1954: Yellow on Blue
1955: White on Green
1956: Green on White
1957: White on Maroon
1958: Black on Gray
1959: Yellow on Green
1960: *Green on Yellow Tab*
1961: *Black on Silver Tab*
1962: Green on White
1963: *White on Green Tab*
1964: *Yellow on Olive Green Tab*
1965: Yellow on Blue
1966: Blue on Tan
1967: Yellow on Blue
1968: Yellow on Green
1969: White on Maroon
1970: White on Yellow-Green
1971: Reflective White on Maroon
1972: *Black on Yellow Sticker*
1973: Reflective White on Dark Blue
1974: *Blue on White Sticker*
1975: *Red on White Sticker*
1976: Reflective White on Red and Blue graphic
1977: *Blue on White Sticker*
1978: *Red on White Sticker*
1979: Reflective White on Black
1980: *White on Red Sticker*
1981: *Black on White Sticker*
1982: *Red on White Sticker*
1983: *White on Red Sticker* on 1979 base
New base issued: Reflective White on Blue undated base made to expire in 1984.
1984: No dated 1984 issue
1985: *Red on White Sticker*
1986: *White on Red Sticker*
1987: *Black on White Sticker*
1988: *Red on White Sticker*
1989: *White on Red Sticker*
1990: *Black on White Sticker*
1991: *Red on White Sticker*
1992: *Green on White Sticker*
1993: *Blue on White Sticker*
1994: *Red on White Sticker*
1995: *Green on White Sticker*

---

[*]1942 Half-Year Plate: White on Dark Green
Those motorists wishing to extend this plate for the remainder of the year received a *White on Green "42" Date Strip*.

MINNESOTA
COLOR CODE

1909: Silver on Red-Orange (Flat)
1910: Gold on Black (Flat)
1911: White on Blue (Porcelain)
1912-13-14: Black on Aluminum
1915-16-17: Red on Aluminum
1918-19-20: White on Black
1920: New registrations received White on Black dated 1920 plate.
1921: Black on Light Blue
1922: Black on Cream
1923: Brown on Gray
1924: White on Blue
1925: Black on Silver
1926: White on Black
1927: Light Green on Dark Green
1928: Black on Tan
1929: White on Black
1930: Black on Silver
1931: White on Black
1932: Deep Yellow on Maroon
1933: Black on Silver
1934: White on Black
1935: Deep Yellow on Maroon
1936: White on Dark Blue
1937: Black on Silver
1938: Silver on Black
1939: Black on Yellow
1940: White on Black
1941: Black on Silver
1942: Red on Cream
1943: *White on Black Tab*
1944: White on Dark Blue
1945: Black on Silver
1946: White on Black
1947: Black on Silver
1948: White on Black
1949: Black on Aluminum
1950: White on Black
1951: Black on Silver
1952: Blue on Orange
1953: White on Black
1954: Blue on Cream
1955: Deep Yellow on Maroon
1956: Green on Reflective White
1957: *Black on Reflective Yellow Tab*
1958: Blue on Reflective White
1959: *Yellow on Reflective Green Tab*
1960: Black on Reflective White
1961: *Yellow on Reflective Blue Tab*

1962: Maroon on Reflective White
1963: *White on Reflective Green Tab*
1964: *Black on Reflective Yellow Tab*
1965: Green on Reflective White
1966: *White on Blue Sticker*
1967: *White on Orange Sticker*
1968: Blue on Reflective White
1969: *White on Pink Sticker or White on Red-Orange Sticker*
1970: *Yellow on Green Sticker*
1971: Green on Reflective White
1972: *White on Blue Sticker*
1973: *White on Red Sticker*
1974: Orange on Reflective White
1975: *Black on White Sticker*
1976: *Olive Green on White Sticker*
1977: *White on Blue Sticker*
1978: Two new bases issued:
    1) Blue on Reflective White undated base* with *White on Blue Sticker*
    2) Blue and Green on Reflective White graphic dated base*
1979: *White on Green Sticker* on both bases
New registrations received Blue and Green on Reflective White graphic undated base.*
1980: *White on Black Sticker*
1981: *White on Red Sticker*
1982: *Black on Yellow Sticker*
New registrations received Blue and Green on Reflective White graphic dated base.*
1983: *White on Blue Sticker*
New registrations received Blue and Green on Reflective White graphic dated base.*
1984: *White on Red Sticker*
1985: *White on Black Sticker*
1986: *White on Green Sticker*
1987: *Black on Yellow Sticker*
New registrations received Blue and Green on Reflective White graphic undated base with above sticker.
1988: *White on Blue Sticker*
All bases but 1987 were replaced during this year.
1989: *White on Red Sticker*
1990: *White on Black Sticker*
1991: *White on Green Sticker*
1992: *White on Red Sticker*
1993: *Black on Gold Sticker*
1994: *White on Blue Sticker*

*Each of these bases remained valid until 1988.

MISSISSIPPI
COLOR CODE

1912: Black on White
1913: Black on White
1914-1918: Black on White (undated)
1919: Light Green on Black
1920: White on Maroon
1921: Red on White
1922: Black on Light Green
1923: Yellow on Black
1924: White on Dark Blue
1925: Black on Yellow
1926: White on Green
1927: Yellow on Blue
1928: White on Black
1929: White on Maroon
1930: Red on Blue
1931: White on Orange
1932: Deep Yellow on Black
1933: White on Green with
    White on Green Lock Strip
1934: White on Black with
    Black on White Lock Strip
1935: Orange on Black with
    Black on Orange Lock Strip
1936: White on Black with
    Black on White Lock Strip
1937: White on Green
1938: White on Dark Blue
1939: Black on Yellow
1940: Yellow on Black
1941: White on Black
1942: Yellow on Blue
1943: Orange on Black
1944: White on Black
1945: Yellow on Black
1946: White on Black
1947: Yellow on Black
1948: White on Black
1949: Orange on Black
1950: Black on Yellow
1951: Yellow on Black
1952: White on Green
1953: Maroon on White
1954: White on Black
1955: White on Blue
1956: Yellow on Black

1957: White on Green
1958: Black on Yellow-Orange
1959: Green on White
1960: Red on White
1961: Black on White
1962: Maroon on White
1963: Blue on White
1964: Red on White
1965: White on Blue
1966: Blue on White
1967: White on Black
1968: Black on Beige
1969: White on Brown
1970: Blue on White
1971: Green on White
1972: Green on Reflective White
1973: Red on Reflective White
1974: Blue on Reflective White
1975: Red on Reflective White
1976: Maroon on Reflective White
1977: Red on Reflective White
1978: *White on Pink Sticker*
1979: *White on Green Sticker*
1980: *White on Green Sticker*
1981: *Black on Yellow Sticker* on 1977 base
    New base issued: Blue and Red on Reflective
    White graphic undated base with 1982 sticker.
1982: *White on Blue Sticker* on 1977 and 1981 bases;
    1977 base phased out.
1983: *Red on White Sticker*
1984: *Black on Yellow Sticker*
1985: *Blue on White Sticker*
1986: *Green on White Sticker*
1987: *Black on White Sticker*
1988: *Red on White Sticker*
1989: *White on Blue Sticker*
1990: *Red on White Sticker*
1991: *Green on White Sticker*
1992: *Purple on White Sticker*
1992: *White on Red Sticker*
    New base issued: Blue on Reflective Blue and
    White graphic undated base with 1993 sticker.
    1981 base phased out.
1993: *Brown on White Sticker*
1994: *Blue on White Sticker*

MISSOURI
COLOR CODE

1911: Aluminum on Yellow
1912: White on Red
1913: White on Blue
1914: Black on White
1915: Black on Green
1916: White on Black
1917: Black on Orange
1918: Blue on White
1919: White on Dark Blue
1920: Black on Light Green
1921: Red on White
1922: White on Brown
1923: Light Blue on Black
1924: Black on Orange
1925: White on Green
1926: Black on Yellow
1927: White on Blue
1928: Blue on Orange
1929: White on Black
1930: White on Brown
1931: Black on Gray
1932: White on Black
1933: Cream on Brown
1934: White on Black
1935: White on Green
1936: Black on White
1937: White on Black
1938: Black on Tan
1939: Tan on Black
1940: Black on White
1941: White on Black
1942: Black on White (some Fiberboard)
1943: *White on Green Date Strip*
1944: Yellow on Black
1945: Black on Tan
1946: White on Black
1947: Black on White
1948: White on Maroon
1949: White on Maroon undated base
  with *White on Orange Tab*
1950: *White on Green Tab*
1951: *Maroon on White Tab*
1952: *White on Black Tab*
1953: *White on Maroon Tab* or
  White on Red Sticker
1954: *Blue on White Sticker*
1955: *Black on Red Sticker*

1956: Yellow on Black undated base
  with *Black on Yellow Sticker*
1957: *Yellow on Black Sticker*
1958: *Black on Yellow Sticker*
1959: *Black on White Sticker*
1960: *Black on Red Sticker*
1961: *Black on Yellow Sticker*
1962: White on Maroon
1963: *White on Green Sticker*
1964: *White on Black Sticker*
1965: *White on Maroon Sticker*
1966: *White on Black Sticker*
  A few new registrations expiring only in
  September received a White on Maroon
  plate with the date embossed.
1967: *Black on Red Sticker* for the first 6 months
  and White on Maroon plate with date embossed
  for the second 6 months
1968: White on Green
1969: Green on White
1970: Black on White
1971: White on Maroon
1972: Blue on Reflective White
1973: Maroon on Reflective White
1974: Black on Reflective White
1975: Blue on Reflective White
1976: Reflective Yellow on Medium Blue or
  Red on Reflective White*
1977: Reflective White on Red
1978: Reflective Yellow on Black
1979: Reflective White on Blue
1980: Reflective White on Maroon
1981: *Black on White Sticker*
1982: *Blue on White Sticker*
1983: *Black on Yellow Sticker*
1984: *Black on Green Sticker*
1985: *Black on White Sticker*
1986: *Black on Orange Sticker*
1987: *Black on Yellow Sticker*
1988: *Black on Green Sticker*
1989: *Black on White Sticker*
1990: *Black on Orange Sticker*
1991: *Black on Yellow Sticker*
1992: *Black on Green Sticker*
1993: *Black on White Sticker*
1994: *Black on Orange Sticker*

*Low-numbered registrations received Red on Reflective
White plates.

MONTANA
COLOR CODE

1915: White on Black
1916: Pale Green on Dark Green
1917: Red on Gray
1918: White on Blue
1919: Dark Green on Light Green
1920: White on Black
1921: White on Maroon
1922: Black on Orange
1923: Red on White
1924: White on Blue
1925: White on Red
1926: White on Black
1927: Black on Green
1928: Black on Orange
1929: Black on White
1930: Black on Orange
1931: Black on White
1932: White on Black
1933: Orange on Maroon
1934: Orange on Black
1935: White on Black
1936: Black on Orange
1937: Black on Green
1938: Black on Orange
1939: Orange on Black
1940: White on Blue
1941: Blue on White
1942: White on Black
1943: *White on Red Tab*
1944: Cream on Green (Fiberboard)
1945: White on Black
1946: Black on White
1947: *Windshield Sticker*
1948: White on Black
1949: Black on White
1950: White on Black
1951: Yellow on Blue
1952: *Windshield Sticker*
1953: White on Black
1954: *Aluminum Tab*
1955: White on Red
1956: *Aluminum Tab*
1957: White on Black
1958: *Aluminum Tab*

1959: Black on Aluminum
1960: *Black on Yellow Tab*
1961: *White on Black Tab*
1962: *White on Blue Tab*
1963: Black on Aluminum
1964: *White on Black Tab*
1965: *White on Blue Tab*
1966: *Black on Yellow Tab*
1967: Reflective Yellow on Blue
1968: Green on Reflective White
1969: *Black on Orange Sticker*
1970: Blue on Reflective White
1971: *White on Gold Sticker*
1972: *White on Blue Sticker*
1973: Reflective White on Green
1974: *White on Green Sticker*
1975: Reflective White on Blue
1976: Blue and Red on Reflective White graphic
1977: *White on Red Sticker*
1978: *White on Blue Sticker*
1979: *White on Green Sticker*
1980: *White on Orange Sticker*
1981: *Blue on White Sticker*
1982: *Green on White Sticker*
1983: *Red on White Sticker*
1984: *Black on Gold Sticker*
1985: *White on Black Sticker*
1986: *Blue on White Sticker*
1987: *White on Green Sticker*
New registrations received Blue and Red on Reflective White and Gold graphic undated base with *Blue on White "87" Sticker.**
1988: *Black on White Sticker* on 1976 and 1987 bases
1989: *White on Black Sticker* on 1976 and 1987 bases
1990: *Red on White Sticker* on 1976 and 1987 bases
1991: *Blue on White Sticker* on 1976 and 1987 bases
New base issued: Blue on Reflective Multicolor and White graphic undated base with above sticker. 1976 base phased out.
1992: *White on Blue Sticker* on 1987 and 1991 bases
1993: *Blue on Yellow Sticker* on 1987 and 1991 bases
1994: *Gold on Lavender Sticker* on 1987 and 1991 bases

---

*This new base was issued to any registrant who requested it.

NEBRASKA
COLOR CODE

1915: Black on White
1916: White on Blue
1917: Black on Cream
1918: Yellow on Black
1919: Black on Light Green
1920: *Cream on Blue Tab*
1921: White on Black
1922: Black on White
1923: Green on Black
1924: White on Black
1925: Black on Orange
1926: White on Green
1927: White on Maroon
1928: White on Blue
1929: White on Black
1930: Cream on Blue
1931: Red on Gray
1932: White on Blue
1933: Dark Blue on Orange
1934: White on Dark Green
1935: Black on Gray
1936: Silver on Black
1937: Black on Gray
1938: Silver on Black
1939: Black on Gray
1940: Orange on Blue
1941: Dark Blue on Orange
1942: Red on White
1943: *White on Dark Blue Tab*
1944: *Black on Orange Tab*
1945: White on Black
1946: White on Oxide Red
1947: *White on Dark Brown Tab*
1948: Blue on Aluminum
1949: Maroon on Aluminum
1950: Blue on White
1951: White on Black
1952: Black on Yellow
1953: *Yellow on Black Tab*
1954: Yellow on Black
1955: Black on Yellow
1956: White on Black
1957: Green on White
1958: Black on Deep Yellow
1959: *Black on Aluminum Tab*
1960: Deep Yellow on Black
1961: *Black on White Sticker*

1962: Green on White (undated)
1963: *White on Red Sticker*
1964: *Green on White Sticker*
1965: Black on White
1966: Red on Reflective White
1967: *Black on Orange Sticker*
1968: *Blue on White Sticker*
1969: Black on Reflective White
1970: *Red on White Sticker*
1971: *Green on White Sticker*
1972: Red on Reflective White
1973: *Black on White Sticker*
1974: *Blue on White Sticker*
1975: *Red on White Sticker*
1976: Red on Reflective Red, Blue and White
graphic base
1977: *White on Red Sticker*
1978: *Blue on White Sticker*
1979: *White on Green Sticker*
1980: *Black on White Sticker*
1981: *Black on Yellow Sticker*
1982: *Black on Blue Sticker (undated)*
1983: *White on Black Sticker*
1984: *White on Red Sticker*
New base issued: Blue on Reflective
White undated base with 1985 sticker.
1985: *Blue on White Sticker*
1986: *White on Green Sticker*
1987: *Black on Yellow Sticker*
New base issued: Red on Reflective Red,
Orange, Yellow, Black and White graphic
undated base with 1988 sticker.
1988: *Red on White Sticker*
1989: *Black on White Sticker*
New registrations received Black on Reflective
Black, Sky Blue, Orange and White graphic
undated base with 1990 sticker.
1990: *Black on Yellow Sticker*
1991: *Black on White Sticker*
1992: *Black on Yellow Sticker*
1993: *Black on Orange Sticker*
New registrations received Blue on Reflective
Black, Red and Gold and White graphic
undated base with 1994 sticker.
1994: *Red on White Sticker*

Note: All bases issued since 1987 remain valid.

NEVADA
COLOR CODE

1916: Yellow on Green (undated)
1917: Silver on Blue (Flat)
1918: Black on Yellow (Flat)
1919: Red on White (Flat)
1920: Yellow on Red (Flat)
1921: Green on White (Flat)
1922: Black on Gray (Flat)
1923: Deep Yellow on Black
1924: White on Light Green
1925: White on Purple
1926: Yellow on Black
1927: Yellow on Green
1928: White on Red
1929: Black on Orange
1930: Orange on Black
1931: Black on Orange
1932: Orange on Black
1933: White on Green
1934: Green on White
1935: White on Green
1936: Silver on Blue
1937: Blue on Silver
1938: Silver on Blue
1939: Blue on Silver
1940: Silver on Blue
1941: Blue on Silver
1942: Silver on Blue
1943: *Yellow on Red Tab*
1944: White on Red
1945: Blue on Silver
1946: Silver on Blue
1947: Blue on Silver
1948: Silver on Blue
1949: Blue on Silver
1950: Silver on Blue
1951: Blue on Silver
1952: Silver on Blue
1953: Gold on Green
1954: Silver on Blue
6/30/55: *Black on Red Sticker*
6/30/56: Blue on Silver
1956-57: Silver on Blue
June 1958: Light Blue on Silver
June 1959: Silver on Light Blue
June 1960: Blue on White
June 1961: Silver on Blue
June 1962: *Aluminum on Red Sticker*

June 1963: *Black on Yellow Sticker*
June 1964: *Silver on Blue Date Strip*
1964: *Black on Yellow Sticker on Date Strip*
1965: Blue on Aluminum
1966: *Black on Orange Sticker*
1967: *Black on Yellow Sticker*
New registrations received Blue on Reflective White 1965 base with above sticker.
1968: *White on Pink Sticker* on 1965 and 1967 bases
1969: Reflective White on Blue
1970: *Black on Reflective Orange Sticker*
1971: *White on Red Sticker*
New registrations received Reflective White on Blue base with above sticker.
1972: *Black on Yellow Sticker*
1973: *White on Green Sticker*
1974: *White on Red Sticker*
1975: *Blue on White Sticker*
New registrations received Reflective White on Blue base with above sticker.
1976: *Black on Yellow Sticker*
1977: *White on Red Sticker*
1978: *White on Green Sticker*
1979: *White on Blue Sticker*
1980: *Black on Yellow Sticker*
1981: *White on Red Sticker*
1982: *Blue on White Sticker*
New registrations received a White on Reflective Blue undated base with above sticker.
1983: *White on Green Sticker*
New registrations received a Blue on Reflective Silver and White graphic undated base with 1984 sticker.
1984: *White on Blue Sticker*
1985: *Black on Yellow Sticker*
1986: *Blue on White Sticker*
1987: *White on Red Sticker*
1988: *White on Green Sticker*
1989: *White on Blue Sticker*
1990: *Black on Orange Sticker*
1991: *Blue on White Sticker*
1992: *White on Green Sticker*
1993: *White on Red Sticker*
1994: *Black on Yellow Sticker*

Note: All bases since 1969 are still valid.

NEW HAMPSHIRE
COLOR CODE

1905-11: White on Green (undated Porcelain)
1912: Green on White
1913: White on Green (Porcelain)
1914: White on Green (Porcelain)
1915: Green on White (Porcelain)
1916: White on Green (Porcelain)
1917: Green on White (Porcelain)
1918: White on Dark Green (Porcelain)*
1919: Green on White (Flat)
1920: White on Green (Flat)
1921: Green on White (Flat)
1922: White on Green
1923: Green on White
1924: White on Dark Green
1925: Green on White
1926: White on Dark Green
1927: Green on White
1928: White on Green
1929: Green on White
1930: White on Dark Green
1931: Green on White
1932: White on Green
1933: Green on White
1934: White on Green
1935: Green on White
1936: White on Green
1937: Green on White
1938-39: White on Green
1939-40: Green on White
1940-41: White on Green
1941-42: Green on White
1942-43: White on Green
1943: *Green on White Date Strip*
1944: Green on White
1945: Black on White
1946: White on Green
1947: Black on White
1948: White on Black
1949: Green on White
1950: White on Green
1951: Green on White
1952: White on Green
1953: Green on White
1954: White on Green
1955: Green on White
1956: White on Green
1957: Green on White
1958: White on Green

1959: Green on White
1960: White on Green
1961: Green on White
1962: White on Green
1963: Green on White
1964: White on Green
1965: Green on White
1966: White on Green
1967: Green on White
1968: White on Green
1969: Green on White
1970: White on Green
1971: Green on White
1972: White on Green
1973: Green on White
1974: *Green on White Sticker*
1975: White on Green
1976: *Blue and Red on White Sticker*
1977: *Red and Blue on White Sticker*
1978: *Light Green on White Sticker*
Red on White undated base issued from December 1977 to April 1978 with 1978 or 1979 stickers.
Green on White undated base issued from April 1978 to January 1979 with 1979 sticker.
1979: *Orange on White Sticker*
New base issued: Green on Reflective White undated base with 1980 sticker.
1980: *White on Green Sticker* on 1978 and 1979 bases
1981: *Black on Orange Sticker* on 1979 base
1982: *Black on Yellow Sticker*
1983: *Black on Green Sticker*
1984: *Black on Red Sticker*
1985: *Black on Blue Sticker*
1986: *Black on Orange Sticker*
1987: *Black on Green Sticker*
New base issued: Green on Reflective White graphic undated base with above sticker.
1988: *Black on Yellow Sticker* on 1979 and 1987 bases
1989: *Black on Red Sticker* on 1979 and 1987 bases
1990: *Black on Blue Sticker* on 1979 and 1987 bases
1991: *Black on Green Sticker* on 1979 and 1987 bases
1992: *Black on Yellow Sticker* on 1987 base
1993: *Black on Red Sticker* on 1987 base
1994: *Black on Blue Sticker* on 1987 base

---

*High-numbered issues were White on Green fiberboard.

NEW JERSEY
COLOR CODE

1908: White on Dark Blue (Flat)
1909: White on Black (Porcelain)
1910: Black on Deep Yellow (Porcelain)
1911: Red on Gray (Porcelain)
1912: Yellow on Blue-Purple (Porcelain)
1913: Red-Orange on White (Porcelain)
1914: White on Red (Porcelain)
1915: White on Dark Green (Porcelain)
1916: White on Brown
1917: White on Blue
1918: Blue on White
1919: White on Gray
1920: White on Red
1921: White on Dark Green
1922: White on Black
1923: Red-Orange on Black
1924: White on Red
1925: Silver on Dark Blue
1926: White on Orange
1927: White on Green
1928: White on Light Blue
1929: White on Dark Gray
1930: White on Gray
1931: White on Dark Red
1932: White on Black
1933: Red on Black
1934: Light Green on Black
1935: Silver on Black
1936: Orange on Black
1937: Light Green on Black
1938: Silver on Black

1939: Orange on Black
1940: Light Green on Black
1941: White on Black
1942: Yellow on Black
1943: *White on Black Tab*
1944: Black on Straw
1945: Blue on Straw
1946: Black on Straw
1947: Blue on Straw
1948: Black on Straw
1949: White on Black
1950: Black on Straw
1951: White on Black
1952: Orange on Black
1953: *Black on Straw Tab*
1954: *Red on Aluminum Tab*
1955: *White on Aluminum Tab*
1956: *Black on Aluminum Tab*
New registrations received Orange on Black undated base, with *Windshield Stickers* issued each year from 1956 to 1959.
1959: Beginning in June, new undated Black on Straw base was issued, phasing out all Orange on Black plates. *Windshield Stickers* were issued each year up to the present.
1979: Straw on Blue undated base with annual *Windshield Stickers* continued.
1991: Black on Reflective Dark Yellow and White graphic undated base with annual *Windshield Stickers* continued.

NEW MEXICO
COLOR CODE

1912-13: Green on White (undated)
1914: White on Green
1915: White on Dark Red
1916: Silver on Blue-Purple
1917: Black on Yellow-Orange
1918: Light Blue on Gray
1919: Black on White
1920: Blue on White (Porcelain)
1921: *Red Diamond Tab*
1922: *Silver Octagon Tab*
1923: *Yellow Star Tab*
1924: Black on Orange
1925: White on Black
1926: Red on Gray
1927: Black on Yellow
1928: Butterscotch on Navy Blue
1929: Red on Cream Yellow
1930: Yellow-Orange on Black
1931: Black on Deep Yellow
1932: White on Green
1933: Red on Yellow
1934: Yellow on Red
1935: White on Dark Blue
1936: Dark Blue on White
1937: Cherry Red on Robin's Egg Blue
1938: Black on Yellow
1939: Black on Yellow-Orange
1940: Deep Yellow on Red
1941: Red on Yellow
1942: Black on White
1943: *Windshield Sticker*
1944: White on Black
1945: White on Blue
1946: Dark Red on Deep Yellow
1947: Yellow on Burnt Red
1948: White on Blue-Gray
1949: Blue on White
1950: White on Blue
1951: Blue on White
1952: Red on White
1953: White on Red
1954: Red on White
1955: Yellow on Maroon
1956: White on Maroon
1957: Green on White
1958: Red on Yellow
1959: Yellow on Dark Red
1960: *Red on White Sticker on Red Tab*
1961: Red on Reflective White (undated)
1962: *Red on Yellow Sticker*
1963: *Red and Blue on White Sticker*
1964: *Silver on Green Sticker*

1965: Red on Reflective Lemon Yellow
Counties 10 to 32 carried 1965 *Red on Lemon Yellow Sticker.*
1966: *Red on White Sticker*
1967: *Silver on Blue Sticker*
1968: *Blue on White Sticker*
1969: *White on Light Green Sticker*
New registrations received Red on Reflective Lemon Yellow base with above sticker.
1970: *Silver on Red Sticker* on 1965 and 1969 bases
1971: *Silver on Blue Sticker* on 1965 and 1969 bases
1972: Red on Reflective White
1973: *Black on Red Sticker*
1974: *Aluminum on Black Sticker*
A few new registrations received Red on Reflective White with "74" embossed.
1975: *Black on White Sticker* on 1972 and 1974 bases
1976: *Blue and Red on White Sticker* on 1972 and 1974 bases
New registrations received Red on Reflective White base (but still with "72" embossed) with above sticker.
1977: *White on Red Sticker* on 1972, 1974 and 1976 bases
New registrations received Red on Reflective Yellow undated base with above sticker.
1978: *White on Blue Sticker*
1979: *Black on White Sticker*
1980: *White on Black Sticker*
1981: *Green on White Sticker*
1982: *White on Brown Sticker*
New registrations received Red on Reflective Lemon Yellow undated base with above sticker.
1983: *White on Red Sticker*
1984: *White on Blue Sticker*
1985: *White on Green Sticker*
1986: *White on Black Sticker*
1987: *White on Dark Blue Sticker*
1988: *White on Brown Sticker*
New registrations received undated Red on Reflective Yellow base with above sticker.
1989: *White on Green Sticker*
1990: *White on Blue Sticker*
1991: *White on Black Sticker*
New base issued: Red on Reflective Turquoise and Yellow graphic undated base with above sticker.
1992: *White on Red Sticker*
1993: *White on Blue Sticker*
1994: *Red on Yellow Sticker*

Note: All bases from 1972 through 1990 remained valid until superceded by the 1991 base.

NEW YORK
COLOR CODE

1910: White on Blue (undated)
1911: White on Maroon (undated
1912: White on Red (undated Porcelain)
1913: White on Blue-Purple
1914: White on Brown
1915: Black on Yellow
1916: Blue on Ivory
1917: White on Olive Green
1918: White on Maroon
1919: White on Black
1920: Black on Light Green
1921: White on Midnight Blue
1922: White on Green
1923: White on Purple
1924: White on Gray
1925: Black on Yellow
1926: White on Dark Blue
1927: Black on Deep Yellow
1928: Deep Yellow on Black
1929: Black on Deep Yellow
1930: Deep Yellow on Black
1931: Black on Deep Yellow
1932: Deep Yellow on Black
1933: Black on Deep Yellow
1934: Deep Yellow on Black
1935: Black on Deep Yellow
1936: Deep Yellow on Black
1937: Black on Deep Yellow
1938: Deep Yellow on Black
1939: Black on Deep Yellow
1940: Deep Yellow on Black
1941: Black on Deep Yellow
1942: Deep Yellow on Black
1943: *Black on Deep Yellow Date Strip*
1944: Black on Deep Yellow
1945: Deep Yellow on Black

1946: Black on Deep Yellow
1947: Deep Yellow on Black
1948: Black on Deep Yellow
1949: *Deep Yellow on Black Tab*
1950: Deep Yellow on Black
1951: Black on Deep Yellow
1952: *Deep Yellow on Black Tab*
1953: Deep Yellow on Black
1954: *Black on Deep Yellow Tab*
1955: Black on Deep Yellow
1956: *Deep Yellow on Black Tab*
1957: Deep Yellow on Black
1958: Black on Deep Yellow
1959: *Deep Yellow on Black Tab*
1960: Deep Yellow on Black
1961: *Black on Deep Yellow Tab*
1962: Black on Deep Yellow
1963: *Deep Yellow on Black Tab*
1964: Light Orange on Black
1965: *Black on Red Sticker*
1966: Orange on Blue undated base with *Red on White Sticker*
1967: *Green on Yellow Sticker*
1968: *Blue on White Sticker*
1969: *Red on Yellow Sticker*
1970: *Black on White Sticker*
1971: *Black on Orange Sticker*
1972: *Red on White Sticker*
1973: *Green on Yellow Sticker or Windshield Sticker*
1974: Blue on Reflective Golden Orange undated base, with *Windshield Stickers* issued each year as of 1993
1986: New registrations received Red and Blue on Reflective White graphic undated base.

NORTH CAROLINA
COLOR CODE

Expires June 30, 1913: White on Black (Porcelain)
Expires June 30, 1914: Red on White (Porcelain)
Expires June 30, 1915: White on Green (Porcelain)
Expires June 30, 1916: Black on Gray (Porcelain)
6/30/17: White on Dark Blue
6/30/18: Blue on White
6/30/19: White on Black
6/30/20: Black on Yellow
6/30/21: White on Brown
6/30/22: Black on White
6/30/23: White on Green
6/30/24: Maroon on Gray
6/30/25: White on Dark Blue
6/30/26: Black on Orange
6/30/27: White on Black
1927: Red on Light Gray
1928: White on Green
1929: White on Light Blue
1930: White on Maroon
1931: Yellow on Black
1932: Black on Yellow
1933: White on Blue
1934: Yellow on Black
1935: Silver on Black
1936: Pea Green on Black
1937: Yellow on Black
1938: Black on Yellow
1939: Silver on Maroon
1940: Maroon on Silver
1941: Yellow-Orange on Black
1942: Black on Yellow-Orange
1943: *Yellow-Orange on Black Tab*
1944: Yellow on Black
1945: Black on Dull Butterscotch
1946: Yellow on Black
1947: Black on Light Orange
1948: Yellow on Black
1949: Black on Yellow-Orange
1950: Yellow on Black
1951: Red on White
1952: White on Dark Red
1953: Yellow-Orange on Black
1954: Black on Yellow-Orange
1955: Yellow-Orange on Black
1956: Black on Yellow-Orange
1957: Yellow-Orange on Black
1958: Black on Yellow-Orange
1959: Yellow-Orange on Black
1960: Black on Yellow-Orange
1961: Yellow-Orange on Black

1962: Black on Yellow-Orange
1963: Yellow-Orange on Black
1964: Black on Yellow-Orange
1965: Yellow-Orange on Black
1966: Black on Yellow-Orange
1967: Green on Reflective White
1968: Red on Reflective White
1969: Green on Reflective White
1970: Red on Reflective White
1971: Green on Reflective White
1972: Blue on Reflective White
1973: Red on Reflective White
1974: Green on Reflective White
1975:. Red on Reflective White
1976: *White on Light Blue Sticker*
1977: *White on Red Sticker*
1978: *White on Green Sticker*
New registrations received Red on Reflective White base with above sticker.
1979: *Black on Orange Sticker* on 1975 and 1978 bases
New registrations received Red on Reflective White base dated "75" with above sticker.
1980: *White on Black Sticker* on 1975, 1978 and 1979 bases
New registrations received Red on Reflective White dated base.
1981: *White on Blue Sticker* on 1975-1980 bases
New registrations received Red on Reflective White dated base or Blue on Reflective Blue, Red and White graphic dated base, some with 1983 stickers.
1982: *White on Red Sticker* on 1975-1981 bases
Red on Reflective White base with embossed date or Blue and Red on Reflective (or not) White graphic dated base
1983: *White on Blue Sticker* on 1975-1982 bases
1984: *Red on Black Sticker* on 1982 graphic base; previous bases phased out.
1985: *White on Blue Sticker*
1986: *White on Black Sticker*
1987: *White on Red Sticker*
1988: *White on Green Sticker*
1989: *Black on Orange Sticker*
1990: *White on Blue Sticker*
1991: *White on Black Sticker*
1992: *White on Red Sticker*
1993: *White on Green Sticker*
1994: *White on Orange Sticker*

NORTH DAKOTA
COLOR CODE

1911: Gold on Black (Flat)
1912: Red on White
1913: Black on Tan
1914: Black on Yellow
1915: Black on Green
1916: Yellow on Black
1917: Black on Off White
1918: Red on Cream
1919: Turquoise on Black
1920: Cream on Green
1921: White on Black
1922: Black on Yellow-Orange
1923: White on Green
1924: Black on Silver
1925: Silver on Black
1926: Red on Gray
1927: Black on Orange
1928: White on Black
1929: Black on Silver
1930: Green on Yellow-Orange
1931: Tan on Dark Blue
1932: White on Maroon
1933: White on Green
1934: Blue on Orange
1935: Orange on Black
1936: Black on Orange
1937: Green on White
1938: Black on Yellow
1939: Red on White
1940: Yellow on Black
1941: Black on Yellow
1942: Yellow on Red
1943: *Windshield Sticker*
New registrations received Yellow on Red 1943 plates.
1944: Yellow on Black
1945: White on Black
1946: Red on Silver
1947: Black on Yellow
1948: Black on Yellow
1949: *Black on White Tab*
New registrations received Black on Yellow 1949 plates.
1950: Black on Orange
1951: White on Black
1952: Black on White
1953: White on Green
1954: White on Black
1955: Yellow on Black

1956: Blue on White
1957: White on Blue
1958: Green on Reflective White
1959: *Black on Reflective Yellow Tab*
1960: *White on Reflective Red-Orange Tab*
1961: *White on Reflective Green Tab*
1962: Black on Reflective White
1963: *Black on Yellow Sticker*
1964: *White on Green Sticker*
1965: *White on Red Sticker*
1966: Red on Reflective White
1967: *White on Red Sticker*
1968: *Black on Yellow Sticker*
1969: *White on Green Sticker*
1970: Dark Blue on Reflective White
1971: *White on Red Sticker*
1972: *Black on Yellow Sticker*
1973: *White on Blue Sticker*
1974: Green on Reflective White
1975: *White on Green Sticker*
1976: *White on Red Sticker*
1977: *Red on White Sticker*
1978: *White on Green Sticker*
1979: *White on Blue Sticker*
1980: Black on Reflective White
1981: *Black on Yellow Sticker*
1982: *White on Red Sticker*
1983: *White on Blue Sticker*
1984: *Black on Orange Sticker*
Optional base introduced: Blue on Reflective Blue, Red and White graphic undated base with above sticker.
1985: *Black on Orange Sticker* on 1980 and 1984 bases
1986: *White on Red Sticker* on 1980 and 1984 bases
1987: *White on Blue Sticker* on 1980 and 1984 bases
New base issued: Black on Reflective Blue, Gold and White graphic undated base with above sticker.
1988: *Black on Yellow Sticker* on 1980 and 1984 bases
1989: *Black on Gold Sticker* on 1988 base; previous bases phased out.
1990: *White on Blue Sticker*
1991: *White on Red Sticker*
1992: *Black on Yellow Sticker*
1993: *White on Blue Sticker*
1994: *Black on Yellow Sticker*

OHIO
COLOR CODE

1908-09: White on Dark Blue (undated Porcelain)
1910: White on Woodgrain (Porcelain)
1911: Black on White (Porcelain)
1912: Green on White (Flat)
1913: Maroon on White (Flat)
1914: Red on White (Flat)
1915: Black on White (Flat)
1916: White on Black (Flat)
1917: Black on Yellow (Flat)
1918: White on Olive Green
1919: White on Maroon
1920: White on Dark Blue
1921: White on Dark Green
1922: Blue on Light Gray
1923: Red on Gray
1924: White on Navy Blue
1925: Black on Cream
1926: White on Brown
1927: Black on Gray
1928: White on Navy Blue
1929: Black on Apple Green
1930: White on Maroon
1931: Black on Gray
1932: White on Navy Blue
1933: Black on Orange
1934: White on Maroon
1935: Yellow on Navy Blue
1936: Blue on White
1937: Maroon on White
1938: Black on White
1939: Blue on White
1940: White on Navy Blue
1941: White on Maroon
1942: Green on White
1943: *Windshield Sticker*
1944: White on Navy Blue
1945: Black on White
1946: Red on White
1947: White on Green
1948: Black on Cream-Yellow
1949: Yellow on Black
1950: Black on Yellow
1951: White on Dark Blue
1952: *Windshield Sticker*
1953: Yellow on Dark Green
1954: White on Maroon
1955: White on Dark Blue
1956: White on Dark Green
1957: White on Maroon
1958: White on Dark Blue

1959: Red on White
1960: Blue on Yellow
1961: White on Green
1962: White on Maroon
1963: White on Dark Blue
1964: White on Green
1965: Red on White
1966: White on Red
1967: White on Blue
1968: Red on White
1969: Blue on White
1970: Scarlet on Gray
1971: Black on Yellow
1972: Yellow on Dark Blue
1973: White on Green
1974: Green on Reflective White
April 1975: *White on Blue Sticker*
May 1975: *White on Green Sticker*
1976: Red on Reflective White (undated)
1977: No dated 1977 issue due to shift from year of use to year of expiration.
April 1978: *White on Blue Sticker*
May 1978: *White on Red Sticker*
April 1979: *White on Gold Sticker*
May 1979: *White on Green Sticker*
1980: *White on Red Sticker*
New base issued: Blue on Reflective White undated base with 1980 or 1981 sticker.
1981: *White on Blue Sticker*
1982: *Black on Orange Sticker*
1983: *Black on Yellow Sticker*
1984: *Black on Green Sticker*
1985: *White on Red Sticker*
New base issued: Green on Reflective White undated base with 1985 or 1986 sticker.
1986: *White on Green Sticker*
1987: *White on Orange Sticker*
1988: *White on Blue Sticker*
1989: *Black on Yellow Sticker*
1990: *White on Red Sticker*
1991: *White on Blue Sticker*
New base issued: Blue on Reflective Blue, Red and White graphic undated base with 1991 or 1992 sticker.
1992: *White on Orange Sticker*
1993: *White on Green Sticker*
1994: *Black on Yellow Sticker*
1995: *White on Black Sticker*
1996: *White on Red Sticker*

OKLAHOMA
COLOR CODE

1915: Blue on White
1916: White on Blue
1917: White on Brown
1918: Yellow on Green
1919: Green on Yellow
1920: White on Blue
1921: White on Brown
1922: Black on Turquoise
1923: White on Maroon
1924: White on Olive Green
1925: Silver on Black
1926: Black on Yellow
1927: Yellow on Black
1928: Black on Yellow
1929: Yellow on Black
1930: Black on Yellow
1931: Yellow on Black
1932: Black on Yellow
1933: Yellow on Black
1934: Black on Yellow
1935: Black on White
1936: Black on Yellow
1937: Yellow on Black
1938: Black on Yellow
1939: Black on Silver
1940: Black on Yellow
1941: White on Black
1942: Blue on White
1943: *Windshield Sticker*
1944: Black on Yellow
1945: Orange on Black
1946: White on Blue-Black
1947: *Black on Yellow Tab*
1948: Black on Yellow
1949: White on Blue-Black
1950: Black on White
1951: Black on Yellow
1952: White on Blue-Black
1953: Black on Yellow
1954: Yellow on Black
1955: White on Black
1956: Black on White
1957: White on Black

1958: Black on White
1959: White on Black
1960: Black on White
1961: White on Black
1962: Black on White
1963: White on Black
1964: Black on White
1965: White on Black
1966: Black on White
1967: Red on Reflective White
1968: Black on Reflective Orange
1969: Red on Reflective White
1970: Green on Reflective White
1971: Red on Reflective White
1972: Green on Reflective White
1973: Red on Reflective White
1974: *White on Green Sticker*
1975: Green on Reflective White
1976: Red on Reflective White
1977: Green on Reflective White
1978: Red on Reflective White
1979: Blue on Reflective White
1980: *White on Blue Sticker*
1981: Green on Reflective White
1982: Green, Black and Yellow on Reflective White graphic undated base with *White on Red Sticker*
1983: *White on Green Sticker*
1984: *Black on White Sticker*
1985: *White on Blue Sticker*
1986: *White on Orange Sticker*
1987: *White on Green Sticker*
1988: *White on Red Sticker*
1989: *Black on Yellow Sticker*
New base issued: Green, Red, Black and Yellow on Reflective White graphic undated base with above sticker.
1990: *White on Green Sticker*
1991: *Black on White Sticker*
1992: *White on Red Sticker*
1993: *Black on Gold Sticker*
1994: *White on Green Sticker*

Note: All bases since 1981 are still valid.

OREGON
COLOR CODE

1908-10: White on Maroon (undated)[*]
1911: Black on Yellow
1912: Black on Light Green
1913: Black on Aluminum
1914: White on Blue
1915: Black on Yellow
1916: White on Dark Red
1917: White on Light Green
1918: Black on Light Blue
1919: Black on Orange
1920: White on Red
1921: White on Green
1922: Black on Deep Yellow
1923: White on Dark Blue
1924: White on Red
1925: Black on Yellow
1926: White on Black
1927: White on Black
1928: Black on White
1929: White on Black
June 30, 1930: *Windshield Sticker*
June 30, 1931: Orange on Black
June 30, 1932: White on Navy Blue
June 30, 1933: White on Black
Dec. 31, 1933: Black on Deep Yellow
1934: Black on Gray
1935: Yellow on Black
1936: Black on Aluminum
1937: White on Black
1938: Black on Aluminum
1939: Black on Yellow
1940: Blue-Purple on White
1941: White on Green
1942: White on Blue
1943: *Windshield Sticker*
1944: *Windshield Sticker*
1945: *Windshield Sticker*
1946: *Windshield Sticker*
   New registrations received Black on Gray dated
   1946 plate.
1947: Black on Aluminum
1948: Red on Aluminum
1949: Black on Aluminum
1950: Black on Aluminum
1951: *Black on Aluminum Tab*
   New registrations received Black on Aluminum
   1951 base.
1952: *Red on Aluminum Tab* on 1950 and 1951 bases
1953: *Yellow on Aluminum Tab* on 1950 and 1951 bases
1954: *Green on Aluminum Tab* on 1950 and 1951 bases
1955: *White on Red Tab* on 1950 and 1951 bases
1956: Yellow on Blue

1957: *Blue on Yellow Tab*
1958: *Blue on Aluminum Tab*
1959: *Black on White Tab*
1960: *White on Red Tab*
1961: *Red on White Sticker*
   New registrations received Yellow on Blue base
   with above sticker.
1962: *Black on White Sticker*
1963: *Dark Green on Yellow Sticker*
1964: *Blue on White Sticker*
1965: *White on Red Sticker*
   New registrations received Yellow on Blue base
   with above sticker.
1966: *White on Green Sticker*
1967: *Dark Green on Yellow Sticker*
1968: *Green on White Sticker*
1969: *Black on Orange Sticker*
1970: *White on Light Green Sticker*
1971: *Green on Deep Yellow Sticker*
1972: *White on Red Sticker*
1973: *Green on White Sticker*
1974: *White on Light Green Sticker*
   New registrations received Blue on Reflective Deep
   Yellow base with above sticker.
1975: *White on Blue Sticker*
1976: *White on Red Sticker*
1977: *Black on White Sticker*
1978: *White on Green Sticker*
1979: *White on Blue Sticker*
1980: *White on Red Sticker*
1981: *Black on White Sticker*
1982: *White on Green Sticker*
1983: *White on Blue Sticker*
1984: *White on Red Sticker*
1985: *Black on White Sticker*
1986: *White on Green Sticker*
1987: *White on Blue Sticker*
1988: *White on Red Sticker*
   New registrations received Blue, Gray and Green on
   Refl. White graphic undated base with above sticker.
1989: *Black on White Sticker*
1990: *White on Green Sticker*
   Previous graphic base modified to Light Blue, Dark
   Blue, Green and Purple on Reflective White undated
   base with above sticker.
1991: *White on Blue Sticker*
1992: *White on Red Sticker*
1993: *Black on White Sticker*
1994: *White on Green Sticker*
1995: *White on Blue Sticker*

Note: All bases from 1956 forward were valid until the early
   1990s, when all but the 1988 and 1990 bases were
   invalidated.

[*]Current information has revealed that this plate was not state issued.

PENNSYLVANIA
COLOR CODE

1906: White on Blue (Porcelain)
1907: White on Red (Porcelain)
1908: Black on Yellow (Porcelain)
1909: Black on White (Porcelain)
1910: White on Blue (Porcelain)
1911: Black on Yellow (Porcelain)
1912: White on Woodgrain (Porcelain)
1913: White on Green (Porcelain)
1914: White on Black (Porcelain)
1915: White on Azure Blue (Porcelain)
1916: Black on Orange
1917: White on Brown
1918: White on Black
1919: Red on Black
1920: White on Blue-Black
1921: Black on Yellow
1922: Brown on Cream
1923: Yellow on Blue-Black
1924: Dark Blue on Yellow-Orange
1925: Orange on Blue-Black
1926: Dark Blue on Yellow-Orange
1927: Yellow-Orange on Blue-Black
1928: Blue-Black on Yellow
1929: Orange on Blue-Black
1930: Blue-Black on Yellow
1931: Orange on Blue-Black
1932: Blue-Black on Yellow
1933: Yellow on Blue-Black
1934: Blue-Black on Yellow
1935: Yellow-Orange on Blue-Black
1936: Dark Blue on Yellow-Orange
1937: Yellow-Orange on Dark Blue
1938: Dark Blue on Yellow-Orange
1939: Yellow-Orange on Dark Blue
1940: Dark Blue on Yellow-Orange
1941: Yellow-Orange on Dark Blue
1942: Dark Blue on Yellow-Orange
1943: *Black on Red Tab*
1944: Yellow-Orange on Dark Blue
1945: Dark Blue on Yellow-Orange
1946: Yellow-Orange on Dark Blue
1947: Dark Blue on Yellow-Orange
1948: Yellow-Orange on Dark Blue
1949: Dark Blue on Yellow-Orange
1950: Yellow-Orange on Dark Blue
1951: Dark Blue on Yellow-Orange
1952: Yellow-Orange on Dark Blue
1953: Dark Blue on Yellow-Orange

1954: Yellow-Orange on Dark Blue
1955: Dark Blue on Yellow-Orange
1956: Yellow-Orange on Dark Blue
1957: Dark Blue on Yellow-Orange
1958: Yellow-Orange on Dark Blue
1959: *Yellow on Dark Blue Sticker*
1960: *White on Green Sticker*
1961: *Yellow on Dark Blue Sticker*
1962: *White on Green Sticker*
1963: *Yellow on Dark Blue Sticker*
1964: *White on Green Sticker*
1965: Dark Blue on Yellow-Orange (undated)
1966: *White on Red Sticker*
1967: *Red on Black Sticker*
1968: *White on Red Sticker*
1969: *White on Blue Sticker*
1970: *White on Red Sticker*
1971: Yellow-Orange on Dark Blue
1972: *White on Blue Sticker*
1973: *White on Red Sticker*
1974: *White on Blue Sticker*
1975: *White on Red Sticker*
1976: *White on Blue Sticker*
1977: Dark Blue on Reflective Yellow-Orange (undated)
1978: *White and Blue Sticker*
1979: *White and Red Sticker*
1980: *Blue on White Sticker*
1981: *Red on White Sticker*
1982: *Blue on White Sticker*
1983: *White on Blue Sticker*
New registrations received Reflective Yellow on Blue undated base with above sticker.
1984: *Black on White Sticker*
1985: *White on Green Sticker*
1986: *Blue on White Sticker*
1987: *White on Red Sticker*
New registrations received Reflective Yellow on Blue undated base with above sticker.
1988: *White on Green Sticker*
1989: *White on Black Sticker*
1990: *Red on White Sticker*
1991: *White on Blue Sticker*
1992: *Black on White Sticker*
1993: *White on Green Sticker*
1994: *Blue on White Sticker*

Note: All bases issued since 1977 are still valid.

RHODE ISLAND
COLOR CODE

1904-07: White on Black (undated Porcelain)
1908-11: White on Black (undated Porcelain)
New registrations only.
1912-17: Black on White (undated Porcelain)
1918: White on Black (Flat)
1919: Black on White (Flat)
1920: White on Black
1921: Black on White
1922: White on Black
1923: Black on White
1924: White on Black
1925: Black on White
1926: White on Black
1927: Black on White
1928: White on Black
1929: Black on White
1930: White on Black
1931: Black on White
1932: White on Black
1933: Black on White
1934: White on Black
1935: Black on White
1936: White on Black
1937: Black on White
1938: White on Black
1939: Black on White
1940: White on Black
1941: Black on White
1942: White on Black
1943: *Windshield Sticker*
1944: White on Black with *Orange Tab*
1945: *Green Tab*
1946: *Red Tab*
Renewals after August 1: Black on Aluminum
undated base with an *Aluminum '46 Tab.*
1947: *White Tab* on 1946 base
1948: Black on White undated base with
Black on White Tab
1949: *Red on White Tab*
1950: *Black on White Tab*
1951: *White on Black Tab*
New registrations received a White on Black
1951 base.
1952: *Windshield Sticker*
New registrations received White on Black
1952 plate.
1953: Black on White
1954: *White on Black Tab*
1955: White on Black
1956: *Black on White Tab*
1957: Black on White
1958: *White on Black Tab*
1959: White on Black
1960: *Black on White Tab*

1961: Black on White undated base with
Black on White Sticker
1962: *Black on Orange Sticker*
1963: *Black on Gold Sticker*
1964: *Black on Green Sticker*
1965: *Black on White Sticker*
1966: *Black on Orange Sticker*
1967: Black on White with *Black on Gold Sticker*
1968: *Black on Red Sticker*
1969: *Black on Green Sticker*
1970: *Blue on White Sticker*
1971: *Black on Deep Yellow Sticker*
1972: *Black on White Sticker*
New registrations received a Black on Reflective
White undated base with above sticker.
1973: *White on Blue Sticker* on 1967 and 1972 bases
1974: *White on Pink Sticker* on 1967 and 1972 bases
1975: *Blue on Deep Yellow Sticker* on 1967 and
1972 bases
1976: *White on Red Sticker* on 1967 and 1972 bases
1977: *White on Blue Sticker* on 1967 and 1972 bases
1978: *Black on Yellow Sticker* on 1967 and 1972 bases
New registrations received a Black on Reflective
White undated base with above sticker.
1979: *White on Green Sticker* on 1967, 1972 and
1978 bases
1980: Blue on Reflective White dated base with
Black on White "80" Stickers used on previous bases
on a temporary basis.
1981: *Red on White Sticker* on 1980 base;
all pre-80 bases invalidated.
1982: *White on Blue Sticker*
New registrations received dated Blue on Reflective
White dated base.
1983: *Red on Yellow Sticker*
New registrations received Blue on Reflective White
dated base.
1984: *Black on White Sticker*
New registrations received Blue on Reflective White
dated base.
1985: *Yellow on Green Sticker*
New registrations received Blue on Reflective White
dated base.
1986: *White on Blue Sticker*
Four variations of new base issued, all Blue on
Reflective White some undated; some dated.
1987: *White on Red Sticker*
1988: *Black on White Sticker*
1989: *White on Blue Sticker*
1990: *White on Green Sticker*
1991: *White on Red Sticker*
1992: *Blue on White Sticker*
1993: *White on Blue Sticker*
1994: *White on Green Sticker*
1995: *White on Black Sticker*

Note: All bases issued since 1980 are still valid.

SOUTH CAROLINA
COLOR CODE

1917: Black on Pale Yellow
1918: White on Green
1919: Blue on White
1920: White on Black
1921: Red on Black
1922: Black on White
1923: White on Black
1924: Black on Orange
1925: White on Green
1926: Red on White
1927: Green on White
1928: Black on Yellow
1929: Black on White
1930: White on Black
1931: Green on Gray
1932: Black on Deep Yellow
1933: Black on White
1934-36: Full-year and half-year plates were issued in different color combinations.

	Full-year Plates *Expiration:* *October 31*	*Half-year Plates* *Expiration:* *April 30*
1934	Yellow on Black	Black on Yellow
1935	Black on White	White on Black
1936	Black on Yellow	Yellow on Black

10/31/37: Black on White
1938: Black on Deep Yellow
1939: Black on White
10/31/40: Yellow on Black
1941: Black on Deep Yellow
1942: Deep Yellow on Black
1943: Black on Deep Yellow
1944: *Yellow on Green Date Strip*
1945: Yellow on Green
1946: Silver on Black
1947: Black on Deep Yellow
1948: Yellow on Black
1949: White on Black
1950: Black on White
1951: White on Black
1952: Yellow on Black
1953: Black on Deep Yellow
1954: White on Black

1955: Black on White
1956: Black on Deep Yellow
1957: White on Blue
1958: Blue on White
1959: White on Blue
1960: Blue on White
1961: Red on White
1962: White on Red
1963: White on Green
1964: White on Black
1965: Black on White
1966: White on Blue
1967: Blue on White
1968: Reflective White on Black
1969: Reflective White on Blue
1970: Reflective White on Green
1971: Reflective White on Brown
1972: Reflective White on Black
1973: Reflective White on Blue
1974: Reflective White on Green
1975: Reflective White on Brown
1976: Blue and Red on Reflective White graphic
1977: *White on Blue Sticker*
1978: *White on Red Sticker*
1979: *White on Black Sticker*
1980: *White on Green Sticker*
1981: Dark Blue on Reflective Light Blue and White graphic undated base
1982: *White on Red Sticker*
1983: *White on Blue Sticker*
1984: *White on Black Sticker*
1985: *White on Green Sticker*
1986: *Red on White Sticker*
New base issued: Blue and Red on Reflective White graphic dated base.
1987: *White on Orange Sticker*
1988: *White on Blue Sticker*
1989: *White on Green Sticker*
1990: *White on Red Sticker*
1991: Black, Brown and Yellow on Reflective White graphic dated "Wren" base
1992: *White on Blue Sticker*
1993: *White on Black Sticker*
1994: *White on Red Sticker*

SOUTH DAKOTA
COLOR CODE

1913: Black on White (undated)
1914: White on Red (undated)
1915: Yellow on Black (undated)
1916: Light Green on Black
1917: Cream on Brown
1918: Brown on Dark Tan
1919: Silver on Olive Green
1920: Maroon on Cream
1921: White on Green
1922: White on Dark Blue
1923: Black on Gray
1924: Silver on Black
1925: Black on Tan
1926: Black on Silver
1927: Black on Light Blue-Green
1928: White on Dark Red
1929: White on Light Green
1930: Black on Yellow
1931: Black on White
1932: Yellow on Black
1933: Black on Yellow
1934: Yellow on Black
1935: Black on Yellow
1936: White on Dark Red
1937: Red on White
1938: White on Blue
1939: Blue on White
1940: Black on Yellow
1941: Yellow on Black
1942: Black on Yellow
1943: *Yellow on Black Tab*
1944: *Windshield Sticker*
1945: Green on White*
1946: White on Black
1947: Black on Aluminum
1948: Red on Aluminum
1949: Blue on Aluminum
1950: Black on Orange
1951: Orange on Black
1952: Maroon on Cream
1953: Cream on Maroon
1954: Black on White
1955: White on Green
1956: Green on Cream
1957: Black on Reflective Gray

1958: *Orange on Maroon Tab*
1959: *Black on Red Tab*
1960: Black on Reflective Tan
1961: Green on Reflective Gray
1962: Black on Reflective White
1963: Red on Reflective White
1964: Blue on Reflective White
1965: Green on Reflective White
1966: Blue on Reflective White
1967: Dark Red on Reflective White
1968: Light Blue on Reflective White
1969: Light Orange on Reflective White
1970: Blue on Reflective White
1971: Green on Reflective White
1972: Black on Reflective White
1973: Red on Reflective White
1974: Blue, Red and Black on Reflective White graphic; late year registrations received Blue on Reflective White plate.
1975: Red, Blue and Black on Reflective White graphic
1976: Blue and Red on Reflective White graphic
1977: *White on Red Sticker*
1978: *White on Blue Sticker*
1979: *White on Green Sticker*
1980: *White on Orange Sticker*
1981: Red and Blue on Reflective White graphic
1982: *White on Red Sticker*
1983: *White on Blue Sticker*
1984: *White on Orange Sticker*
1985: *White on Green Sticker*
1986: *White on Red Sticker*
1987: Red and Blue on Reflective White graphic
1988: *White on Red Sticker*
1989: *White on Blue Sticker*
1990: *Black on Yellow Sticker*
New base issued: Green and Red on Reflective Tan, Brown and White graphic undated base with above sticker.
1991: *White on Pale Green Sticker* on 1987 and 1990 bases
1992: *White on Red Sticker* on 1987 and 1990 bases
1993: *White on Blue Sticker* on 1987 and 1990 bases
1994: *White on Pink Sticker* on 1987 and 1990 bases

---

*In 1945 a windshield sticker was issued in leiu of a front plate.

TENNESSEE
COLOR CODE

1915: White on Dark Blue
1916: Black on Cream
1917: White on Black
1918: Black on Light Green
1919: White on Black
1920: Black on Gray
1921: Black on Orange
1922: White on Dark Green
1923: Blue on Gray
1924: Black on Yellow
1925: White on Maroon
1926: White on Black
1927: White on Lavender
1928: White on Black
1929: White on Green
1930: *Blue-Black on Silver*
1931: *Yellow on Black*
1932: *White on Black*
1933: *Cream on Brown*
1934: *White on Light Blue*
1935: *White on Black*
1936: *Blue on White*
1937: *Black on Yellow*
1938: *Blue on Silver*
1939: *Red on Silver*
1940: *Orange on Black*
1941: *White on Black*
1942: *Black on White*
1943: *Yellow on Black Tab*
1944: *White on Black*
1945: *Blue on Silver*
1946: *Green on Silver*
1947: *White on Black*
1948: *Black on Pale Yellow*
1949: *Pale Yellow on Black*
1950: *Black on Silver*
1951: *White on Orange*
1952: *Black on White*
1953: *Blue on Silver*
1954: *Yellow on Black*
1955: *Red on White*
1956: *White on Blue-Black*
1957: *White on Black*
1958: *Black on White*
1959: *White on Black*

1960: Black on White
1961: White on Black
1962: Black on White
1963: *White on Green Sticker*
New registrations received Black on White 1963 base.
1964: *Black on Orange Sticker* on 1962 and 1963 bases
New registrations received Black on White 1964 base.
1965: *White on Blue Sticker* on 1962, 1963, and 1964 bases
New registrations received Black on White 1965 plate.
1966: Black on White
1967: *Black on White Sticker*
1968: *Black on Deep Yellow Sticker*
1969: *Green on White Sticker*
1970: *Red on White Sticker*
1971: Black on White
1972: *Blue on White Sticker*
1973: *Orange on White Sticker*
1974: *Green on White Sticker*
1975: *White on Red Sticker*
1976: *Black "76" on White map on Light Blue Sticker*
1977: Blue on Reflective Blue, Yellow and White graphic
1978: *White on Dark Blue Sticker*
1979: *White on Red Sticker*
1980: *White on Green Sticker*
1981: *Black on Yellow Sticker*
1982: *White on Red Sticker*
1983: *White on Black Sticker*
1984: Blue on Reflective Green and White graphic
1985: *White on Blue Sticker*
1986: *Green on White Sticker*
1987: *White on Blue Sticker*
1988: *White on Green Sticker*
1989: Red on Reflective Blue and White graphic
1990: *Blue on White Sticker*
1991: *White on Red Sticker*
1992: *Blue on White Sticker*
1993: *Black on Orange Sticker*
1994: *Black on Green Sticker*

TEXAS
COLOR CODE

1917-22: White on Dark Blue (undated)
1917: *White on Red Metal Seal*
1918: *Blue on White Metal Seal*
1919: *White on Blue Metal Seal*
1920: *White on Black Metal Seal*
1921: *White on Olive Green Metal Seal*
1922: *Black on Yellow Metal Seal*
1923: White on Black (undated)
1924: *White on Red Metal Seal*
1925: White on Maroon
1926: Black on Gray
1927: White on Green
1928: White on Brown
1929: Orange on Black
1930: Blue on Deep Yellow
1931: White on Black
1932: White on Green
1933: Orange on White
1934: Black on Orange
1935: White on Maroon
1936: Dark Blue on Cream
1937: Ivory on Black
1938: Black on White
1939: Purple on Yellow-Orange
1940: Purple on White
1941: Yellow-Orange on Black
1942: Black on Yellow-Orange
1943: *Yellow-Orange on Black Tab*
1944: *Cream on Green Tab*
1945: Black on Yellow-Orange
1946: Cream on Black
1947: White on Black
1948: Yellow on Black
1949: Black on Yellow-Orange
1950: Yellow on Black
1951: Black on Yellow-Orange
1952: Yellow on Black
1953: Black on Yellow-Orange
1954: Yellow on Black
1955: Black on Yellow-Orange
1956: Yellow on Black
1957: Black on White
1958: White on Black
1959: Black on White
1960: White on Black

1961: Black on White
1962: White on Black
1963: Black on White
1964: White on Black
1965: Black on White
1966: White on Black
1967: Black on White
1968: White on Black
1969: Black on Reflective White
1970: Blue on Reflective White
1971: Black on Reflective White
1972: Green on Reflective White
1973: Black on Reflective White
1974: Red on Reflective White
1975: Black on Reflective White with date faintly embossed
1976: *White on Blue Sticker*
1977: *White on Red Sticker*
1978: *White on Green Sticker*
1979: *Black on Yellow Sticker*
1980: *White on Red Sticker*
1981: *White on Green Sticker*
1982: *Blue on Yellow Sticker*
1983: *White on Red Sticker*
1984: *White on Green Sticker*
1985: *Black on Yellow Sticker*
New registrations received Red and Blue on Reflective White graphic undated base with above sticker.
1986: *White on Red Sticker* on 1975 and 1985 bases
1987: *White on Green Sticker* on 1975 and 1985 bases
1988: *Black on Yellow Sticker* on 1975 and 1985 bases
1989: *White on Red Sticker* on 1975 and 1985 bases
New registrations received Blue and Red on Reflective White graphic undated base with above sticker.
1990: *White on Green Sticker* on 1975, 1985 and 1989 bases
1991: *Black on Yellow Sticker* on 1985 and 1989 bases; 1975 base invalidated.
1992: *White on Red Sticker* on 1985 and 1989 bases
1993: *White on Blue Sticker* on 1985 and 1989 bases
1994: *Red on White Sticker* on 1985 and 1989 bases

UTAH
COLOR CODE

1915: Dark Green on White
1916: Cream on Brown
1917: Blue on Gray
1918: White on Blue
1919: White on Dark Olive Green
1920: White on Blue
1921: Orange on Black
1922: White on Black
1923: White on Red
1924: White on Blue
1925: White on Green
1926: Black on Silver
1927: White on Dark Blue
1928: Black on Yellow
1929: Black on Green
1930: White on Black
1931: Black on Silver
1932: White on Black
1933: White on Black
1934: Black on Silver
1935: White on Black
1936: Black on Silver
1937: White on Black
1938: Maroon on White
1939: White on Blue-Black
1940: Orange on Dark Blue
1941: White on Black
1942: Black on White
1943: *Windshield Sticker*
1944: Black on White (Patterned Paper on Fiberboard)
1945: White on Maroon
1946: White on Black
1947: Yellow on Black
1948: White on Black
1949: White on Black
1950: Orange on Black
1951: White on Green
1952: White on Blue
1953: Yellow on Black
1954: White on Dark Green
1955: White on Black
1956: White on Dark Red
1957: White on Dark Blue
1958: Yellow on Dark Blue
1959: White on Red-Orange
1960: Red-Orange on Off White
1961: Dark Blue on Off White
1962: Red on Light Gray
1963: Reflective White on Dark Blue

1964: Reflective White on Green
1965: Reflective White on Blue
1966: Reflective White on Black
1967: Reflective White on Green
1968: Reflective White on Black with "68" very faintly embossed
1969: *Yellow on Red Sticker*
1970: *White on Black Sticker*
1971: *Black on Yellow Sticker*
1972: *Red on White Sticker*
1973: Black on Reflective White dated base
1974: *Black on Yellow Sticker*
New registrations received Black on Reflective White undated base with above sticker.
1975: *White on Green Sticker*
New registrations received Black on Reflective White base with above sticker and beehive in the center.
1976: *White on Blue Sticker*
1977: *White on Red Sticker*
1978: *White on Green Sticker*
1979: *White on Blue Sticker*
New registrations received a Black on Reflective White graphic undated base with above sticker.
1980: *White on Red Sticker*
1981: *White on Green Sticker*
1982: *Black on Yellow Sticker*
1983: *White on Blue Sticker*
New registrations received a Black on Reflective White graphic undated base with above sticker.
1984: *White on Red Sticker*
1985: *White on Green Sticker*
New registrations received a Red and Blue on Reflective White graphic undated base with above sticker.
1986: *Black on Yellow Sticker*
1987: *White on Blue Sticker*
1988: *White on Red Sticker*
1989: *White on Green Sticker*
1990: *Black on Yellow Sticker* on 1985 base
1991: *Black on Green Sticker*
1992: *White on Red Sticker*
1993: *White on Blue Sticker*
1994: *Black on Yellow Sticker*

Note: All bases from 1973 to 1985 remained valid until 1990. Since then, the 1985 base has been used.

VERMONT
COLOR CODE

1905-06: White on Blue (undated Porcelain)
1907-08: Black on White (undated Porcelain)
1909: Black on White (Porcelain)
1910: Black on White (Porcelain)
1911: Black on White (Porcelain)
1912: Black on White (Porcelain)
1913: Black on White (Porcelain)
1914: Black on White (Porcelain)
1915: Black on White (Porcelain)
1916: White on Blue-Black (undated)
1917: Blue on White (Undated)
1918: Yellow-Orange on Dark Green (undated)
1919: Blue on Light Cream
1920: White on Black
1921: Black on White
1922: Blue on Light Cream
1923: Black on Yellow
1924: Black on Silver
1925: Deep Yellow on Green
1926: Green on Deep Yellow
1927: Deep Yellow on Green
1928: Green on Deep Yellow
1929: Tan on Maroon
1930: Maroon on Dark Cream
1931: White on Dark Blue
1932: Dark Blue on White
1933: White on Dark Blue
1934: Dark Blue on White
1935: White on Dark Blue
3/31/37: Dark Blue on White
4/01/38: White on Dark Blue
1938: Dark Blue on White
1939: White on Dark Blue
1940: Dark Blue on White
1941: White on Dark Blue
1942: Dark Blue on White
1943: *Black on Yellow Tab*
1944: Black on White
1945: White on Dark Blue
1946: Black on White
1947: White on Black
1948: Yellow on Green
1949: Green on White
1950: White on Green
1951: White on Green
1952: Green on White
1953: White on Green

1954: Green on White
1955: White on Green
1956: Green on White
1957: White on Green
1958: Green on White
1959: White on Green
1960: Green on White
1961: White on Green
1962: Green on White
1963: White on Green
1964: Green on White
1965: White on Green
1966: Green on White
1967: Reflective White on Reflective Green
1968: *Black on Yellow Sticker*
1969: Reflective White on Reflective Green (undated)
1970: *White on Red Sticker*
1971: *Black on White Sticker*
1972: Reflective White on Reflective Green
1973: *Black on Yellow Sticker*
1974: *Blue on White Sticker*
1975: *White on Red Sticker*
1976: *White on Blue and Red Sticker*
1977: Reflective White on Reflective Green (undated)
1978: *White on Red Sticker*
1979: *Black on Yellow Sticker*
1980: *Blue on White Sticker*
1981: *White on Red Sticker*
1982: *White on Black Sticker*
1983: *White on Blue Sticker*
1984: *White on Red Sticker*
1985: *Yellow on Black Sticker*
New registrations received a Reflective White on Reflective Green graphic undated base with above sticker.
1986: *Green on Gold Sticker* on 1977 and 1985 bases
1987: *Gold on Green Sticker* on 1977 and 1985 bases
1988: *Green on White Sticker* on 1977 and 1985 bases
1989: *Blue on White Sticker* on 1977 and 1985 bases
1990: *Red on White Sticker* on 1985 base; 1977 base invalidated
1991: *Black on Green Sticker*
1992: *Gold on Black Sticker*
1993: *Green on White Sticker*
1994: *White on Blue Sticker*

VIRGINIA
COLOR CODE

1906-09: White on Black (undated Porcelain)
1910: Red on White (Porcelain)
1911: White on Blue (Porcelain)
1912: White on Green (Porcelain)
1913: White on Dark Red (Porcelain)
1914: Blue on White
1915: White on Green
1916: Dark Blue on Orange
1917: White on Black
1918: Black on White
1919: White on Black
1920: White on Green
1921: Black on Orange
1922: White on Dark Blue
1923: White on Green
1924: White on Dark Red
1925: Black on White
1926: Yellow-Orange on Dark Blue
1927: Red on Green
1928: Yellow-Orange on Black
1929: Black on Orange
1930: Orange on Black
1931: Black on Orange
1932: White on Black
1933: Black on White
1934: White on Black
1935: Black on White
1936: Orange on Dark Blue
1937: White on Black
1938: Black on White
1939: White on Black
1940: Black on White
1941: White on Black
1942: Black on White
1943: *White on Black Tab*
1944: Black on Yellow (Fiberboard)
1945: Black on White
1946: White on Black
1947: Black on Aluminum
1948: White on Black
1949: Black on Aluminum
1950: White on Black
1951: Black on White
1952: *White on Black Tab*
1953: Orange on Blue
1954: White on Black
1955: Black on White

1956: White on Black
1957: Black on White
1958: White on Black
1959: Black on White
1960: White on Black
1961: Black on White
1962: White on Black
1963: Black on White
1964: White on Black
1965: Black on White
1966: White on Black
1967: Black on White
1968: White on Black
1969: Black on White
1970: White on Black
1971: Black on White or
Black on Reflective White
1972: White on Black
1973: Blue on White undated base with
White on Red Sticker
1974: *White on Blue Sticker*
1975: *White on Green Sticker*
1976: *White on Red Sticker*
1977: *White on Blue Sticker*
1978: *Red on White Sticker*
1979: *Green on White Sticker*
New registrations received a Blue on
Reflective White graphic undated base
with 1980 sticker.
1980: *White on Blue Sticker*
1981: *Red on White Sticker*
1982: *White on Green Sticker*
1983: *Blue on White Sticker*
1984: *White on Red Sticker*
1985: *Green on White Sticker*
1986: *White on Blue Sticker*
1987: *Red on White Sticker*
1988: *White on Green Sticker*
1989: *Blue on White Sticker*
1990: *White on Red Sticker*
1991: *Green on White Sticker*
1992: *White on Blue Sticker*
1993: *Red on White Sticker*
1994: *White on Green Sticker*
1995: *Blue on White Sticker*

Note: All general issue bases since 1973 remain valid.

WASHINGTON
COLOR CODE

1916: White on Dark Blue (Exp. 2/29/16)
1917: White on Lavender (Exp. 2/28/17)
1918: White on Black (Exp. 2/28/18)
1919: Black on Yellow (Exp. 2/28/19)
1920: *Black on White Porcelain Tab* (Exp. 2/29/20)
New registrations received Black on Yellow and White 1920 plates, some of which were porcelain.
1921: White on Green (Exp. 2/28/21)
Black on Gray (3/01/21 to 12/31/21)
1922: White on Brown
1923: Blue on White
1924: White on Blue
1925: Blue on White
1926: White on Green
1927: Green on White
1928: Black on Orange
1929: White on Green
1930: Green on White
1931: White on Green
1932: Green on White
1933: White on Green
1934: Green on White
1935: White on Blue
1936: Blue on White
1937: White on Blue
1938: Green on White
1939: Yellow on Green
1940: Green on White
1941: White on Green
1942: Green on White
1943: *Windshield Sticker*
1944: *Windshield Sticker*
New registrations received Green on White 1944 plate.
1945: Green on White
1946: *Windshield Sticker*
1947: Green on Aluminum
1948: *Windshield Sticker*
1949: Green on Aluminum
1950: Green on White
1951: *Green on Aluminum Tab*
New registrations received Green on White 1951 plate.
1952: *Windshield Sticker*
1953: *Reflective Green Tab*
1954: White on Green
1955: *Red on Aluminum Tab*
1956: *Green on White Tab*
1957: *White on Green Tab*
1958: White on Green with *Aluminum on Green Sticker*

1959: *Green on White Sticker*
1960: *Aluminum on Green Sticker*
1961: *Green on Aluminum Sticker*
1962: *White on Green Sticker*
1963: Green on White
1964: *White on Green Sticker*
1965: *Green on White Sticker*
New registrations received Green on White undated base with above sticker.
1966: *White on Green Sticker*
1967: *Green on Gold Sticker*
1968: *Yellow on Red Sticker*
New registrations received Green on Reflective White undated base with above sticker.
1969: *Blue on Yellow Sticker*
1970: *White on Red Sticker*
1971: *Half Black on Yellow, Half Yellow on Black Sticker*
1972: *Green on White Sticker*
1973: *Red on White Sticker*
1974: *Yellow on Black Sticker*
1975: *Black on White Sticker*
1976: *Red on White Sticker*
1977: *White on Blue Sticker*
1978: *White on Red Sticker*
New registrations received Green on Reflective White undated base with above sticker.
1979: *Green on White Sticker*
1980: *White on Blue Sticker*
1981: *Red on White Sticker*
1982: *White on Green Sticker*
1983: *Blue on White Sticker*
1984: *White on Red Sticker*
1985: *White on Green Sticker*
1986: *White on Blue Sticker*
1987: *White on Red Sticker*
New registrations received Dark Blue and Red on Reflective Light Blue and White graphic undated base with above sticker.
1988: *White on Green Sticker*
1989: *Green on White Sticker*
1990: *White on Blue Sticker*
1991: *White on Red Sticker*
New registrations received Blue on Reflective Blue, Red and White undated base with above sticker.
1992: *White on Green Sticker*
1993: *White on Blue Sticker*
1994: *White on Red Sticker*

Note: 1963 bases were valid until 1985. All other bases issued since 1968 remain valid.

WEST VIRGINIA
COLOR CODE

1906: White on Dark Blue (3-7/8" X 6-3/4")
1907-08: Black on White (undated Porcelain)
1909: Black on Red (Porcelain)
1910: White on Dark Blue (Porcelain)
1911: Black on White (Porcelain)
1912: White on Green (Porcelain)
July 1914: Yellow on Black (Porcelain)
1914-15: White on Light Blue (Porcelain)
1915-16: White on Red (Porcelain)
1916-17: Blue on White (Flat)
1917-18: Yellow on Black
1918-19: Black on White
1919-20: White on Black
1921: White on Dark Blue
1922: Black on Tan
1923: Red on White
1924: White on Maroon
1925: Black on Orange
1926: Ivory on Dark Blue
1927: Black on Gray
1928: White on Dark Green
1929: Orange on Black
1930: Black on Gray
1931: Yellow on Black
1932: White on Black
1933: Yellow on Black
1934: *Six-Month Windshield Sticker*
1934-35: Black on Yellow
1935-36: Yellow on Black
1936-37: Black on Yellow
1937-38: Yellow on Black
1938-39: Black on Yellow
1939-40: Yellow on Black
1940-41: Black on Yellow
6/30/42: Yellow on Black
6/30/43: *Black on White Tab*
6/30/44: *Windshield Sticker*
6/30/45: Black on Yellow
6/30/46: Yellow on Black
6/30/47: Black on Deep Yellow
6/30/48: Deep Yellow on Black
6/30/49: Black on Deep Yellow
6/30/50: Yellow on Black
6/30/51: Black on Yellow
6/30/52: Yellow on Black
6/30/53: Black on Yellow
6/30/54: Yellow on Black
1954: Black on Yellow
1955: No dated 1955 issue due to change in system of dating.
1956: White on Green
1957: Yellow on Dark Blue
1958: Green on White

1959: White on Green
1960: Red on White
1961: White on Maroon or Reflective White on Reflective Dark Red
1962: Green on Reflective White
1963: Reflective Deep Yellow on Blue
1964: Blue on Reflective Deep Yellow
1965: Reflective Deep Yellow on Blue
1966: Blue on Reflective Deep Yellow
1967: Reflective Deep Yellow on Blue
1968: Blue on Reflective Deep Yellow
1969: Reflective Deep Yellow on Blue
1970: Blue on Reflective Deep Yellow
1971: Blue on Reflective Deep Yellow undated base with *White on Blue Sticker*
1972: *White on Red Sticker*
1973: *White on Green Sticker*
1974: *White on Black Sticker*
1975: *Yellow on Red Sticker*
1976: *Yellow on Green Sticker* on 1971 base
Early in 1976, a new base was introduced, Dark Blue, Light Blue and Deep Yellow on Reflective White graphic. Additionally a *Blue, Red and Black on White "76" Sticker* covered the date on base.
1977: No dated 1977 issue due to extended expiration of 1976 base
1978: *White on Red Sticker*
1978: *Yellow on Green Sticker* (actually used in 1979)
1979: No dated 1979 issue due to manufacturing error; thus two different 1978 stickers!
1980: *White on Blue Sticker*
1981: *White on Red Sticker*
1982: *White on Black Sticker*
New registrations received a Blue and Yellow on White graphic dated base with no sticker.
1983: *White on Green Sticker*
1984: *White on Brown Sticker*
1985: *White on Orange Sticker*
New registrations received Blue and Yellow on Reflective White graphic dated base with no sticker.
1986: *White on Blue Sticker*
1987: *White on Green Sticker*
1988: *White on Red Sticker*
1989: *Yellow on Blue Sticker*
1990: *Orange on Black Sticker*
1991: *Blue on Yellow Sticker*
1992: *White on Green Sticker*
1993: *Black on Red Sticker*

Note: All bases issued since 1976 remain valid.

WISCONSIN
COLOR CODE

1905-1911: Silver on Black
New registrations in 1911 received a dated Aluminum on Green plate.
1912: Aluminum on Red
1913: Aluminum on Blue
1914: Black on White
1915: White on Black
1916: Red on White
1917: White on Olive Green
1918: Black on Beige
1919: Yellow on Green
1920: White on Maroon
1921: Black on Gray
1922: White on Olive Green
1923: Red on White
1924: White on Black
1925: Yellow on Blue
1926: Black on Cream
1927: White on Blue-Black
1928: Black on Orange
1929: White on Light Green
1930: Black on Gray
1931: Yellow on Blue
1932: Blue on Yellow
1933: White on Blue-Black
1934: Black on White
1935: White on Black
1936: Green on White
1937: White on Blue
1938: Black on Silver
1939: White on Black
1940: Red on White
1941: Black on Yellow
1942: Yellow on Black
1943: *Black on White Tab*
1944: *White on Green Tab*
1945: *Red on White Tab*
1946: White on Black
1947: *Black on Orange Tab*
New registrations received White on Black 1947 base.
1948: *Black on Yellow Tab*
1949: *White on Green Tab*
1950: *Yellow on Light Blue Tab*
New registrations received White on Black undated base with above tab.
1951: *Dark Red on White Tab*
1952: *Black on Yellow Tab*
1953: Black on Yellow

1954: *White on Red Tab*
1955: Green on White
1956: *Blue on Yellow Tab*
1957: Black on Yellow
1958: *Red on White Tab*
1959: Green on White
1960: *Black on Orange Tab*
1961: Black on Pale Yellow
1962: *Black on Red Sticker*
1963: Blue on White
1964: *Silver on Red Sticker*
1965: White on Maroon
1966: *Black on Deep Yellow Sticker*
1967: *Silver on Green Sticker*
1968: Black on Reflective Lemon Yellow
1969: *Red on White Sticker*
1970: *Black on Orange Sticker*
1971: *Black on Green Sticker*
1972: *Black on Red Sticker*
1973: Red on Reflective White
1974: *Black on Green Sticker*
1975: *Black on Orange Sticker*
1976: *Yellow on Blue Sticker*
1977: *White on Red Sticker*
1978: *White on Blue Sticker*
1979: *Yellow on Black Sticker*
1980: Black on Reflective Yellow
1981: *White on Green Sticker*
1982: *White on Red Sticker*
1983: *White on Blue Sticker*
1984: *Blue on Silver Sticker*
1985: *Yellow on Green Sticker*
1986: *Black on Red Sticker*
New registrations received a Blue on Reflective Blue, Red, Black, Green and White graphic undated base with above sticker.
1987: *Silver on Blue Sticker*
New registrations received a Red on Reflective Blue, Red, Black, Green and White graphic undated base with above sticker.
1988: *Blue on White Sticker*
1989: *Black on Green Sticker*
1990: *Black on Red Sticker*
1991: *Black on Yellow Sticker*
1992: *Black on Blue Sticker*
1993: *Red on White Sticker*
1994: *Black on Orange Sticker*

Note: All bases since 1980 remain valid.

166

WYOMING

1913: Red on White (undated)
1914: White on Blue (undated)
1915: White on Black (undated)
1916: Blue on White (undated Porcelain)
1917: Brown on Light Buff (undated)
1918: White on Maroon
1919: Black on Light Green
1920: White on Dark Olive Green
1921: *Black on Pea Green Tab with*
Brass Number Insert
New registrations received Black
on Orange 1921 plates.
1922: Blue on Cream
1923: White on Blue
1924: White on Red
1925: Black on White
1926: White on Green
1927: Black on Yellow
1928: Yellow on Dark Blue
1929: Red on Light Gray
1930: White on Black
1931: Green on Gray
1932: Cream on Light Brown
1933: Black on Ivory
1934: White on Dark Red
1935: Blue on White
1936: Black on White
1937: Yellow on Brown
1938: Yellow on Dark Blue
1939: Dark Blue on Yellow-Orange
1940: White on Light Blue
1941: Red on Cream
1942: Black on White
1943: Orange on Black
1944: Black on Orange (Fiberboard)
1945: Black on White
1946: Green on Cream
1947: White on Black
1948: Brown on Pale Yellow
1949: Red on Cream
1950: White on Black
1951: Black on White
1952: Yellow on Black

1953: White on Black
1954: Black on White
1955: Yellow on Black
1956: White on Black
1957: Reflective Yellow on Black
1958: Reflective Yellow on Green
1959: Reflective White on Black
1960: Reflective Yellow on Black
1961: Reflective White on Red
1962: Reflective White on Light Blue
1963: Reflective White on Black
1964: Reflective White on Red
1965: Reflective Yellow on Black
1966: Reflective White on Green
1967: Reflective White on Red
1968: Reflective Yellow on Brown
1969: Reflective White on Dark Blue
1970: Reflective Yellow on Green
1971: Reflective White on Black
1972: Brown on Reflective Yellow
1973: Black on Reflective White
1974: Brown on Reflective Yellow
1975: Blue and Red on Reflective White graphic
1976: *White on Blue Sticker*
1977: *Black on White Sticker*
1978: Brown and Yellow on Reflective White graphic
1979: *White on Green Sticker*
1980: *White on Red Sticker*
1981: *White on Blue Sticker*
1982: *Black on White Sticker*
1983: Brown on Reflective Yellow graphic
1984: *Blue on White Sticker*
1985: *White on Green Sticker*
1986: *Black on White Sticker*
1987: *White on Blue Sticker*
1988: Red and Blue on Reflective White graphic
1989: *White on Blue Sticker*
1990: *Blue on White Sticker*
1991: *Blue on White Sticker*
1992: Multicolored graphic undated base with
White on Red Sticker
1993: *Black on Green Sticker*
1994: *Black on Orange Sticker*

Afterword

As a precocious lad of six, I started collecting stamps and license plates at about the same time, eventually amassing a valuable collection of both. The only stamps I have kept to this day are limited to those from Tibet. I disposed of my 11,000-plus license plate collection in 1949 and the 1950s but still maintain a small collection consisting of those which interest me, especially with an eye for harmonious arrangement. Thus, I've kept up my interest and study in both philatelic and license plate subjects. There has been so much license plate lore which has been uncovered in those nearly 63 years, and much of this I have both discovered and chronicled since I was seven years old and had learned to read.

License plate collecting and stamp collecting invite comparison. Except for weight and convenience (or inconvenience) of carting stamps or license plates around, there are more similarities than differences between the two. Stamps are easier to deal with because of their size and weight. And yet, I've lost one or two valuable specimens in my own collection due to an unfriendly breeze which whisked them away to God knows where. On the other hand, although plates can be heavy to transport, it takes a tornado or similar disaster to take them to kingdom come.

They both deal in colors, shapes, sizes, commemoratives (special issues available for a limited period), inverts, comparative rarity and/or condition, essays or experimental designs, prototypes—essays which have won the approval for a forthcoming series but in different colors, reprints and repaints in the stamp world and license plate milieu respectively, and counterfeits. Other similarities may be noted in specialty subjects of both areas. In philately, collectors may specialize in air mail stamps, first-day covers, postage-due varieties and subjects such as those featuring animals, birds, flowers, statesmen and so on. In license plates, collectors may confine their main interest to procuring one plate for each state and Canadian province for every year of issue, obtaining at least one example from every country and territory, from the largest to each city, state or political enclave known to issue or have issued plates at one time or another, including those changes in type or design caused by governmental upheavals, invasions or simply the revamping of a style by a government on replacing one registration system with a newer one or adding or deleting series from the existing one. Some collectors specialize in military-type plates; other predilections include birth-year examples, commercial or motorcycle plates and many, many more.

The first license plates were unconsciously collected by motorists who nailed them on the walls inside their garages or barns upon the plates' expiration. When I began collecting them, generally just asking for them got them. By 1939 I knew perhaps a dozen other collectors in the various states, and plates were either traded or sold between us. The price seldom varied—samples, 10¢ each; "regular" plates, seven or eight for $1; porcelains, 35¢ each; and foreign, 75¢—regardless of whether the plate was from Great Britain, Danzig or Sarawak!

In those halcyon times, the aim of "tin collectors" was to get one plate from each state, each Canadian province and as many foreign countries as possible. But even then, there were the specialists who recognized that all plates weren't created equal and that some were rarer than others, which I recognized when most of my compatriots did not or would not. This realization was the direct result of my stamp collecting experience and realizing a stamp's value by reading the current stamp catalogue.

No better an example of this could be found than from a trip my late brother and I made in 1941 to the Province of New Brunswick, Canada, where I proceeded to fill the trunk of his '36 Ford coupe with New Brunswick license plates dating back to 1910. There was an obvious difference in worth between New York State and New Brunswick porcelain plates which most other collectors could neither understand nor accept. They just could not see why I felt that one of these Canadian issues was much rarer, despite the fact that 107,262 passenger cars were registered in New York State in 1912, whereas New Brunswick boasted a mere 700 of all types of motor vehicles that same year. One for one—that seemed to be the accepted rule for most collectors. I couldn't make them understand that the value of the plate should be predicated on many things, including the number of plates issued, the known or estimated rate of survival, the condition and the other lesser-known but equally important considerations. That was 52 years ago, and my fellow hobbyists thought I was crazy. They were right. I was, like a fox. I hung on to such trading stock until a transaction could be made satisfactory to both parties.

We have been on the threshold of a renaissance in our chosen field for far too many years. We have become more particular in our plate interests for the last generation or so. The formation of the Automobile License Plate Collectors Association and its bi-monthly newsletter have spurred the cause and rekindled for many collectors their initial flame of interest, which may have been initially sparked by such items as the Shell road maps of 1932 and 1933; the License Plate Gum cards of 1936 through 1939; the Atlas tire ads of the 1950s and 1960s; later on, the metal miniature plates which came in cereal boxes; and for many years, the color charts printed by the Department of Transportation as well as the Polk's License Plate Guides, which are issued annually now.

A gap of 18 years existed before the introduction of the first adhesive postage stamp in 1840 in Great Britain and the first U.S. stamp catalog which portrayed known stamps and quoted their estimated values. Philately has grown immensely since then.

I fervently believe that this book is going to serve as a sort of catalyst to the growth of interest in the license plate field. And it is my personal opinion that this book will be the major factor in the further development of the study and collecting of license plates as the years give up hidden treasures and we accumulate additional history on them.

Keith Marvin
Menands, New York

Automobile License Plate Collectors Association
A Brief History of ALPCA

There were certainly license plate collectors before ALPCA was founded. In fact, there were plate collectors almost as soon as there were plates! Some of the earliest of these pioneers will remain forever nameless, but there were collectors known to have begun their hobby as early as the 1920s and 1930s. There was Robert Julian of Omaha, Nebraska, Art Keck of Buffalo, New York, Bill Swigart and Earl Fuller of Pennsylvania, and of course, Keith Marvin of Albany, New York. In The Netherlands, Karel Stoel, Jan Erkelens, and H.F.J. Hesselfelt even formed an unofficial group called the "BBTBBA," which *very* loosely translated stood for, "The group who helps foreign tourists find their way around The Netherlands." While it was true that these young schoolboys did indeed assist foreign motorists in getting around in The Netherlands, their *real* purpose was to try to talk these motorists out of their plates! Such was the state of plate collecting in the early days. Loosely organized, each of these pioneers discovered each other only by accident, if at all. By 1953, there were several hundred collectors roaming the globe in search of plates, most totally unknown to the others.

In 1954, a psychologist named Dr. Cecil George of Massachusetts read an article in a Boston newspaper about a man in New Hampshire who collected license plates. Dr. George had a mild interest in license plates, too, and as a psychologist, felt strongly that hobbies contributed to good mental health. He wrote the man from New Hampshire, a postmaster from Rumney Depot named Asa Colby, and together, the two men set about finding as many license plate collectors as they could, with the intention of forming a fraternal organization based on a common interest in plates. Shortly, a "newsletter" was mailed to about 40 known collectors, consisting of names and addresses and brief statements of collecting interests of the various people involved. When the responses came in, George and Colby were happy to find that the list had expanded to several dozen people, and in December of 1954, the *Automobile License Plate Collectors Association* was founded. Actually, the name was chosen later, as the group began its life with no name at all! Dr. George issued himself the #1 membership and Mr. Colby took #2. By the end of 1954, four members were enrolled, and by the end of 1955, the number had grown to 108. Among those receiving the lowest numbers were Roy Carson, Shib Pixley, Robert Tuthill, Bogart Seamen and Tom Chilton, who became key players in the development of the new organization. ALPCA passed the 1,000 member mark in 1969, and in 1993, the membership numbers being issued are in the 6,500 range. Of course, members have died, lost interest and dropped out over its 40-year history, too, and active membership is at about 2,700 today.

ALPCA has a national convention every June, and many regional groups have plate meets at various times of the year. ALPCA publishes a newsletter six times each year, and it is full of articles on plates, photographs of plates, ads to buy, sell and trade plates, etc. Though Asa Colby has passed on, Dr. George remains a member and seems surprised that his innocent inquiry to Colby has spawned such a boom in our hobby. For information on ALPCA or instructions on how to join the Club, contact the ALPCA Secretary-Treasurer, Gary Brent Kincade, P.O. Box 77, Horner, WV 26372.

Collection of Peter Kanze

Collection of Charles Gauthier
Photo by Howard S. Fisk on 9-9 1909 Speedway (Car make)
D.C. Porcelain   VA. Porcelain   MD. Leather

Collection of Peter Kanze

Collection of Peter Kanze

173

Acknowledgments

As with most projects of this magnitude, there are a great many people to thank. To Keith Marvin and Arthur Keck, my mentors; to Carole Gilligan, who has helped to drag me, kicking and screaming, into the computer age, this book is better for her help; to Tom Murray, who once said, "You know, you oughtta write a *book*"; to Dan Morgan at Straight Shooter Photography in Cleveland, Ohio, and his assistants Jesse Kramer, Laura Flaws and Rich Jochems, who are responsible for 99% of the photos in this book; and to Joe Walsh, who never fails to bring me plates: "How ya *doin'*, Joe?"

Lastly, a sincere and boundless thanks to the members of the Automobile License Plate Collectors Association, whose members have played a continuing role in my understanding and appreciation of license plates. I could name literally hundreds of members who have provided me with information over the years, but special thanks are due to the following members who have contributed their expertise directly to this book: Tom Allen, Jim Benjaminson, Roy Carson, Richard Dragon, Charles Gauthier, Denny Huron, Gary Kincade, Roy Klotz, Dave Lincoln, Don Merrill, Jeff Minard, Cecil Presnell and Steve Raiche.

About the Author

Jim Fox was born in Cleveland, Ohio, in 1947. After a career in music as founder, leader and drummer for the rock group The James Gang, he turned his attention to the research and study of license plates. He has written a monthly column on license plates for *Car Collector* magazine, and is a regular contributor to the ALPCA newsletter. In 1993, he was elected to his third term as ALPCA president and chairman of the Board of Directors. He lives in Mentor, Ohio, with his wife, two daughters and three dogs. He is always interested in corresponding with other collectors or with people who have questions or comments about license plates or their history. He can be reached at: Oakmont, Mentor, OH 44060-6816.